CRAYON Shinchan

By Yoshito Usui

Volume 7

CRAYON Shinchan

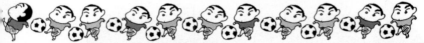

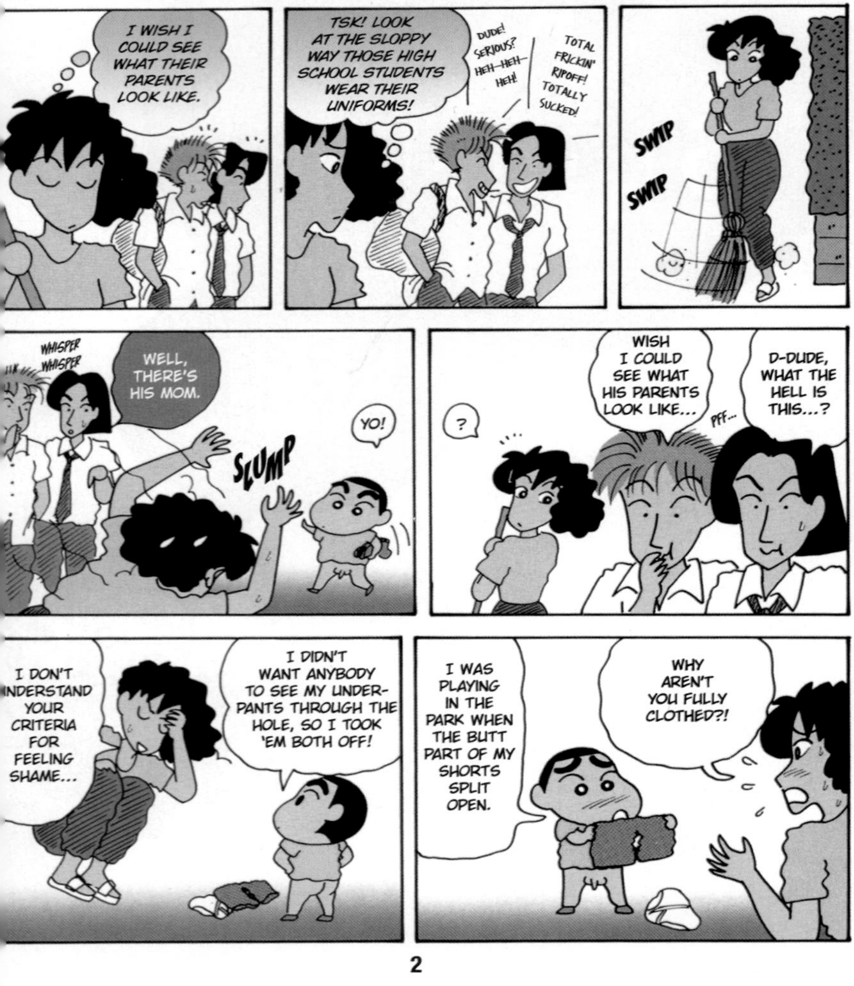
SWIP
SWIP
TOTAL FRICKIN' RIPOFF! TOTALLY SUCKED!
DUDE! SERIOUS? HEH-HEH-HEH!
TSK! LOOK AT THE SLOPPY WAY THOSE HIGH SCHOOL STUDENTS WEAR THEIR UNIFORMS!
I WISH I COULD SEE WHAT THEIR PARENTS LOOK LIKE.
D-DUDE, WHAT THE HELL IS THIS...?
WISH I COULD SEE WHAT HIS PARENTS LOOK LIKE...
PFF...
?
YO!
WELL, THERE'S HIS MOM.
WHISPER WHISPER
SLUMP
WHY AREN'T YOU FULLY CLOTHED?!
I WAS PLAYING IN THE PARK WHEN THE BUTT PART OF MY SHORTS SPLIT OPEN.
I DIDN'T WANT ANYBODY TO SEE MY UNDER-PANTS THROUGH THE HOLE, SO I TOOK 'EM BOTH OFF!
I DON'T UNDERSTAND YOUR CRITERIA FOR FEELING SHAME...

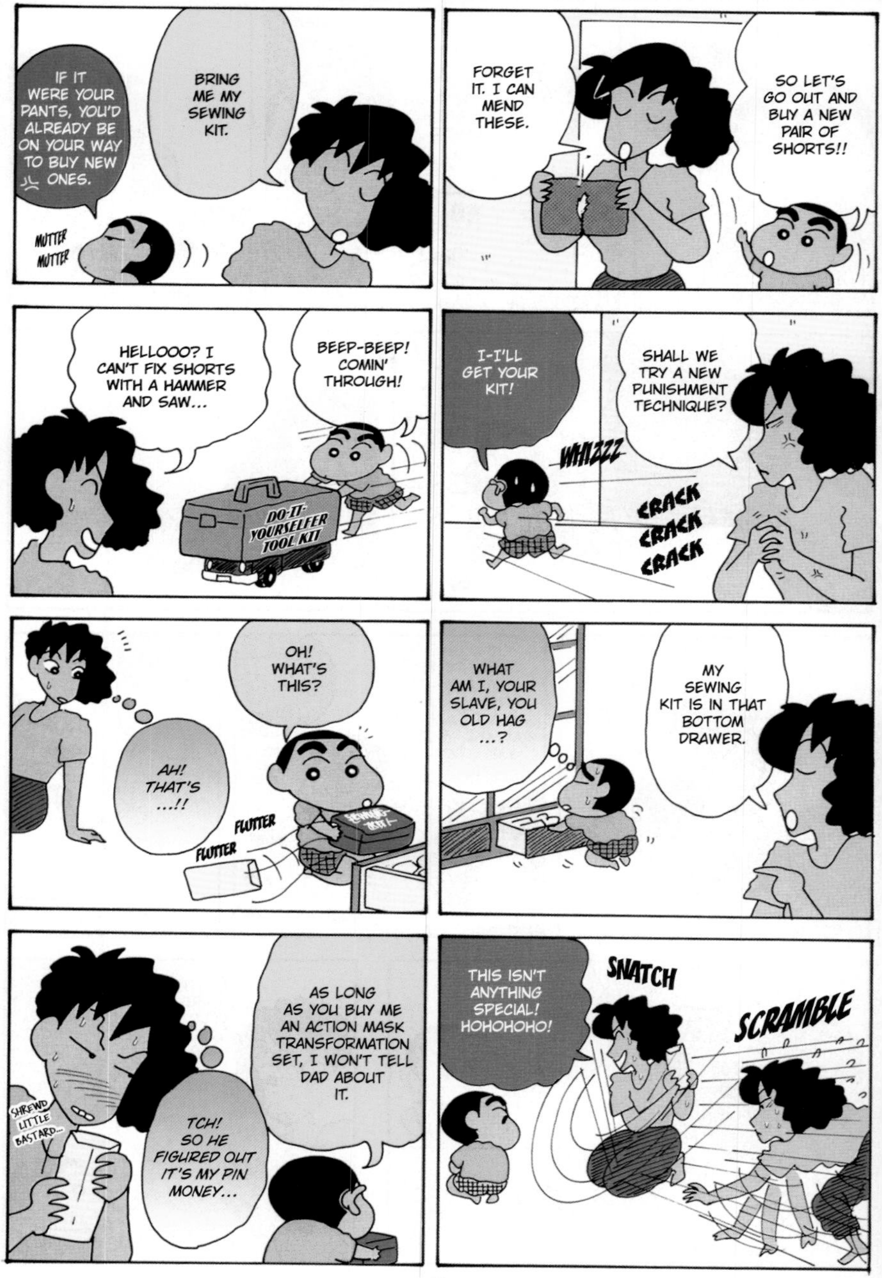
SO LET'S GO OUT AND BUY A NEW PAIR OF SHORTS!!
FORGET IT. I CAN MEND THESE.
BRING ME MY SEWING KIT.
IF IT WERE YOUR PANTS, YOU'D ALREADY BE ON YOUR WAY TO BUY NEW ONES.
MUTTER MUTTER
SHALL WE TRY A NEW PUNISHMENT TECHNIQUE?
I-I'LL GET YOUR KIT!
WHIZZZ
CRACK CRACK CRACK
BEEP-BEEP! COMIN' THROUGH!
HELLOOO? I CAN'T FIX SHORTS WITH A HAMMER AND SAW...
DO-IT-YOURSELFER TOOL KIT
MY SEWING KIT IS IN THAT BOTTOM DRAWER.
WHAT AM I, YOUR SLAVE, YOU OLD HAG ...?
OH! WHAT'S THIS?
AH! THAT'S ...!!
FLUTTER
FLUTTER
SCRAMBLE
SNATCH
THIS ISN'T ANYTHING SPECIAL! HOHOHOHO!
AS LONG AS YOU BUY ME AN ACTION MASK TRANSFORMATION SET, I WON'T TELL DAD ABOUT IT.
TCH! SO HE FIGURED OUT IT'S MY PIN MONEY...
SHREWD LITTLE BASTARD...

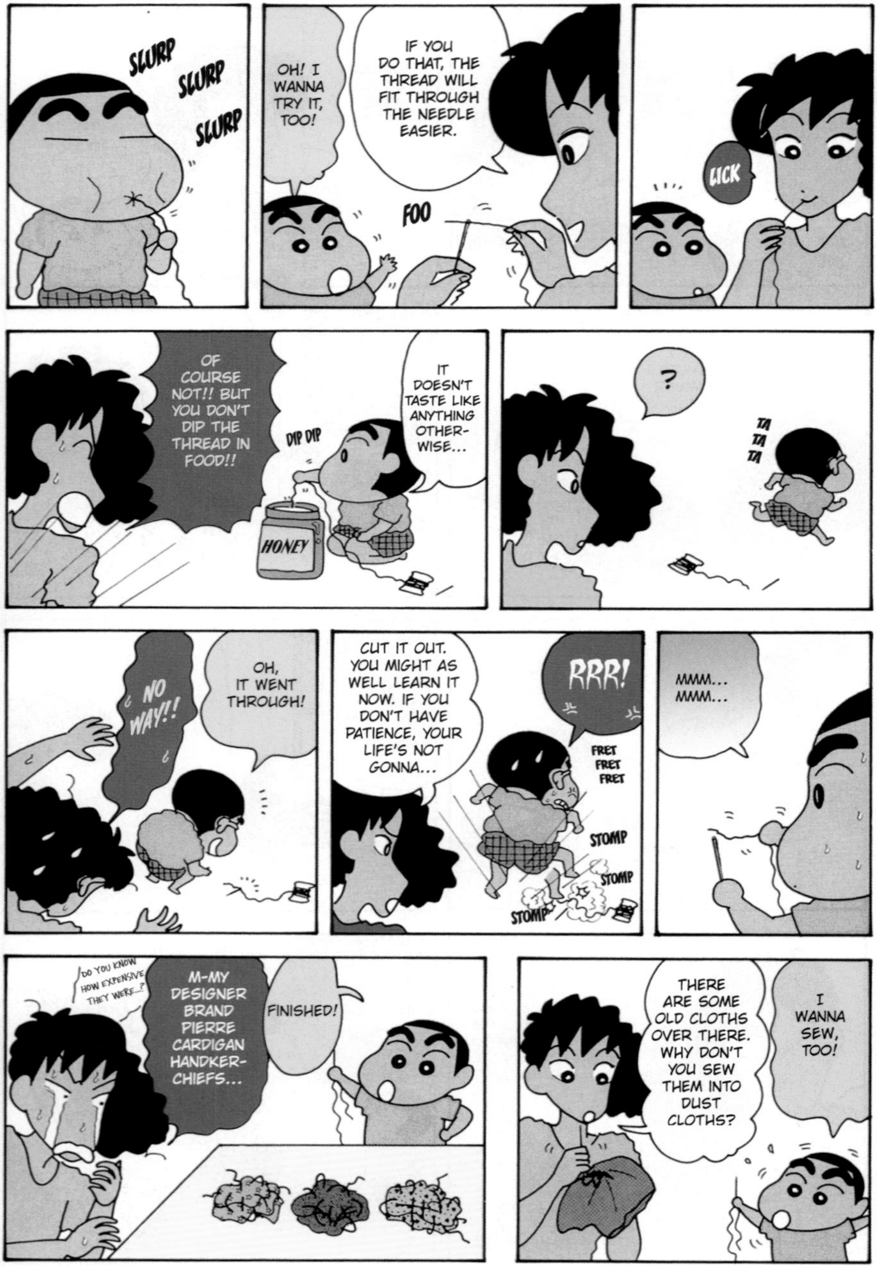
LICK
IF YOU DO THAT, THE THREAD WILL FIT THROUGH THE NEEDLE EASIER.
OH! I WANNA TRY IT, TOO!
FOO
SLURP
SLURP
SLURP
?
TA TA TA
IT DOESN'T TASTE LIKE ANYTHING OTHER-WISE...
OF COURSE NOT!! BUT YOU DON'T DIP THE THREAD IN FOOD!!
DIP DIP
HONEY
MMM... MMM...
RRR!
CUT IT OUT. YOU MIGHT AS WELL LEARN IT NOW. IF YOU DON'T HAVE PATIENCE, YOUR LIFE'S NOT GONNA...
FRET FRET FRET
STOMP
STOMP
STOMP
OH, IT WENT THROUGH!
NO WAY!!
I WANNA SEW, TOO!
THERE ARE SOME OLD CLOTHS OVER THERE. WHY DON'T YOU SEW THEM INTO DUST CLOTHS?
FINISHED!
M-MY DESIGNER BRAND PIERRE CARDIGAN HANDKER-CHIEFS...
DO YOU KNOW HOW EXPENSIVE THEY WERE...?

SUNFLOWER CLASS

CRAYON Shinchan

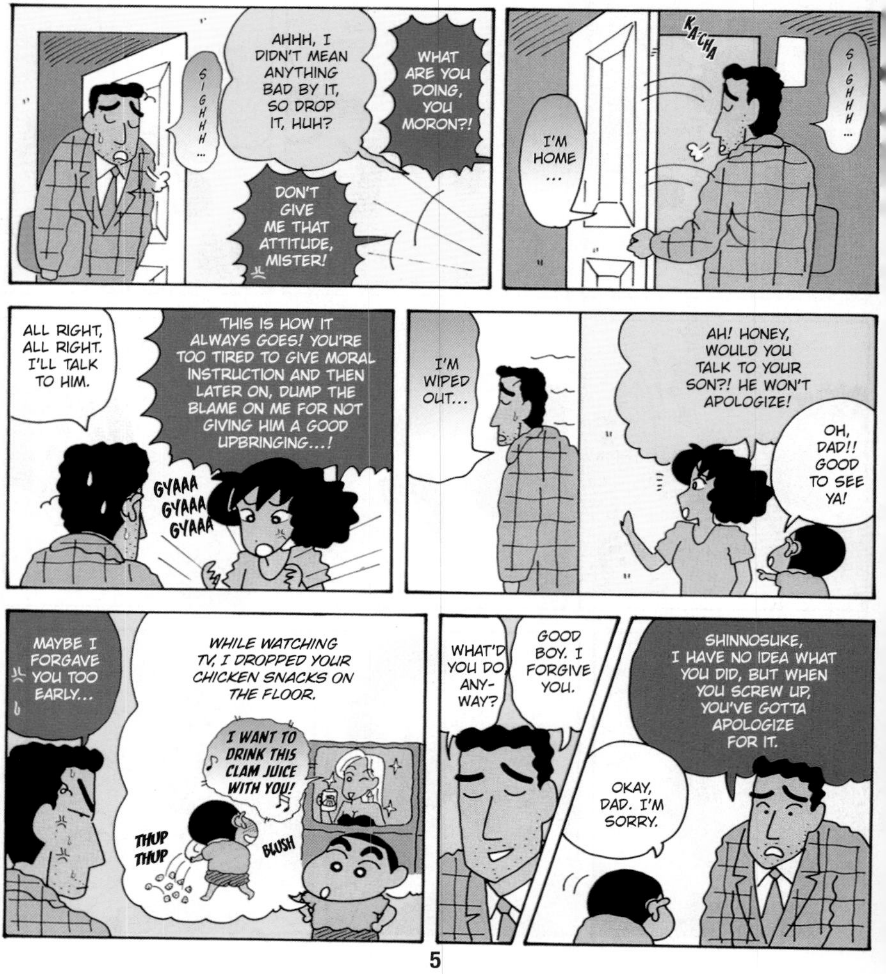
KA-CHA
SIGHHH...
I'M HOME...
WHAT ARE YOU DOING, YOU MORON?!
DON'T GIVE ME THAT ATTITUDE, MISTER!
AHHH, I DIDN'T MEAN ANYTHING BAD BY IT, SO DROP IT, HUH?
SIGHHH...
AH! HONEY, WOULD YOU TALK TO YOUR SON?! HE WON'T APOLOGIZE!
OH, DAD!! GOOD TO SEE YA!
I'M WIPED OUT...
THIS IS HOW IT ALWAYS GOES! YOU'RE TOO TIRED TO GIVE MORAL INSTRUCTION AND THEN LATER ON, DUMP THE BLAME ON ME FOR NOT GIVING HIM A GOOD UPBRINGING...!
ALL RIGHT, ALL RIGHT. I'LL TALK TO HIM.
GYAAA GYAAA GYAAA
SHINNOSUKE, I HAVE NO IDEA WHAT YOU DID, BUT WHEN YOU SCREW UP, YOU'VE GOTTA APOLOGIZE FOR IT.
OKAY, DAD. I'M SORRY.
GOOD BOY. I FORGIVE YOU.
WHAT'D YOU DO, ANYWAY?
WHILE WATCHING TV, I DROPPED YOUR CHICKEN SNACKS ON THE FLOOR.
I WANT TO DRINK THIS CLAM JUICE WITH YOU!
BLUSH
THUP THUP
MAYBE I FORGAVE YOU TOO EARLY...

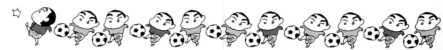

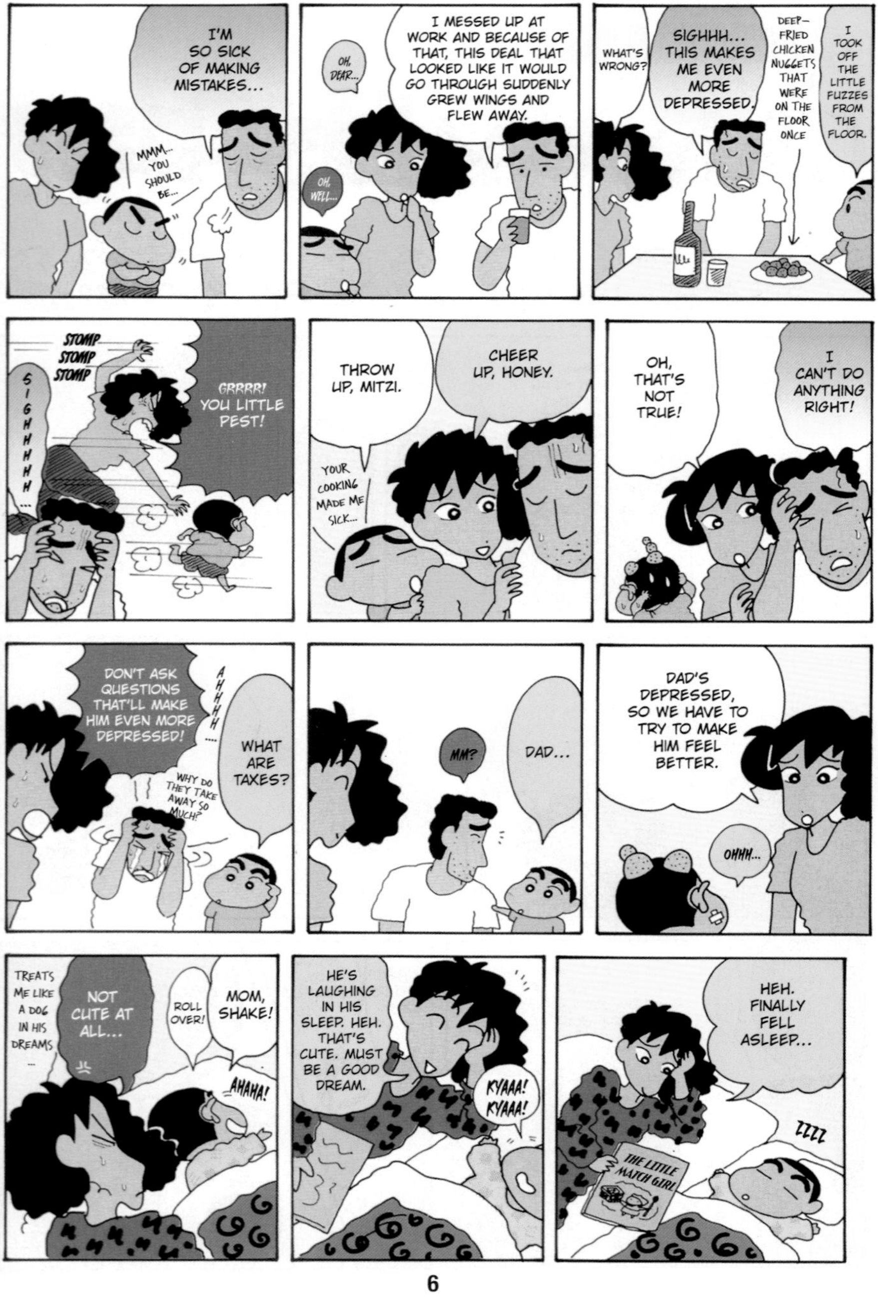
I TOOK OFF THE LITTLE FUZZES FROM THE FLOOR.
DEEP-FRIED CHICKEN NUGGETS THAT WERE ON THE FLOOR ONCE
SIGHHH... THIS MAKES ME EVEN MORE DEPRESSED.
WHAT'S WRONG?
I MESSED UP AT WORK AND BECAUSE OF THAT, THIS DEAL THAT LOOKED LIKE IT WOULD GO THROUGH SUDDENLY GREW WINGS AND FLEW AWAY.
OH, DEAR...
OH, WELL...
I'M SO SICK OF MAKING MISTAKES...
MMM... YOU SHOULD BE...
I CAN'T DO ANYTHING RIGHT!
OH, THAT'S NOT TRUE!
CHEER UP, HONEY.
THROW UP, MITZI.
YOUR COOKING MADE ME SICK...
GRRRR! YOU LITTLE PEST!
STOMP STOMP STOMP
SIGHHHHHH...
DAD'S DEPRESSED, SO WE HAVE TO TRY TO MAKE HIM FEEL BETTER.
OHHH...
DAD...
MM?
WHAT ARE TAXES?
AHHHH...
DON'T ASK QUESTIONS THAT'LL MAKE HIM EVEN MORE DEPRESSED!
WHY DO THEY TAKE AWAY SO MUCH?
HEH. FINALLY FELL ASLEEP...
ZZZZ
THE LITTLE MATCH GIRL
KYAAA! KYAAA!
HE'S LAUGHING IN HIS SLEEP. HEH. THAT'S CUTE. MUST BE A GOOD DREAM.
MOM, SHAKE!
ROLL OVER!
AHAHA!
NOT CUTE AT ALL...
TREATS ME LIKE A DOG IN HIS DREAMS...

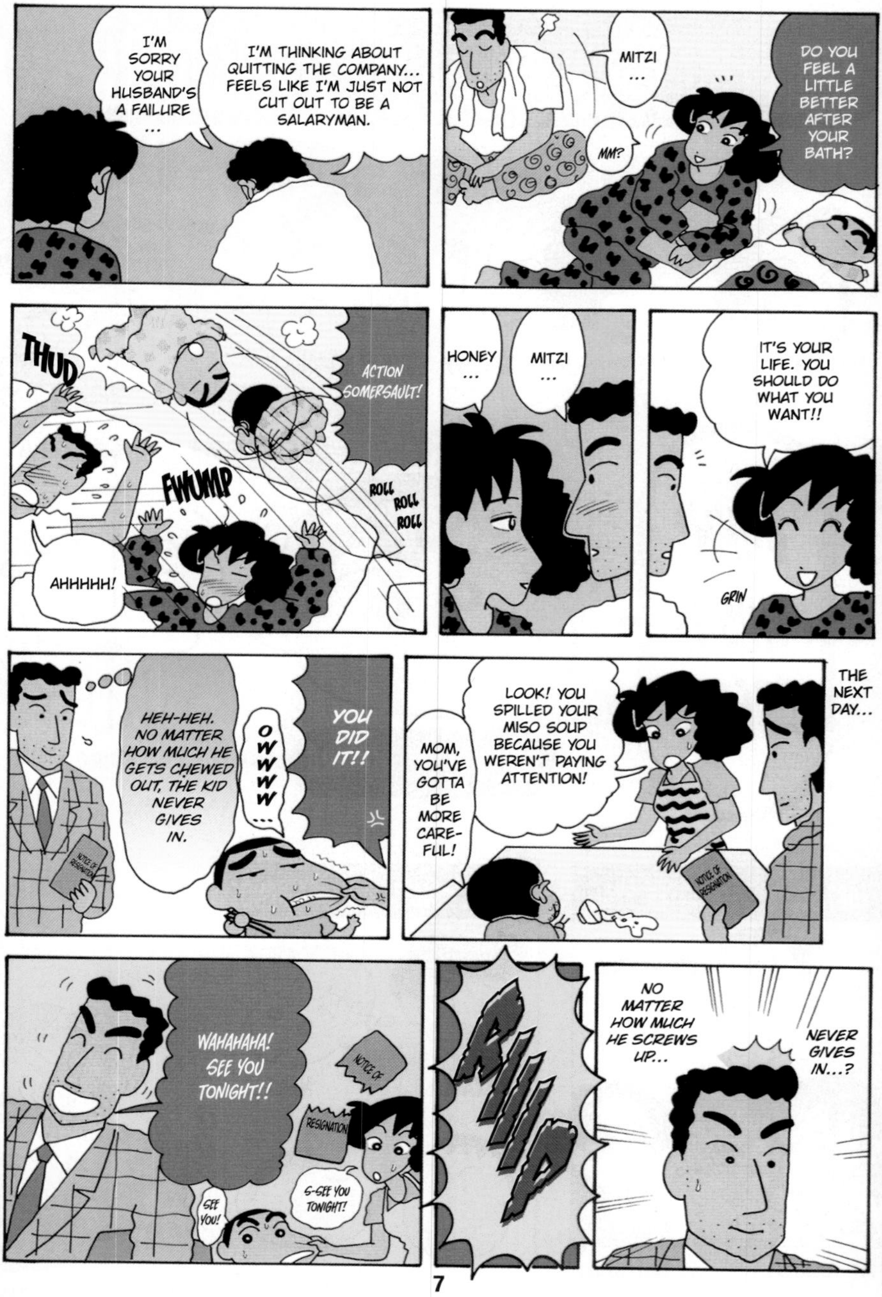
DO YOU FEEL A LITTLE BETTER AFTER YOUR BATH?
MITZI ...
MM?
I'M THINKING ABOUT QUITTING THE COMPANY... FEELS LIKE I'M JUST NOT CUT OUT TO BE A SALARYMAN.
I'M SORRY YOUR HUSBAND'S A FAILURE ...
IT'S YOUR LIFE. YOU SHOULD DO WHAT YOU WANT!!
GRIN
MITZI ...
HONEY ...
ACTION SOMERSAULT!
THUD
FWUMP
ROLL ROLL ROLL
AHHHHH!
THE NEXT DAY...
LOOK! YOU SPILLED YOUR MISO SOUP BECAUSE YOU WEREN'T PAYING ATTENTION!
MOM, YOU'VE GOTTA BE MORE CARE-FUL!
NOTICE OF RESIGNATION
YOU DID IT!!
OWWWWW ...
HEH-HEH. NO MATTER HOW MUCH HE GETS CHEWED OUT, THE KID NEVER GIVES IN.
NOTICE OF RESIGNATION
NEVER GIVES IN...?
NO MATTER HOW MUCH HE SCREWS UP...
RIIIP
WAHAHAHA! SEE YOU TONIGHT!!
NOTICE OF
RESIGNATION
S-SEE YOU TONIGHT!
SEE YOU!

SHIN-CHAN'S COMPLETE RELATIONSHIP CHART

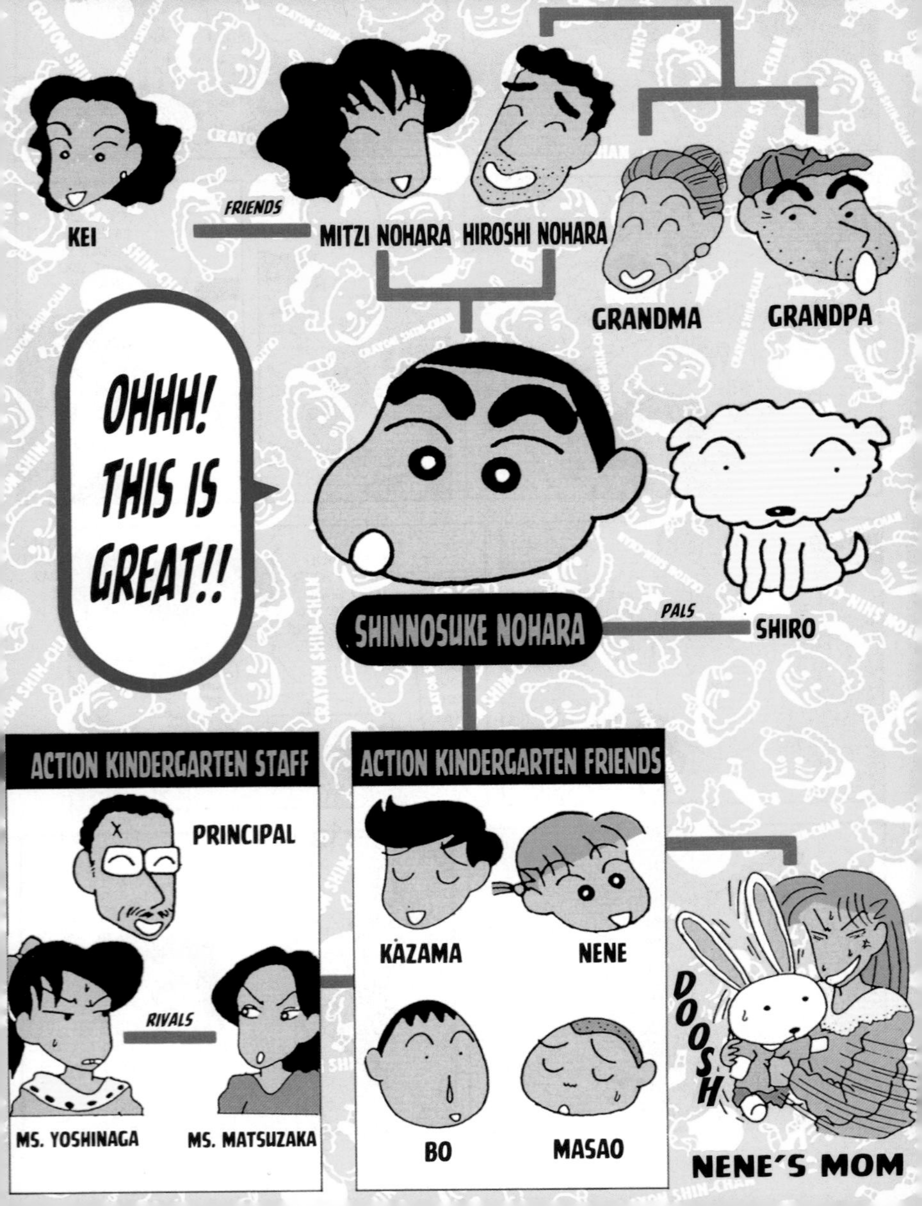

KEI
FRIENDS
MITZI NOHARA
HIROSHI NOHARA
GRANDMA
GRANDPA
OHHH! THIS IS GREAT!!
SHINNOSUKE NOHARA
PALS
SHIRO
ACTION KINDERGARTEN STAFF
PRINCIPAL
RIVALS
MS. YOSHINAGA
MS. MATSUZAKA
ACTION KINDERGARTEN FRIENDS
KAZAMA
NENE
BO
MASAO
DOOSH
NENE'S MOM

SHIN GIVES HIS ALL AND NEVER QUITS!

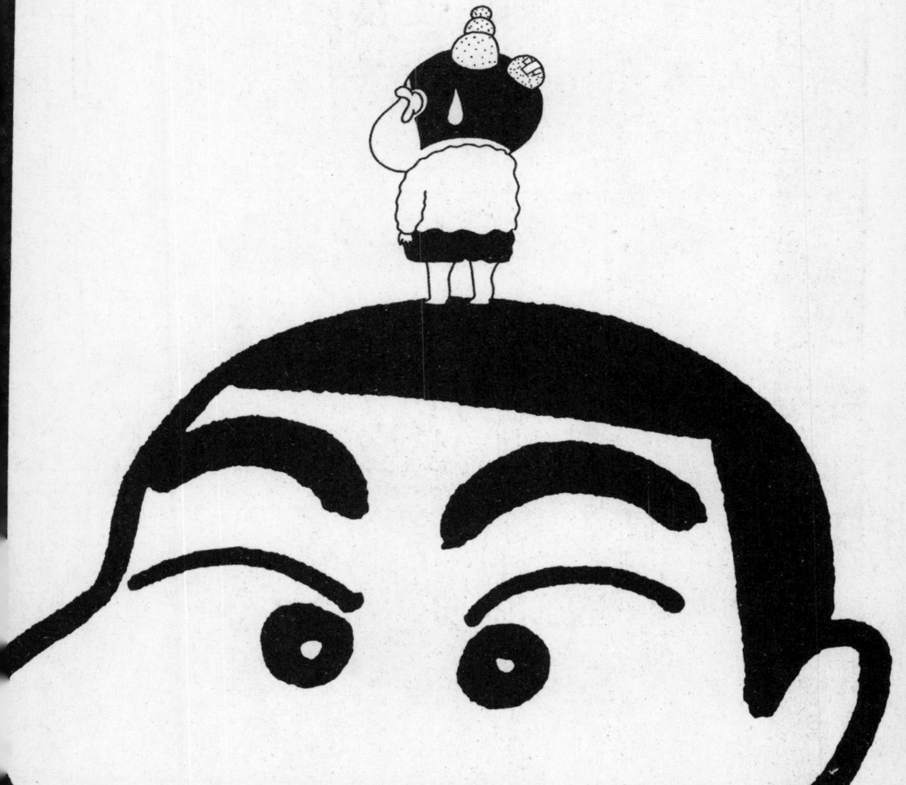

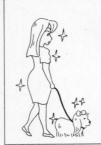

SHIN GIVES HIS ALL AND NEVER QUITS!

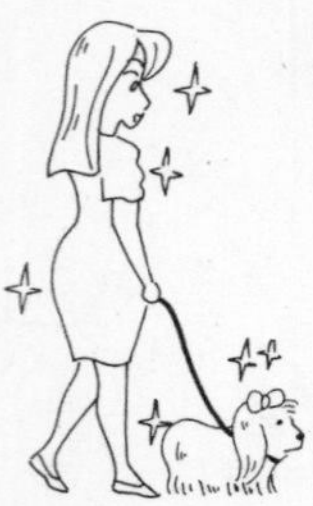

CHAPTER 1

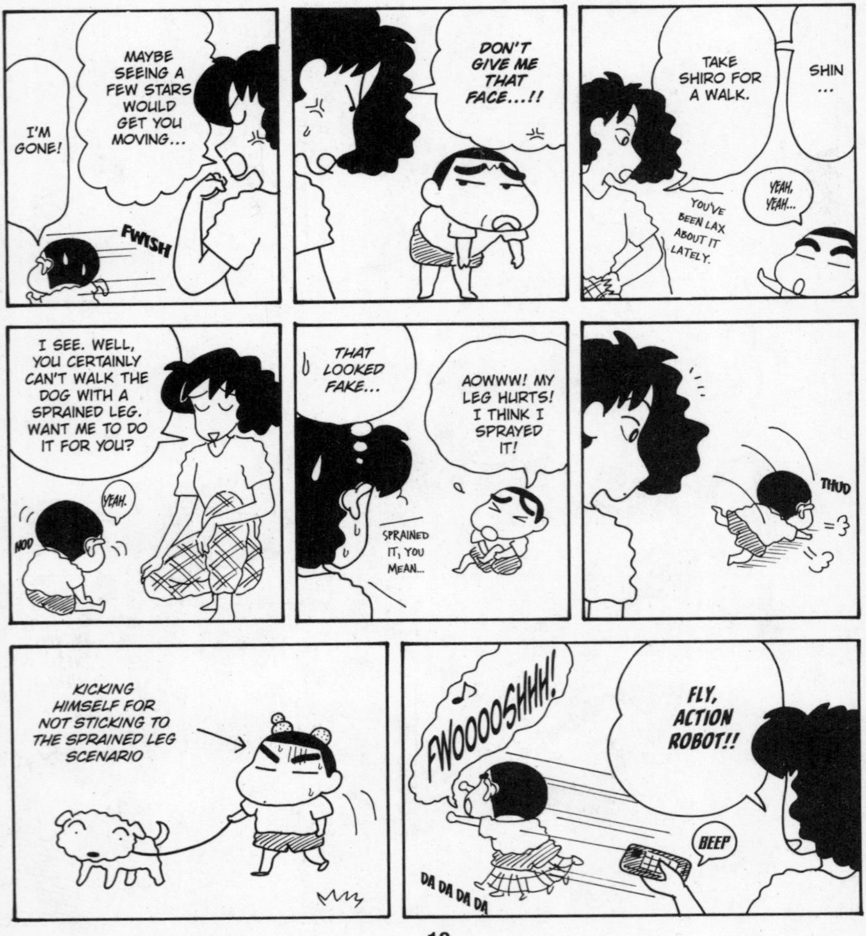
SHIN ...
TAKE SHIRO FOR A WALK.
YOU'VE BEEN LAX ABOUT IT LATELY.
YEAH, YEAH...
DON'T GIVE ME THAT FACE...!!
MAYBE SEEING A FEW STARS WOULD GET YOU MOVING...
I'M GONE!
FWISH
THUD
AOWWW! MY LEG HURTS! I THINK I SPRAYED IT!
THAT LOOKED FAKE...
SPRAINED IT, YOU MEAN...
I SEE. WELL, YOU CERTAINLY CAN'T WALK THE DOG WITH A SPRAINED LEG. WANT ME TO DO IT FOR YOU?
YEAH.
NOD
FLY, ACTION ROBOT!!
FWOOOOSHHH!
BEEP
DA DA DA DA
KICKING HIMSELF FOR NOT STICKING TO THE SPRAINED LEG SCENARIO

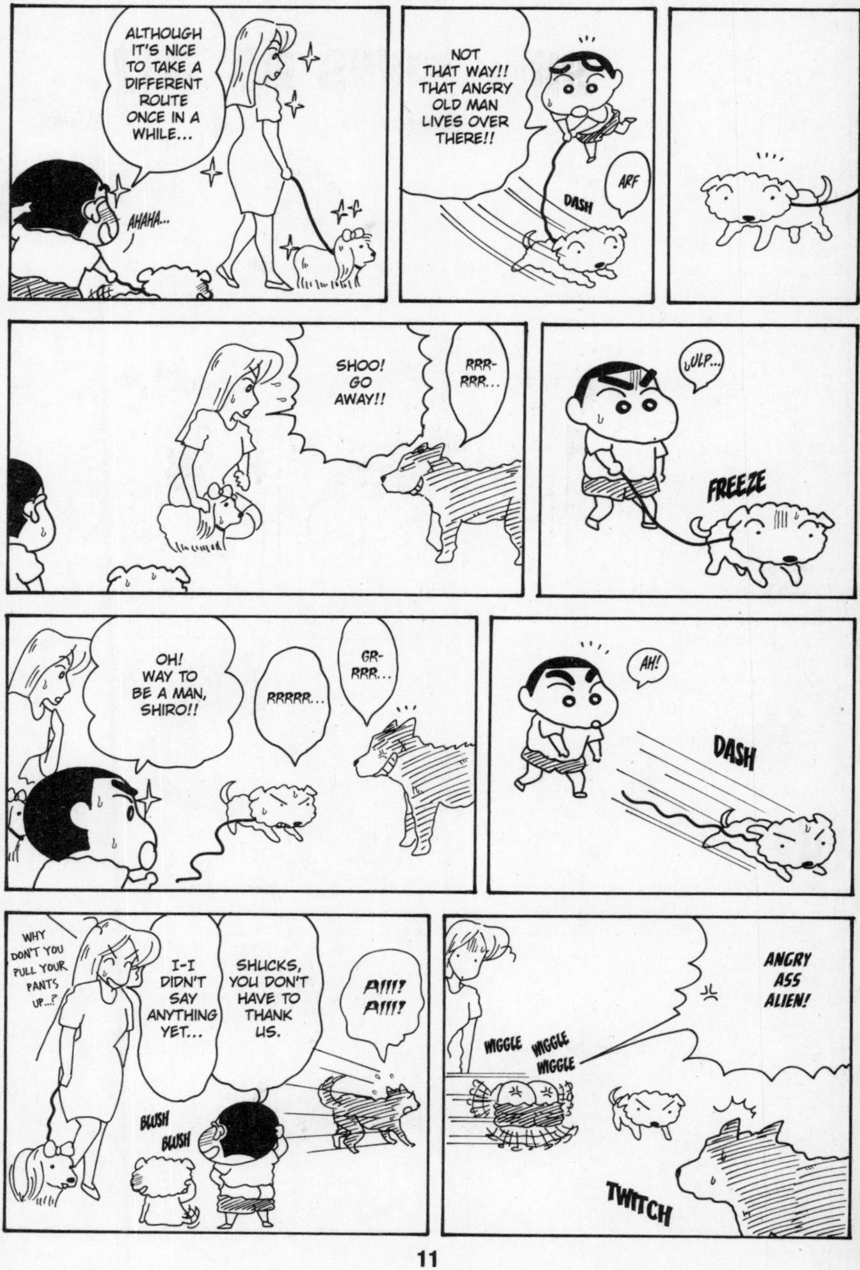
NOT THAT WAY!! THAT ANGRY OLD MAN LIVES OVER THERE!!
ARF
DASH
ALTHOUGH IT'S NICE TO TAKE A DIFFERENT ROUTE ONCE IN A WHILE...
AHAHA...
¿ULP...
FREEZE
RRR-RRR...
SHOO! GO AWAY!!
AH!
DASH
GR-RRR...
RRRRR...
OH! WAY TO BE A MAN, SHIRO!!
ANGRY ASS ALIEN!
WIGGLE
WIGGLE WIGGLE
TWITCH
AIII! AIII!
SHUCKS, YOU DON'T HAVE TO THANK US.
I-I DIDN'T SAY ANYTHING YET...
WHY DON'T YOU PULL YOUR PANTS UP...?
BLUSH
BLUSH

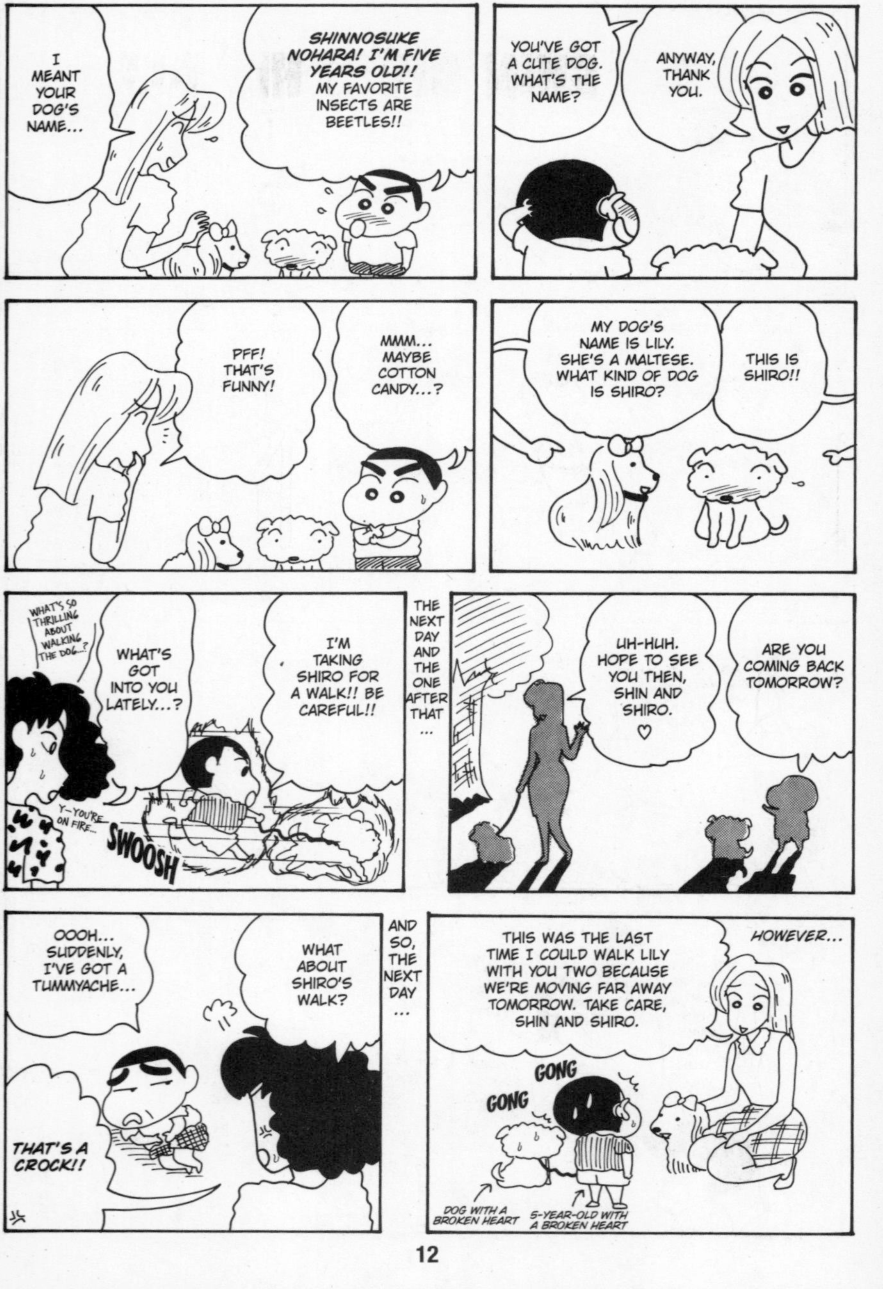
ANYWAY, THANK YOU.
YOU'VE GOT A CUTE DOG. WHAT'S THE NAME?
SHINNOSUKE NOHARA! I'M FIVE YEARS OLD!! MY FAVORITE INSECTS ARE BEETLES!!
I MEANT YOUR DOG'S NAME...
THIS IS SHIRO!!
MY DOG'S NAME IS LILY. SHE'S A MALTESE. WHAT KIND OF DOG IS SHIRO?
MMM... MAYBE COTTON CANDY...?
PFF! THAT'S FUNNY!
THE NEXT DAY AND THE ONE AFTER THAT...
ARE YOU COMING BACK TOMORROW?
UH-HUH. HOPE TO SEE YOU THEN, SHIN AND SHIRO. ♡
I'M TAKING SHIRO FOR A WALK!! BE CAREFUL!!
WHAT'S GOT INTO YOU LATELY...?
WHAT'S SO THRILLING ABOUT WALKING THE DOG...?
Y-YOU'RE ON FIRE...
SWOOSH
AND SO, THE NEXT DAY...
HOWEVER...
THIS WAS THE LAST TIME I COULD WALK LILY WITH YOU TWO BECAUSE WE'RE MOVING FAR AWAY TOMORROW. TAKE CARE, SHIN AND SHIRO.
GONG
GONG
5-YEAR-OLD WITH A BROKEN HEART
DOG WITH A BROKEN HEART
WHAT ABOUT SHIRO'S WALK?
OOOH... SUDDENLY, I'VE GOT A TUMMYACHE...
THAT'S A CROCK!!

SHIN GIVES HIS ALL AND NEVER QUITS!

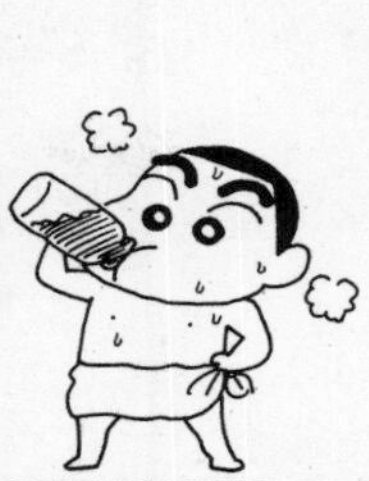

CHAPTER 2

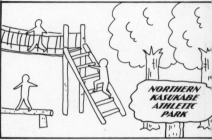

NORTHERN KASUKABE ATHLETIC PARK
OKAY, EVERYONE! TODAY WE'RE REALLY GONNA WORK UP A SWEAT EXERCISING!!
OOOH...
I'D RATHER WORK UP A SWEAT AT A SAUNA!
THEN, AFTER I'M DONE, I'LL GRAB A COLD MILK COFFEE AND...
AHHHH! YEAH, THAT'S THE STUFF!!
G-GO SLOWLY, THOUGH, SO YOU DON'T GET HURT.
IGNORE HIM, IGNORE HIM...
GULP
EVERYONE WHO COMPLETES THE COURSE WILL GET A PRIZE FOR THEIR EFFORT!
OHHH!
PRIZES FOR EFFORT
8 DAY, 7 NIGHT TRIP TO THE U.S.
1 YEAR SUPPLY OF RACE QUEENS WITH CHOCO-BEES.
BE PICKED UP BY ANGELINA JOLIE.
P-PRINCIPAL, SHIN'S LETTING HIS IMAGINATION RUN WILD.
JUST LEAVE HIM BE...

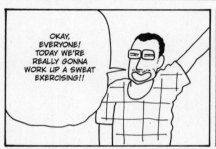

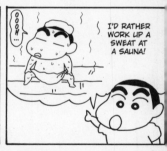

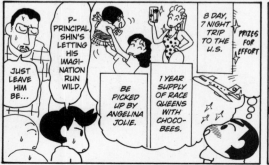

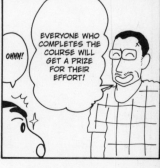

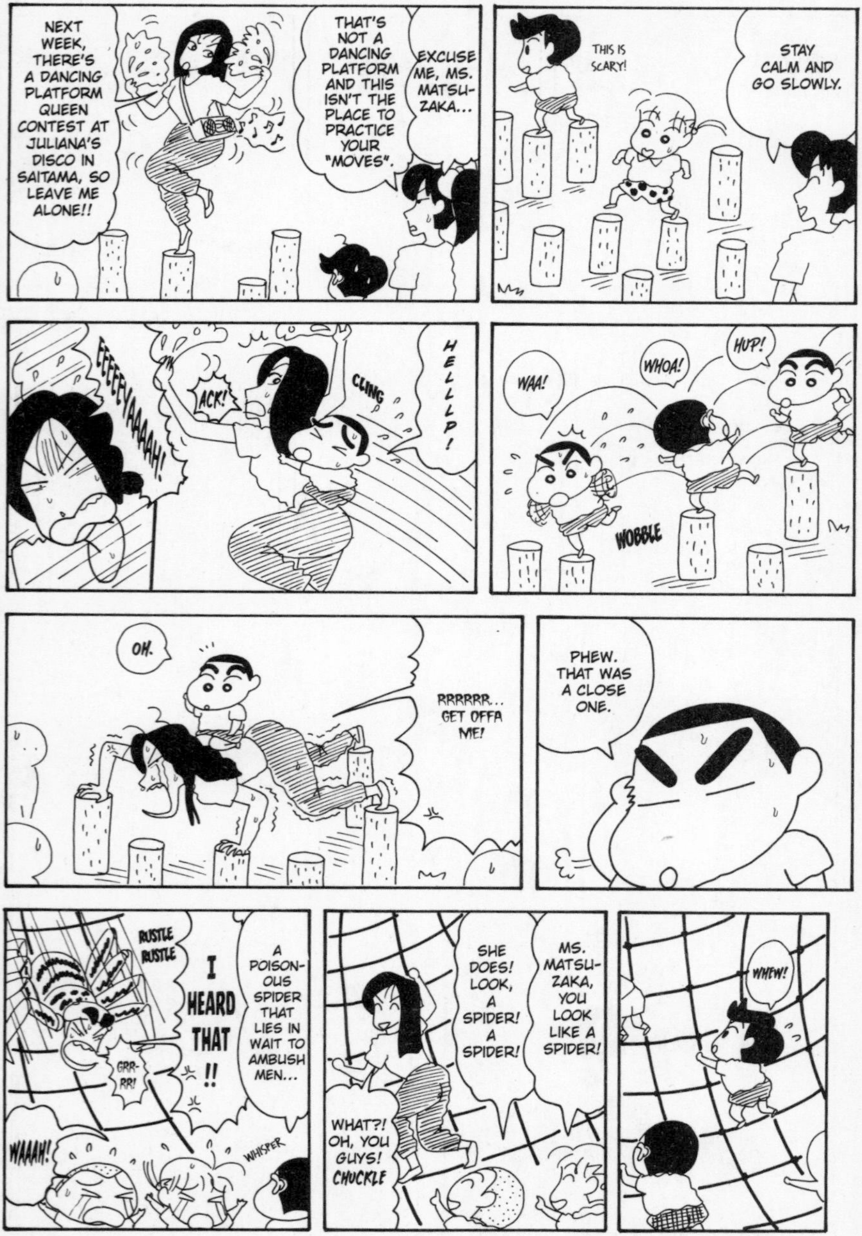
STAY CALM AND GO SLOWLY.
THIS IS SCARY!
EXCUSE ME, MS. MATSU-ZAKA...
THAT'S NOT A DANCING PLATFORM AND THIS ISN'T THE PLACE TO PRACTICE YOUR "MOVES".
NEXT WEEK, THERE'S A DANCING PLATFORM QUEEN CONTEST AT JULIANA'S DISCO IN SAITAMA, SO LEAVE ME ALONE!!
HUP!
WHOA!
WAA!
WOBBLE
HELLLP!
CLING
ACK!
EEEEEYAAAAAH!
PHEW. THAT WAS A CLOSE ONE.
RRRRRR... GET OFFA ME!
OH.
WHEW!
MS. MATSU-ZAKA, YOU LOOK LIKE A SPIDER!
SHE DOES! LOOK, A SPIDER! A SPIDER!
WHAT?! OH, YOU GUYS! CHUCKLE
A POISON-OUS SPIDER THAT LIES IN WAIT TO AMBUSH MEN...
RUSTLE RUSTLE
I HEARD THAT !!
GRR-RR!
WHISPER
WAAAH!

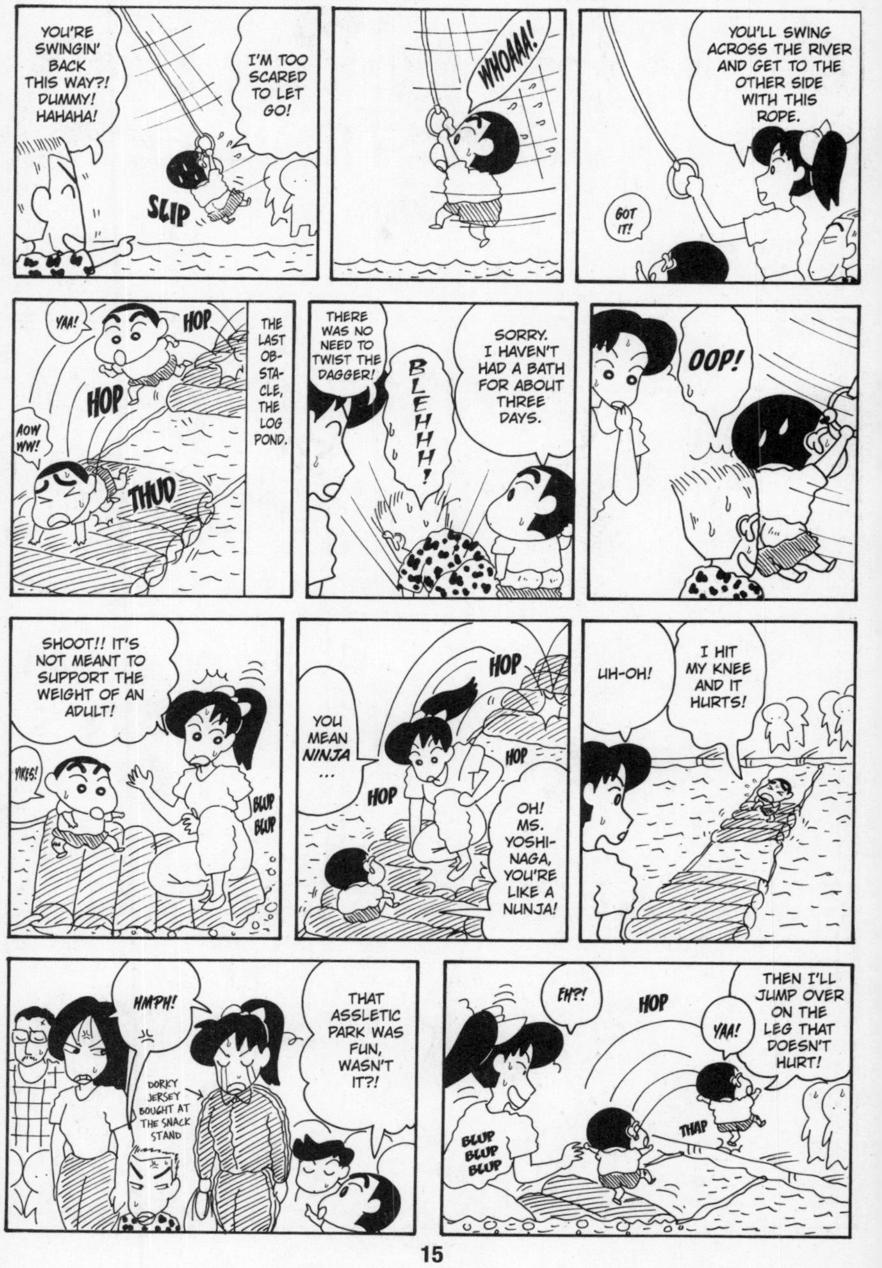
YOU'LL SWING ACROSS THE RIVER AND GET TO THE OTHER SIDE WITH THIS ROPE.
GOT IT!
WHOAAA!
I'M TOO SCARED TO LET GO!
YOU'RE SWINGIN' BACK THIS WAY?! DUMMY! HAHAHA!
SLIP
OOP!
SORRY. I HAVEN'T HAD A BATH FOR ABOUT THREE DAYS.
BLEHHH!
THERE WAS NO NEED TO TWIST THE DAGGER!
THE LAST OB-STA-CLE, THE LOG POND.
HOP
YAA!
HOP
AOWWW!
THUD
I HIT MY KNEE AND IT HURTS!
UH-OH!
HOP
OH! MS. YOSHI-NAGA, YOU'RE LIKE A NUNJA!
HOP
YOU MEAN NINJA ...
HOP
BLUP BLUP
SHOOT!! IT'S NOT MEANT TO SUPPORT THE WEIGHT OF AN ADULT!
YIKES!
THEN I'LL JUMP OVER ON THE LEG THAT DOESN'T HURT!
YAA!
HOP
EH?!
THAP
BLUP BLUP BLUP
THAT ASSLETIC PARK WAS FUN, WASN'T IT?!
HMPH!
DORKY JERSEY BOUGHT AT THE SNACK STAND

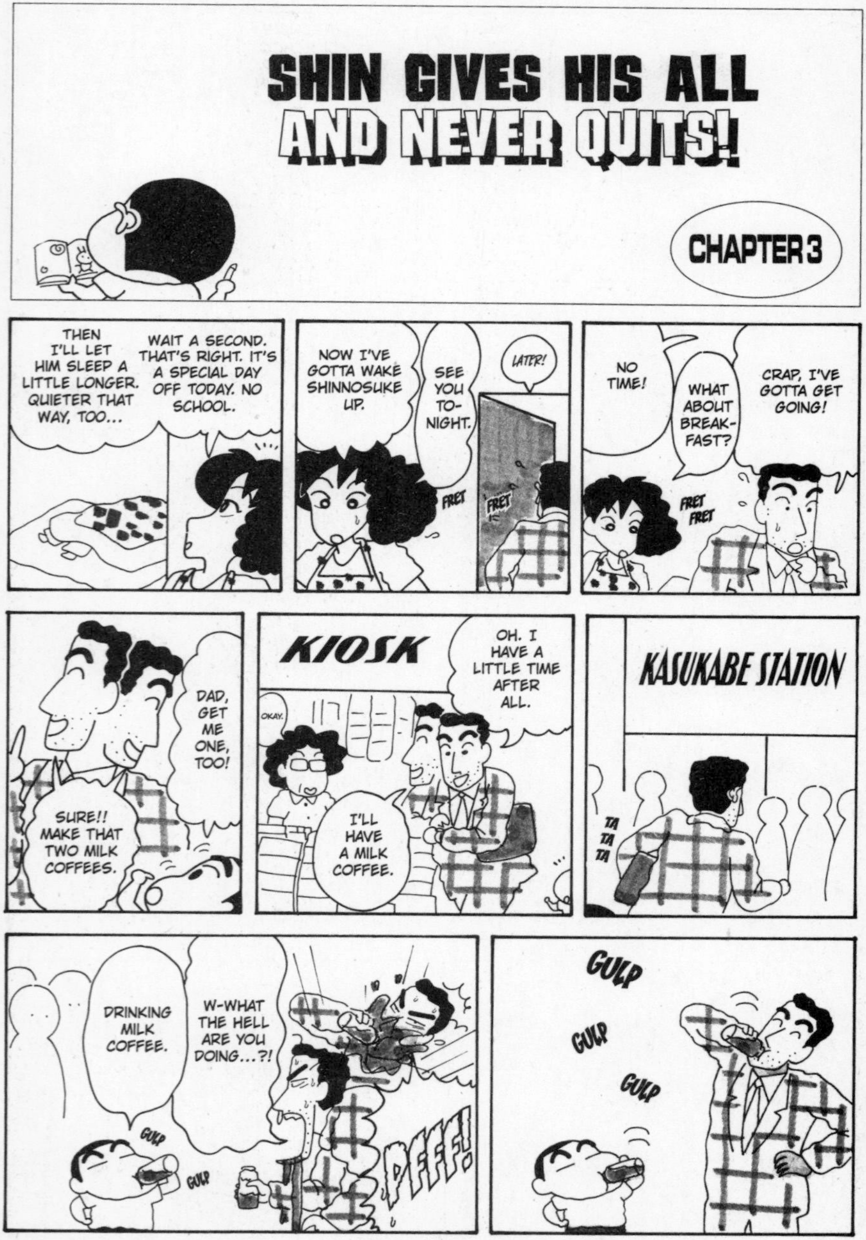
SHIN GIVES HIS ALL AND NEVER QUITS!
CHAPTER 3
CRAP, I'VE GOTTA GET GOING!
WHAT ABOUT BREAK-FAST?
NO TIME!
FRET FRET
LATER!
SEE YOU TO-NIGHT.
NOW I'VE GOTTA WAKE SHINNOSUKE UP.
FRET
FRET
WAIT A SECOND. THAT'S RIGHT. IT'S A SPECIAL DAY OFF TODAY. NO SCHOOL.
THEN I'LL LET HIM SLEEP A LITTLE LONGER. QUIETER THAT WAY, TOO...
KASUKABE STATION
TA TA TA
KIOSK
OH. I HAVE A LITTLE TIME AFTER ALL.
OKAY.
I'LL HAVE A MILK COFFEE.
DAD, GET ME ONE, TOO!
SURE!! MAKE THAT TWO MILK COFFEES.
GULP
GULP
GULP
W-WHAT THE HELL ARE YOU DOING...?!
DRINKING MILK COFFEE.
PFFF!
GULP
GULP

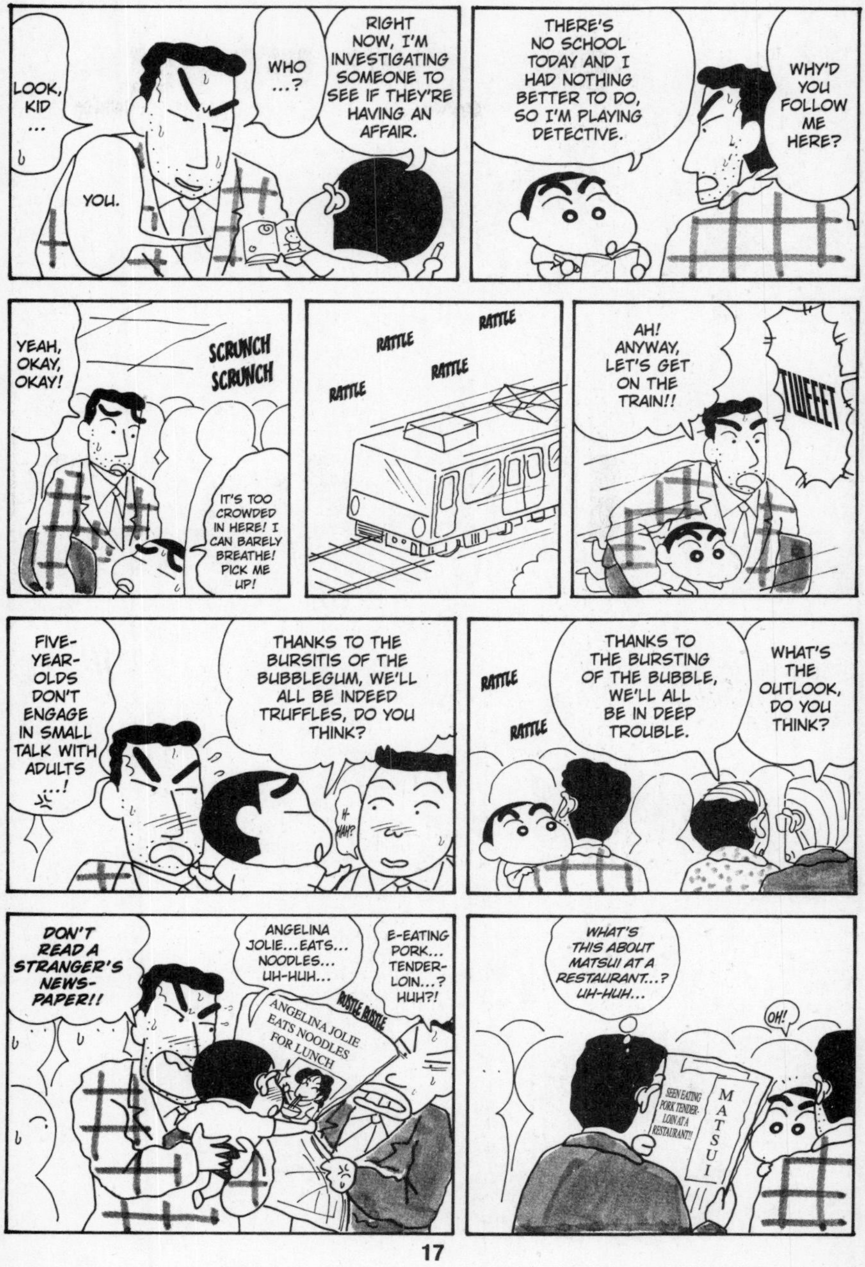
WHY'D YOU FOLLOW ME HERE?
THERE'S NO SCHOOL TODAY AND I HAD NOTHING BETTER TO DO, SO I'M PLAYING DETECTIVE.
RIGHT NOW, I'M INVESTIGATING SOMEONE TO SEE IF THEY'RE HAVING AN AFFAIR.
WHO ...?
LOOK, KID ...
YOU.
TWEEET
AH! ANYWAY, LET'S GET ON THE TRAIN!!
RATTLE
RATTLE
RATTLE
RATTLE
SCRUNCH SCRUNCH
YEAH, OKAY, OKAY!
IT'S TOO CROWDED IN HERE! I CAN BARELY BREATHE! PICK ME UP!
WHAT'S THE OUTLOOK, DO YOU THINK?
THANKS TO THE BURSTING OF THE BUBBLE, WE'LL ALL BE IN DEEP TROUBLE.
RATTLE
RATTLE
THANKS TO THE BURSITIS OF THE BUBBLEGUM, WE'LL ALL BE INDEED TRUFFLES, DO YOU THINK?
H-HAH?
FIVE-YEAR-OLDS DON'T ENGAGE IN SMALL TALK WITH ADULTS ...!
OH!
WHAT'S THIS ABOUT MATSUI AT A RESTAURANT...? UH-HUH...
MATSUI
SEEN EATING PORK TENDER-LOIN AT A RESTAURANT!!
E-EATING PORK... TENDER-LOIN...? HUH?!
RUSTLE RUSTLE
ANGELINA JOLIE...EATS... NOODLES... UH-HUH...
ANGELINA JOLIE EATS NOODLES FOR LUNCH
DON'T READ A STRANGER'S NEWS-PAPER!!

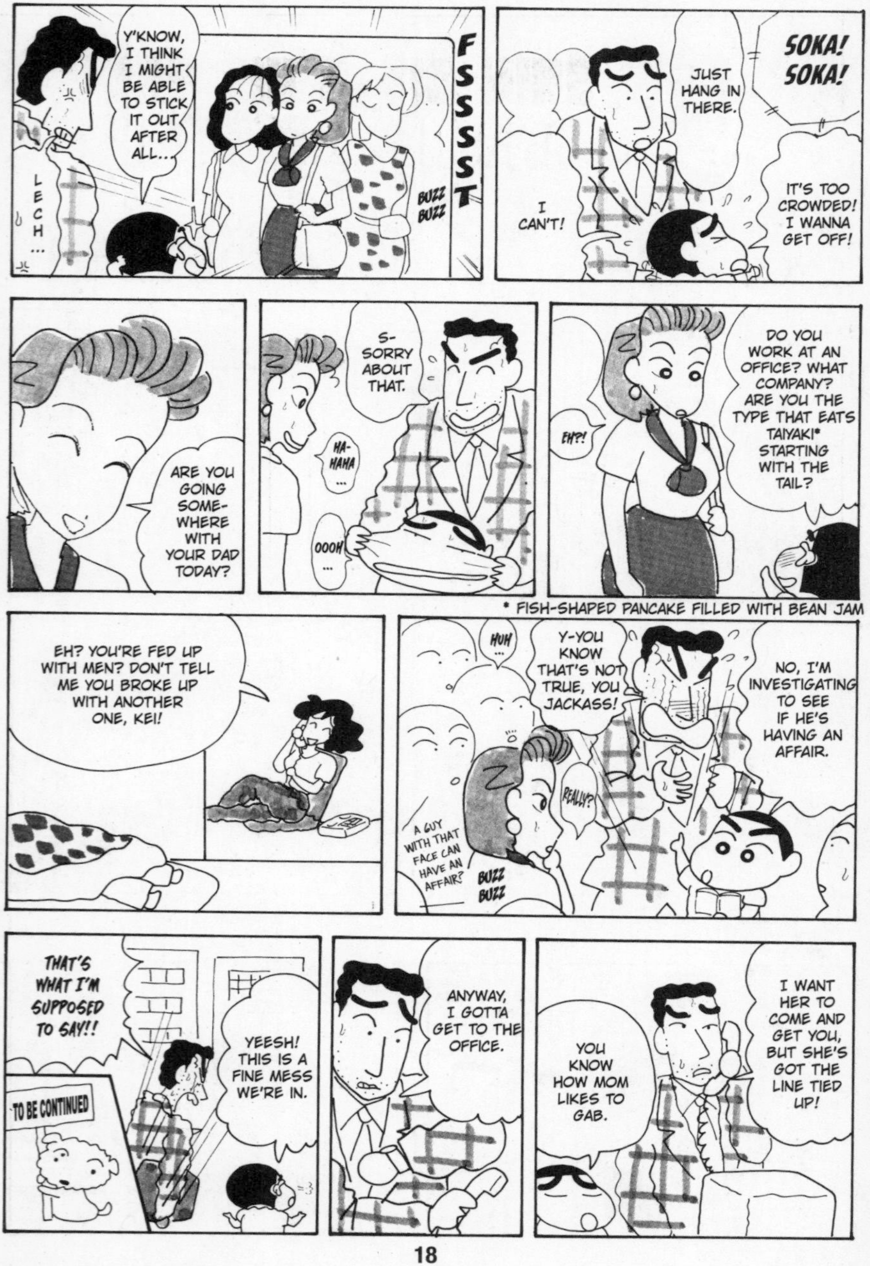
SOKA! SOKA!
JUST HANG IN THERE.
IT'S TOO CROWDED! I WANNA GET OFF!
I CAN'T!
FSSSST
Y'KNOW, I THINK I MIGHT BE ABLE TO STICK IT OUT AFTER ALL...
BUZZ BUZZ
LECH...
DO YOU WORK AT AN OFFICE? WHAT COMPANY? ARE YOU THE TYPE THAT EATS TAIYAKI* STARTING WITH THE TAIL?
EH?!
S-SORRY ABOUT THAT.
HA-HAHA...
OOOH...
ARE YOU GOING SOME-WHERE WITH YOUR DAD TODAY?
NO, I'M INVESTIGATING TO SEE IF HE'S HAVING AN AFFAIR.
Y-YOU KNOW THAT'S NOT TRUE, YOU JACKASS!
HUH...
REALLY?
A GUY WITH THAT FACE CAN HAVE AN AFFAIR?
BUZZ BUZZ
EH? YOU'RE FED UP WITH MEN? DON'T TELL ME YOU BROKE UP WITH ANOTHER ONE, KEI!
I WANT HER TO COME AND GET YOU, BUT SHE'S GOT THE LINE TIED UP!
YOU KNOW HOW MOM LIKES TO GAB.
ANYWAY, I GOTTA GET TO THE OFFICE.
YEESH! THIS IS A FINE MESS WE'RE IN.
THAT'S WHAT I'M SUPPOSED TO SAY!!
TO BE CONTINUED

* FISH-SHAPED PANCAKE FILLED WITH BEAN JAM

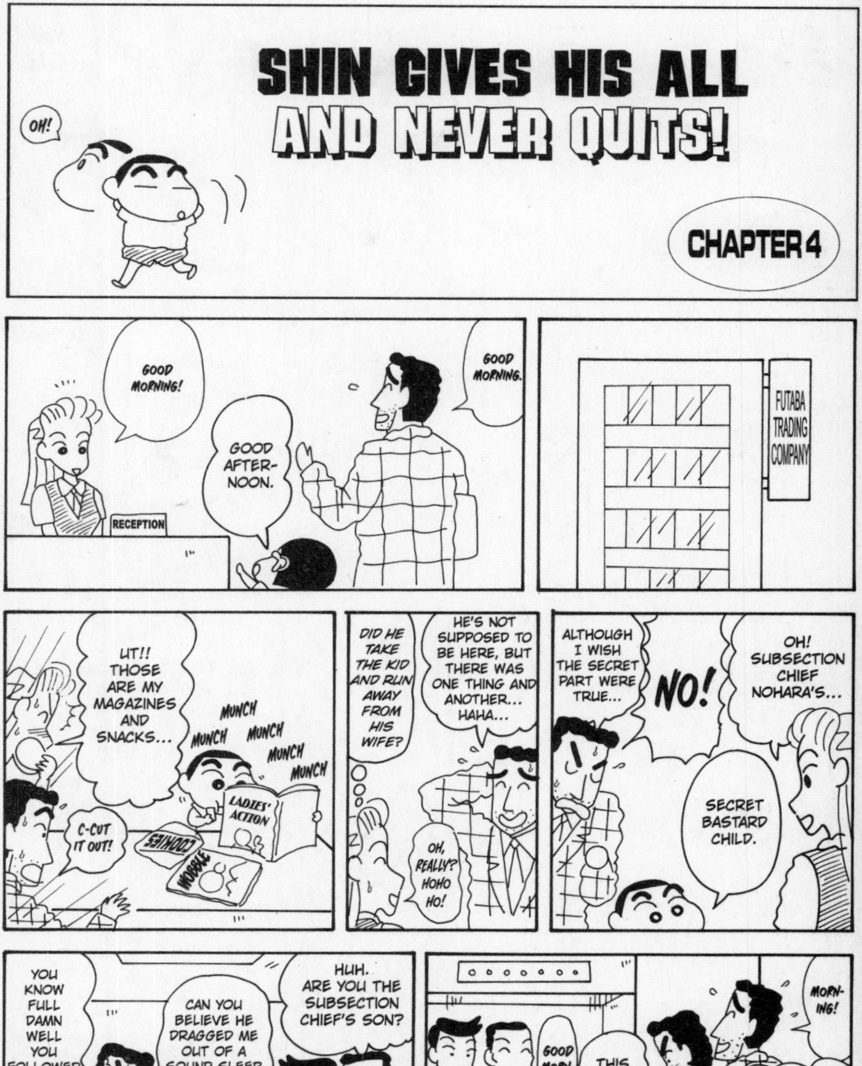
SHIN GIVES HIS ALL AND NEVER QUITS!
OH!
CHAPTER 4
FUTABA TRADING COMPANY
GOOD MORNING.
GOOD MORNING!
GOOD AFTERNOON.
RECEPTION
OH! SUBSECTION CHIEF NOHARA'S...
SECRET BASTARD CHILD.
NO!
ALTHOUGH I WISH THE SECRET PART WERE TRUE...
HE'S NOT SUPPOSED TO BE HERE, BUT THERE WAS ONE THING AND ANOTHER... HAHA...
DID HE TAKE THE KID AND RUN AWAY FROM HIS WIFE?
OH, REALLY? HOHO HO!
UT!! THOSE ARE MY MAGAZINES AND SNACKS...
MUNCH
MUNCH
MUNCH
MUNCH
MUNCH
LADIES' ACTION
COOKIES
WOBBLE
C-CUT IT OUT!
MORN-ING!
YAYYY! FIFTH FLOOR, PLEASE! I WANNA GO TO THE TOY DEPARTMENT!
THIS IS NOT A DEPART-MENT STORE!
GOOD MORN-ING.
HUH. ARE YOU THE SUBSECTION CHIEF'S SON?
CAN YOU BELIEVE HE DRAGGED ME OUT OF A SOUND SLEEP TO COME HERE, FOR CRYIN' OUT LOUD...?
YOU KNOW FULL DAMN WELL YOU FOLLOWED ME!
I SAY "FOR CRYIN' OUT LOUD"!!

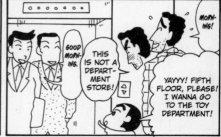

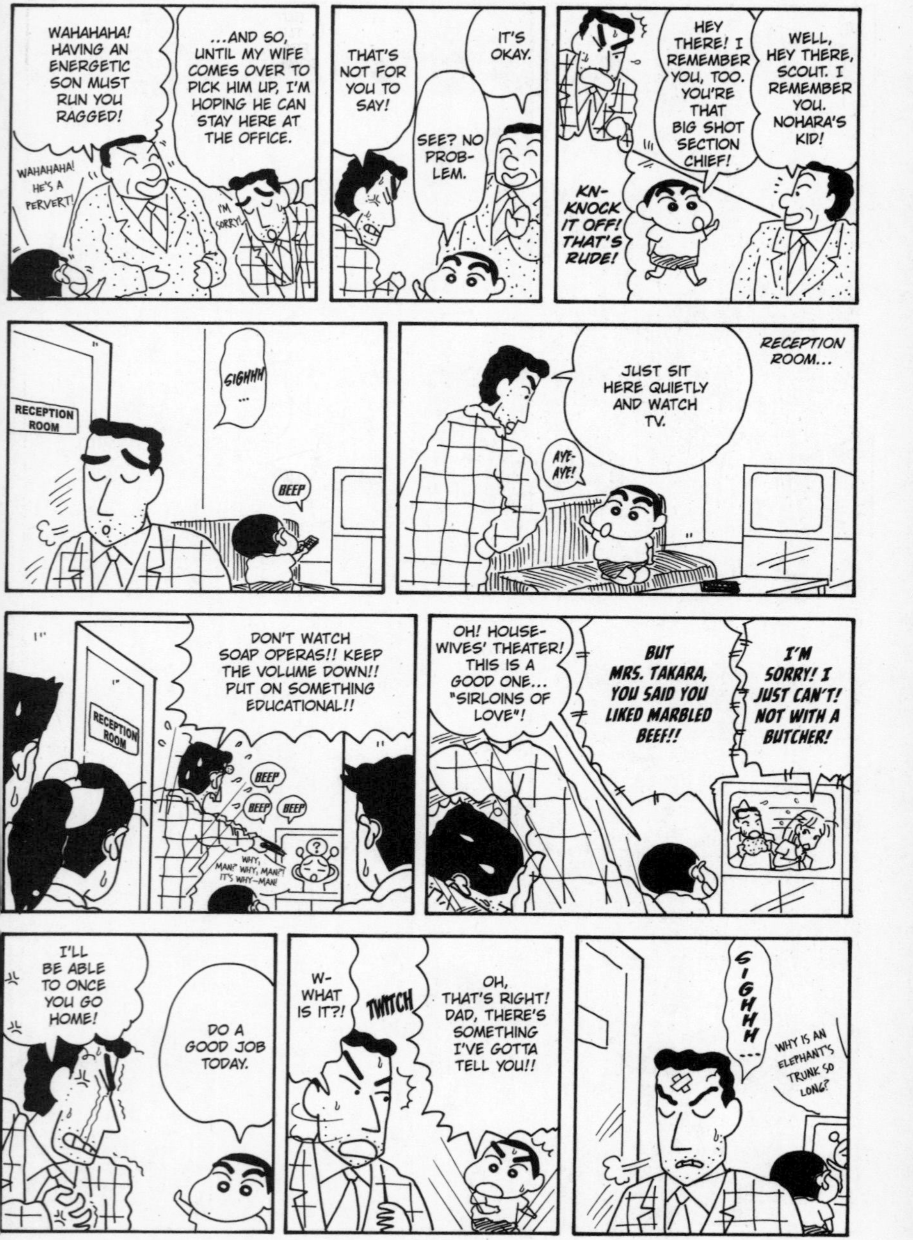
WELL, HEY THERE, SCOUT. I REMEMBER YOU. NOHARA'S KID!
HEY THERE! I REMEMBER YOU, TOO. YOU'RE THAT BIG SHOT SECTION CHIEF!
KN-KNOCK IT OFF! THAT'S RUDE!
IT'S OKAY.
SEE? NO PROB-LEM.
THAT'S NOT FOR YOU TO SAY!
...AND SO, UNTIL MY WIFE COMES OVER TO PICK HIM UP, I'M HOPING HE CAN STAY HERE AT THE OFFICE.
WAHAHAHA! HAVING AN ENERGETIC SON MUST RUN YOU RAGGED!
I'M SORRY!
WAHAHAHA! HE'S A PERVERT!
RECEPTION ROOM...
JUST SIT HERE QUIETLY AND WATCH TV.
AYE-AYE!
SIGHHH ...
RECEPTION ROOM
BEEP
I'M SORRY! I JUST CAN'T! NOT WITH A BUTCHER!
BUT MRS. TAKARA, YOU SAID YOU LIKED MARBLED BEEF!!
OH! HOUSE-WIVES' THEATER! THIS IS A GOOD ONE... "SIRLOINS OF LOVE"!
DON'T WATCH SOAP OPERAS!! KEEP THE VOLUME DOWN!! PUT ON SOMETHING EDUCATIONAL!!
RECEPTION ROOM
BEEP
BEEP
BEEP
WHY, MAN? WHY, MAN?! IT'S WHY-MAN!
SIGHHH ...
WHY IS AN ELEPHANT'S TRUNK SO LONG?
OH, THAT'S RIGHT! DAD, THERE'S SOMETHING I'VE GOTTA TELL YOU!!
TWITCH
W-WHAT IS IT?!
DO A GOOD JOB TODAY.
I'LL BE ABLE TO ONCE YOU GO HOME!

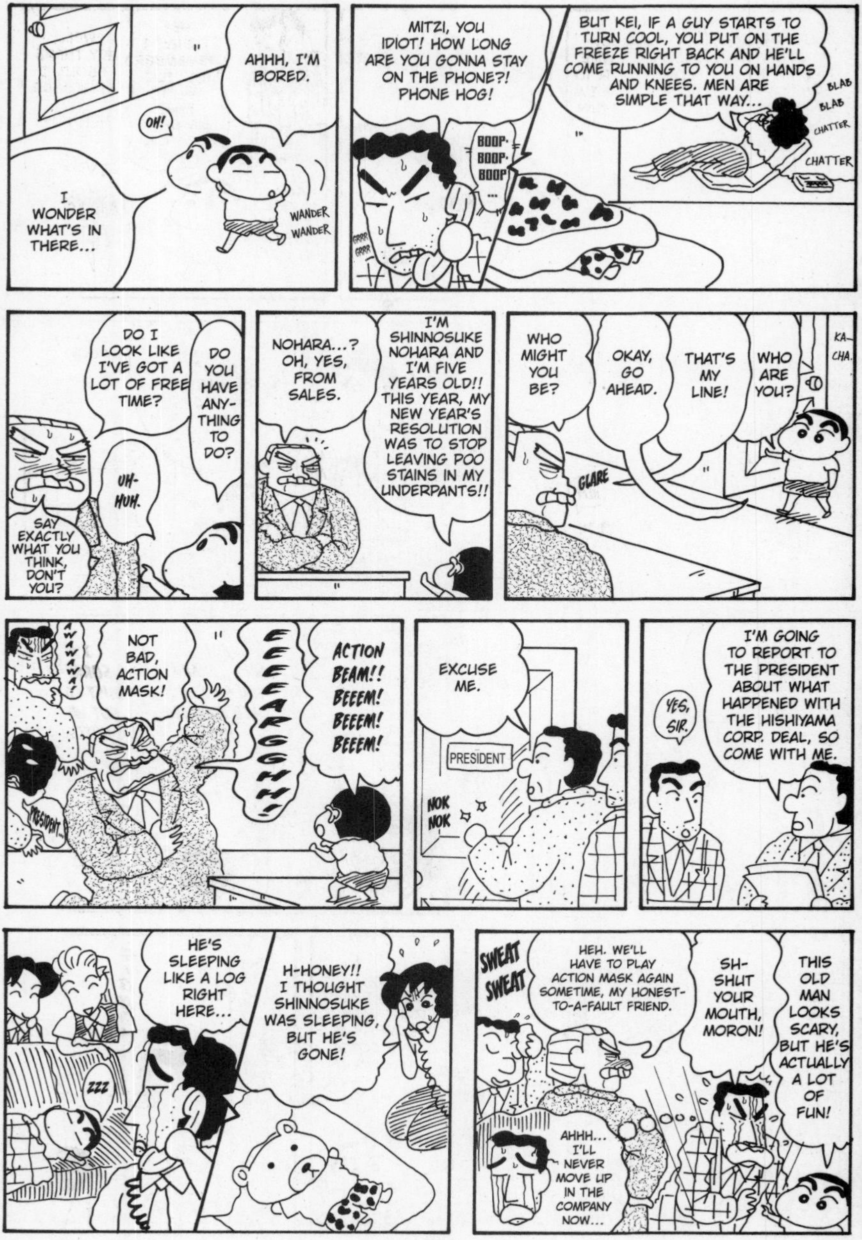
BUT KEI, IF A GUY STARTS TO TURN COOL, YOU PUT ON THE FREEZE RIGHT BACK AND HE'LL COME RUNNING TO YOU ON HANDS AND KNEES. MEN ARE SIMPLE THAT WAY...
BLAB
BLAB
CHATTER
CHATTER
MITZI, YOU IDIOT! HOW LONG ARE YOU GONNA STAY ON THE PHONE?! PHONE HOG!
BOOP-BOOP-BOOP...
GRRR GRRR
AHHH, I'M BORED.
OH!
WANDER WANDER
I WONDER WHAT'S IN THERE...
KA-CHA.
WHO ARE YOU?
THAT'S MY LINE!
OKAY, GO AHEAD.
WHO MIGHT YOU BE?
GLARE
I'M SHINNOSUKE NOHARA AND I'M FIVE YEARS OLD!! THIS YEAR, MY NEW YEAR'S RESOLUTION WAS TO STOP LEAVING POO STAINS IN MY UNDERPANTS!!
NOHARA...? OH, YES, FROM SALES.
DO YOU HAVE ANYTHING TO DO?
DO I LOOK LIKE I'VE GOT A LOT OF FREE TIME?
UH-HUH.
SAY EXACTLY WHAT YOU THINK, DON'T YOU?
I'M GOING TO REPORT TO THE PRESIDENT ABOUT WHAT HAPPENED WITH THE HISHIYAMA CORP. DEAL, SO COME WITH ME.
YES, SIR.
EXCUSE ME.
PRESIDENT
NOK NOK
ACTION BEAM!! BEEEM! BEEEM! BEEEM!
EEEEARGGHH!
NOT BAD, ACTION MASK!
AWAWAWA!
PRESIDENT...
THIS OLD MAN LOOKS SCARY, BUT HE'S ACTUALLY A LOT OF FUN!
SH-SHUT YOUR MOUTH, MORON!
HEH. WE'LL HAVE TO PLAY ACTION MASK AGAIN SOMETIME, MY HONEST-TO-A-FAULT FRIEND.
SWEAT SWEAT
AHHH... I'LL NEVER MOVE UP IN THE COMPANY NOW...
H-HONEY!! I THOUGHT SHINNOSUKE WAS SLEEPING, BUT HE'S GONE!
HE'S SLEEPING LIKE A LOG RIGHT HERE...
ZZZ

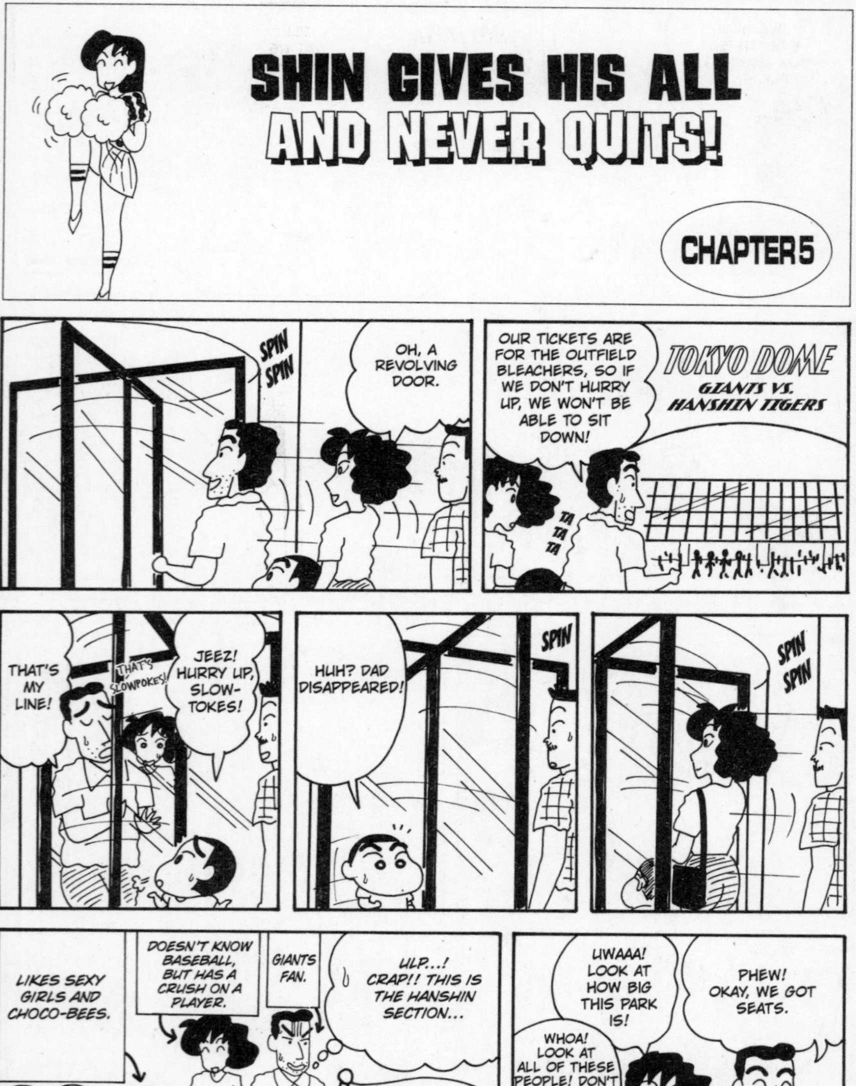
SHIN GIVES HIS ALL AND NEVER QUITS!
CHAPTER 5
TOKYO DOME
GIANTS VS. HANSHIN TIGERS
OUR TICKETS ARE FOR THE OUTFIELD BLEACHERS, SO IF WE DON'T HURRY UP, WE WON'T BE ABLE TO SIT DOWN!
TA TA TA
OH, A REVOLVING DOOR.
SPIN SPIN
SPIN SPIN
SPIN
HUH? DAD DISAPPEARED!
JEEZ! HURRY UP, SLOW-TOKES!
THAT'S SLOWPOKES!
THAT'S MY LINE!
PHEW! OKAY, WE GOT SEATS.
UWAAA! LOOK AT HOW BIG THIS PARK IS!
WHOA! LOOK AT ALL OF THESE PEOPLE! DON'T THEY HAVE ANYTHING BETTER TO DO?
ULP...! CRAP!! THIS IS THE HANSHIN SECTION...
GIANTS FAN.
DOESN'T KNOW BASEBALL, BUT HAS A CRUSH ON A PLAYER.
LIKES SEXY GIRLS AND CHOCO-BEES.
Tigers
TIGER POWER

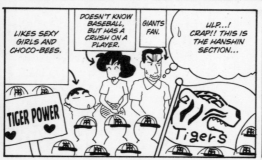

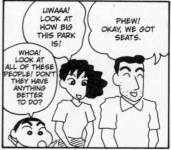

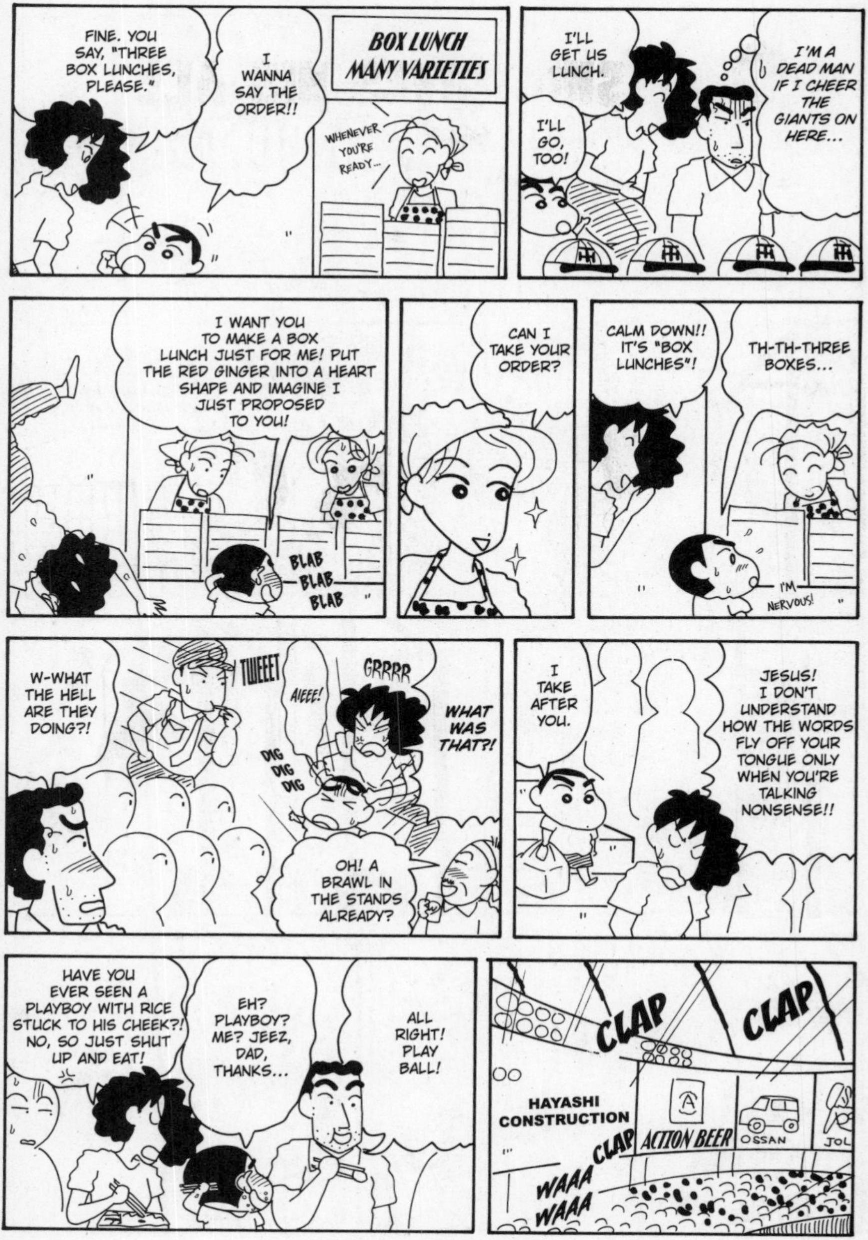
I'M A DEAD MAN IF I CHEER THE GIANTS ON HERE...
I'LL GET US LUNCH.
I'LL GO, TOO!
BOX LUNCH
MANY VARIETIES
I WANNA SAY THE ORDER!!
FINE. YOU SAY, "THREE BOX LUNCHES, PLEASE."
WHENEVER YOU'RE READY...
TH-TH-THREE BOXES...
CALM DOWN!! IT'S "BOX LUNCHES"!
I'M NERVOUS!
CAN I TAKE YOUR ORDER?
I WANT YOU TO MAKE A BOX LUNCH JUST FOR ME! PUT THE RED GINGER INTO A HEART SHAPE AND IMAGINE I JUST PROPOSED TO YOU!
BLAB BLAB BLAB
JESUS! I DON'T UNDERSTAND HOW THE WORDS FLY OFF YOUR TONGUE ONLY WHEN YOU'RE TALKING NONSENSE!!
I TAKE AFTER YOU.
WHAT WAS THAT?!
GRRRR
AIEEE!
TWEEET
W-WHAT THE HELL ARE THEY DOING?!
DIG DIG DIG
OH! A BRAWL IN THE STANDS ALREADY?
CLAP
CLAP
HAYASHI CONSTRUCTION
ACTION BEER
OSSAN
CLAP
WAAA WAAA
ALL RIGHT! PLAY BALL!
EH? PLAYBOY? ME? JEEZ, DAD, THANKS...
HAVE YOU EVER SEEN A PLAYBOY WITH RICE STUCK TO HIS CHEEK?! NO, SO JUST SHUT UP AND EAT!

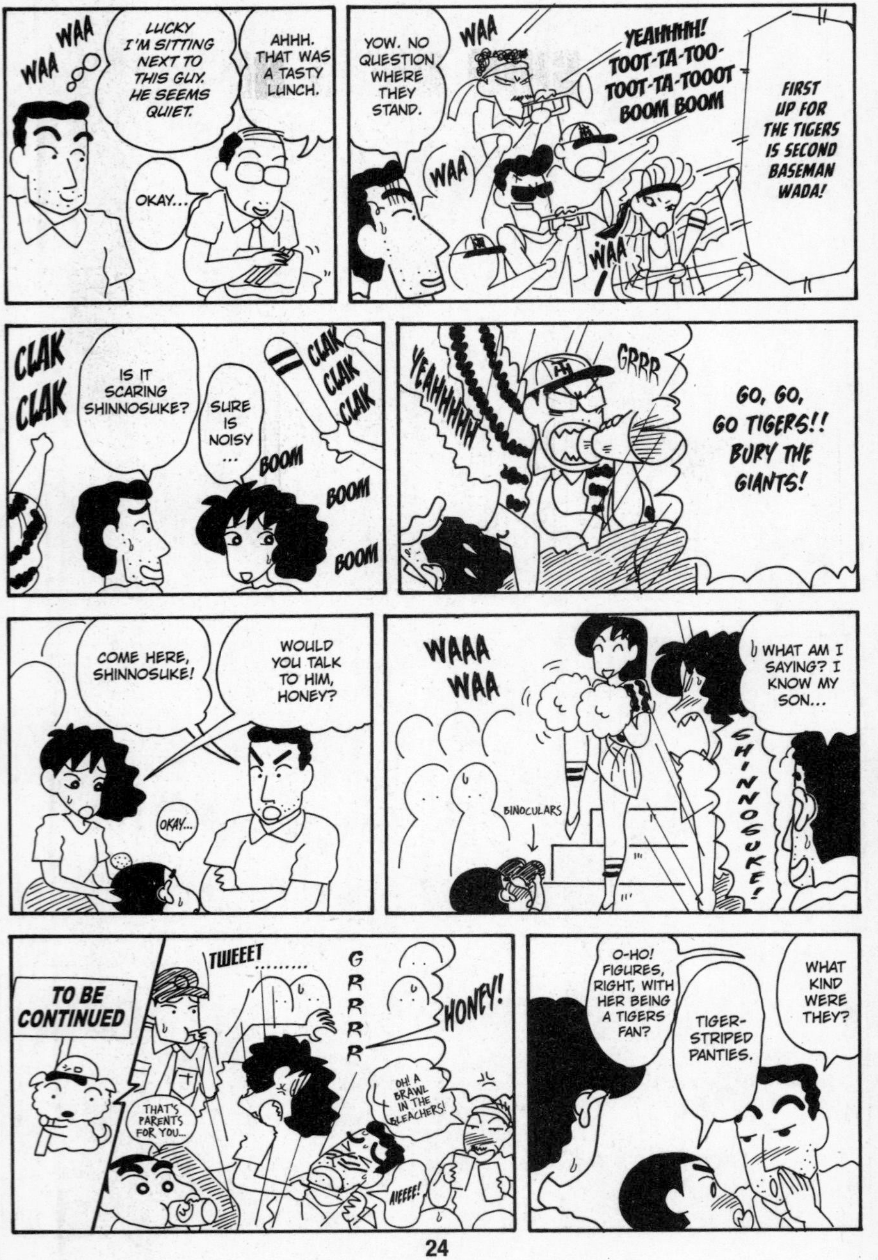
FIRST UP FOR THE TIGERS IS SECOND BASEMAN WADA!
YEAHHHH! TOOT-TA-TOO-TOOT-TA-TOOOT BOOM BOOM
WAA
YOW. NO QUESTION WHERE THEY STAND.
WAA
WAA
AHHH. THAT WAS A TASTY LUNCH.
LUCKY I'M SITTING NEXT TO THIS GUY. HE SEEMS QUIET.
WAA WAA
OKAY...
GO, GO, GO TIGERS!! BURY THE GIANTS!
GRRR
YEAHHHHH
CLAK CLAK CLAK
SURE IS NOISY ...
IS IT SCARING SHINNOSUKE?
CLAK CLAK
BOOM
BOOM
BOOM
WHAT AM I SAYING? I KNOW MY SON...
SHINNOSUKE!
WAAA WAA
BINOCULARS
WOULD YOU TALK TO HIM, HONEY?
COME HERE, SHINNOSUKE!
OKAY...
WHAT KIND WERE THEY?
O-HO! FIGURES, RIGHT, WITH HER BEING A TIGERS FAN?
TIGER-STRIPED PANTIES.
HONEY!
GRRRR
TWEEET ....
OH! A BRAWL IN THE BLEACHERS!
AIEEEE!
TO BE CONTINUED
THAT'S PARENTS FOR YOU...

BOXING

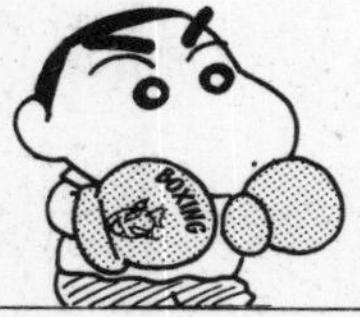

SHIN GIVES HIS ALL AND NEVER QUITS!

CHAPTER 6

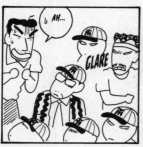

KRAKKK
YESSS!
CHOOF
AH...
GLARE
YOU GIANTS OUTFIELDER MORON! WHY'D YOU HAVE TO CATCH THE BALL?! NEXT TIME, YOU BETTER DROP IT OR I'M COMIN' OUT THERE! GIANTS SUCK!
THAT'S GOING A LITTLE TOO FAR...
OH, LOOK! A GIANT TV!
YEP. IT SHOWS PEOPLE IN THE STANDS.
FLASH
HEY, LOOK! WE'RE ON THE SCREEN!
OH, NO!
OH!
YEP, THAT'S ME ALL RIGHT!
PULL UP YOUR PANTS, IDIOT!!
DUN
HAH HAH

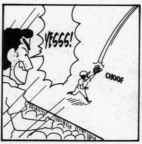

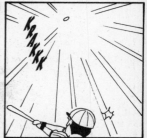

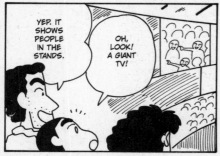

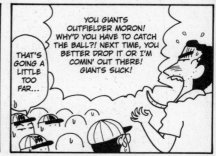

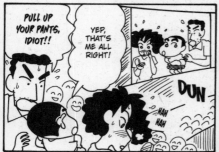

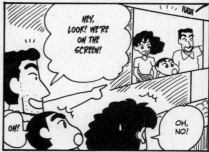

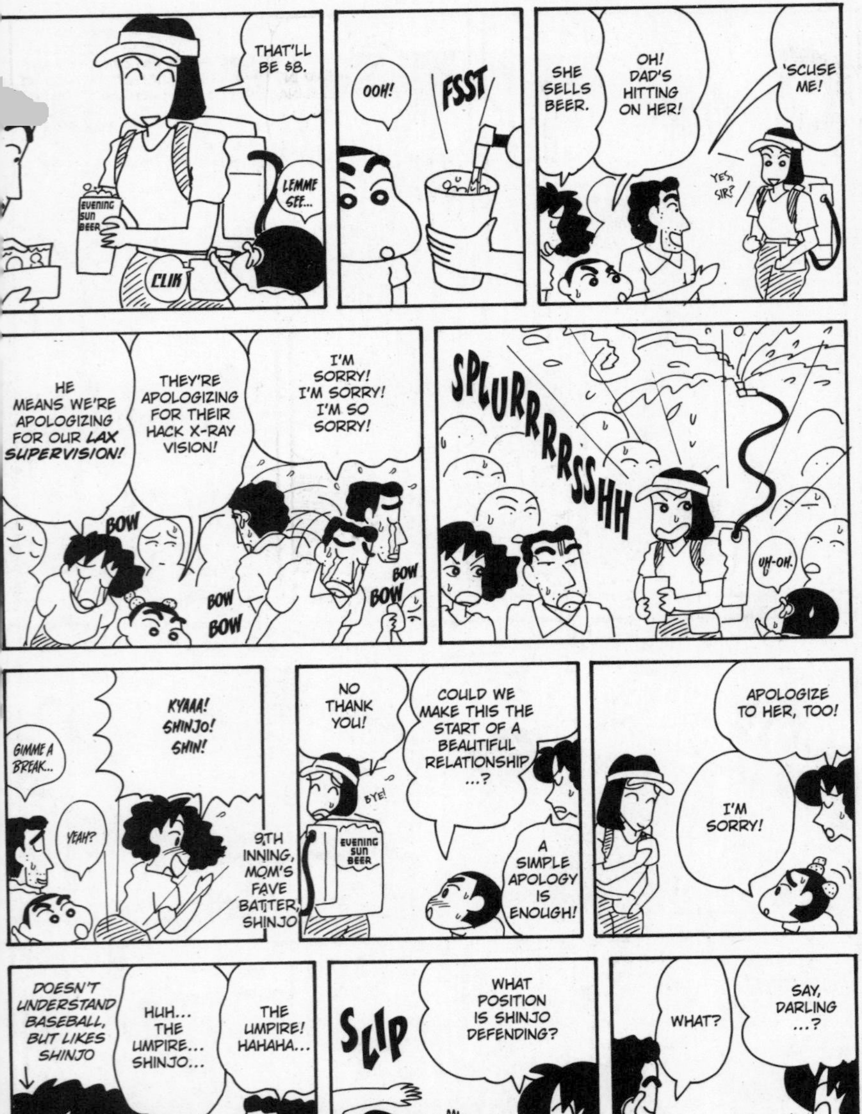
'SCUSE ME!
YES, SIR?
OH! DAD'S HITTING ON HER!
SHE SELLS BEER.
FSST
OOH!
THAT'LL BE $8.
LEMME SEE...
EVENING SUN BEER
CLIK
SPLURRRRRSSHH
UH-OH.
I'M SORRY! I'M SORRY! I'M SO SORRY!
THEY'RE APOLOGIZING FOR THEIR HACK X-RAY VISION!
HE MEANS WE'RE APOLOGIZING FOR OUR LAX SUPERVISION!
BOW
BOW
BOW
BOW
BOW
APOLOGIZE TO HER, TOO!
I'M SORRY!
COULD WE MAKE THIS THE START OF A BEAUTIFUL RELATIONSHIP ...?
NO THANK YOU!
BYE!
EVENING SUN BEER
A SIMPLE APOLOGY IS ENOUGH!
KYAAA! SHINJO! SHIN!
GIMME A BREAK...
YEAH?
9TH INNING, MOM'S FAVE BATTER, SHINJO
SAY, DARLING ...?
WHAT?
WHAT POSITION IS SHINJO DEFENDING?
SLIP
DEPENDING?
THE UMPIRE! HAHAHA...
HUH... THE UMPIRE... SHINJO...
DOESN'T UNDERSTAND BASEBALL, BUT LIKES SHINJO
VAMPIRE?

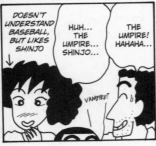

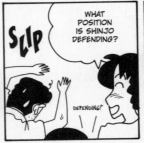

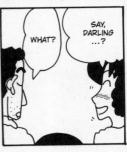

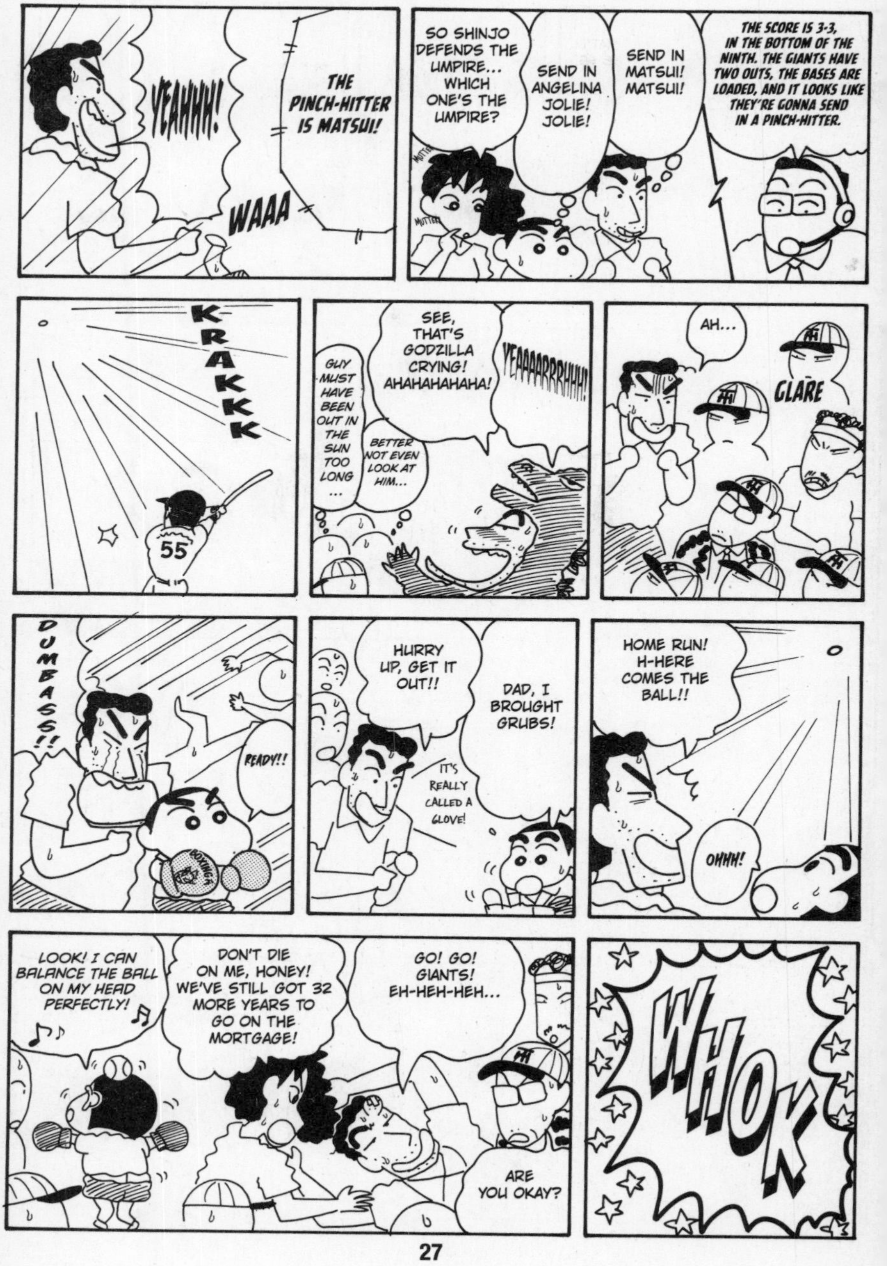
THE SCORE IS 3-3, IN THE BOTTOM OF THE NINTH. THE GIANTS HAVE TWO OUTS, THE BASES ARE LOADED, AND IT LOOKS LIKE THEY'RE GONNA SEND IN A PINCH-HITTER.
SEND IN MATSUI! MATSUI!
SEND IN ANGELINA JOLIE! JOLIE!
SO SHINJO DEFENDS THE UMPIRE... WHICH ONE'S THE UMPIRE?
MUTTER
MUTTER
THE PINCH-HITTER IS MATSUI!
YEAHHH!
WAAA
AH...
GLARE
YEAAAARRRHHH!
SEE, THAT'S GODZILLA CRYING! AHAHAHAHAHA!
GUY MUST HAVE BEEN OUT IN THE SUN TOO LONG...
BETTER NOT EVEN LOOK AT HIM...
KRAKKK
HOME RUN! H-HERE COMES THE BALL!!
OHHH!
HURRY UP, GET IT OUT!!
DAD, I BROUGHT GRUBS!
IT'S REALLY CALLED A GLOVE!
DUMBASS!!
READY!!
WHOK
GO! GO! GIANTS! EH-HEH-HEH...
ARE YOU OKAY?
DON'T DIE ON ME, HONEY! WE'VE STILL GOT 32 MORE YEARS TO GO ON THE MORTGAGE!
LOOK! I CAN BALANCE THE BALL ON MY HEAD PERFECTLY!

SHIN GIVES HIS ALL AND NEVER QUITS!

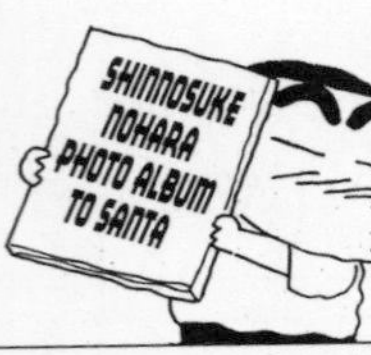

SHINNOSUKE NOHARA PHOTO ALBUM TO SANTA

CHAPTER 7

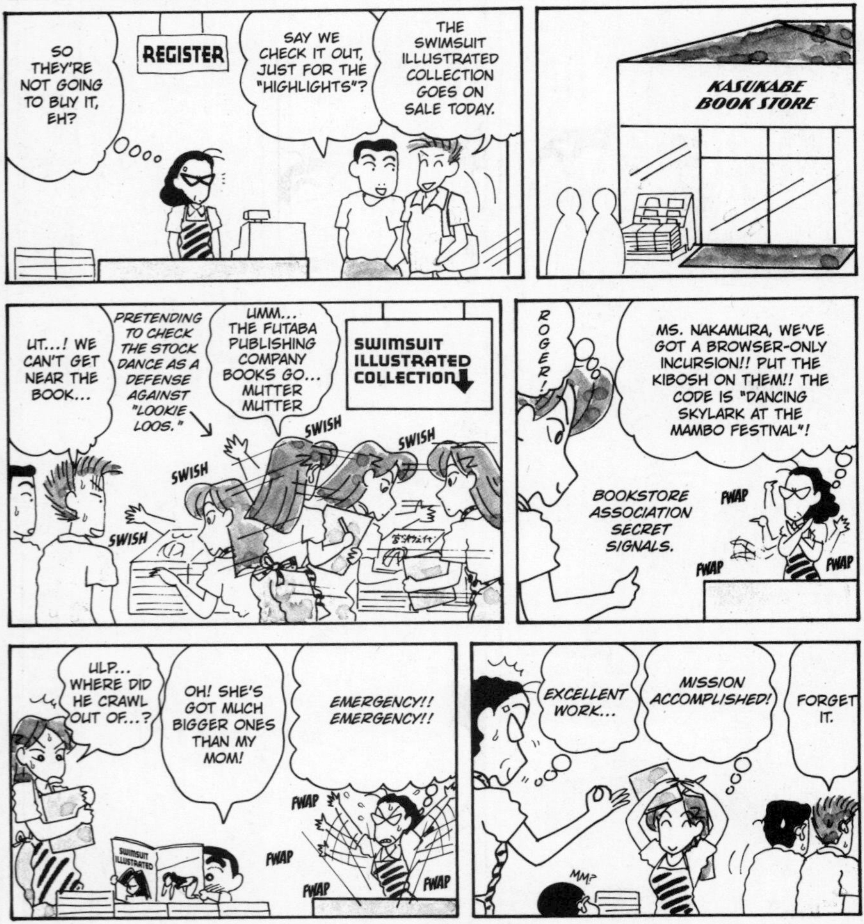

KASUKABE BOOK STORE
THE SWIMSUIT ILLUSTRATED COLLECTION GOES ON SALE TODAY.
SAY WE CHECK IT OUT, JUST FOR THE "HIGHLIGHTS"?
REGISTER
SO THEY'RE NOT GOING TO BUY IT, EH?
ROGER!
MS. NAKAMURA, WE'VE GOT A BROWSER-ONLY INCURSION!! PUT THE KIBOSH ON THEM!! THE CODE IS "DANCING SKYLARK AT THE MAMBO FESTIVAL"!
FWAP
BOOKSTORE ASSOCIATION SECRET SIGNALS.
FWAP
FWAP
SWIMSUIT ILLUSTRATED COLLECTION
UMM... THE FUTABA PUBLISHING COMPANY BOOKS GO... MUTTER MUTTER
PRETENDING TO CHECK THE STOCK DANCE AS A DEFENSE AGAINST "LOOKIE LOOS."
UT...! WE CAN'T GET NEAR THE BOOK...
SWISH
SWISH
SWISH
SWISH
FORGET IT.
MISSION ACCOMPLISHED!
EXCELLENT WORK...
MMP
EMERGENCY!! EMERGENCY!!
OH! SHE'S GOT MUCH BIGGER ONES THAN MY MOM!
ULP... WHERE DID HE CRAWL OUT OF...?
FWAP
FWAP
FWAP
FWAP
SWIMSUIT ILLUSTRATED

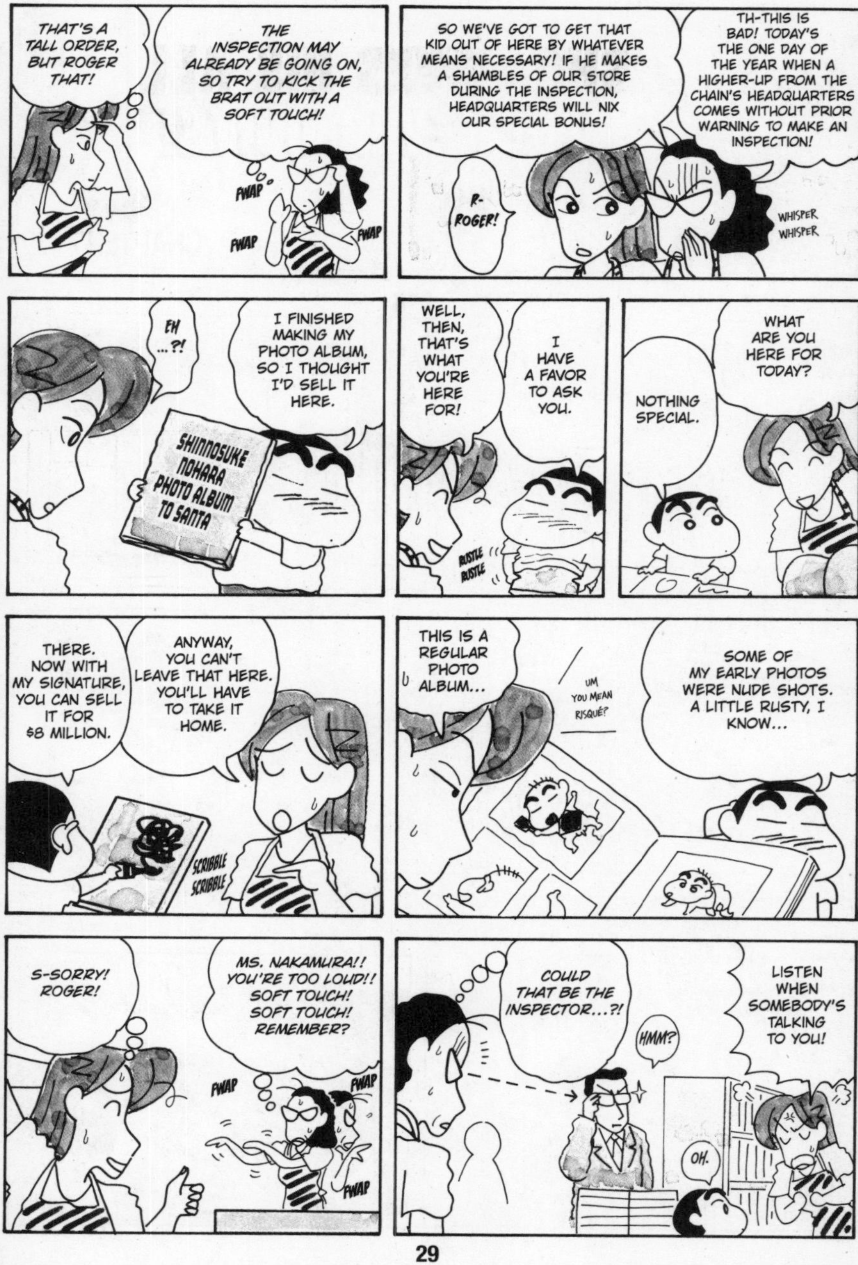
TH-THIS IS BAD! TODAY'S THE ONE DAY OF THE YEAR WHEN A HIGHER-UP FROM THE CHAIN'S HEADQUARTERS COMES WITHOUT PRIOR WARNING TO MAKE AN INSPECTION!
SO WE'VE GOT TO GET THAT KID OUT OF HERE BY WHATEVER MEANS NECESSARY! IF HE MAKES A SHAMBLES OF OUR STORE DURING THE INSPECTION, HEADQUARTERS WILL NIX OUR SPECIAL BONUS!
WHISPER WHISPER
R-ROGER!
THE INSPECTION MAY ALREADY BE GOING ON, SO TRY TO KICK THE BRAT OUT WITH A SOFT TOUCH!
THAT'S A TALL ORDER, BUT ROGER THAT!
FWAP
FWAP
FWAP
WHAT ARE YOU HERE FOR TODAY?
NOTHING SPECIAL.
I HAVE A FAVOR TO ASK YOU.
WELL, THEN, THAT'S WHAT YOU'RE HERE FOR!
BUSTLE BUSTLE
I FINISHED MAKING MY PHOTO ALBUM, SO I THOUGHT I'D SELL IT HERE.
EH ...?!
SHINNOSUKE NOHARA PHOTO ALBUM TO SANTA
SOME OF MY EARLY PHOTOS WERE NUDE SHOTS. A LITTLE RUSTY, I KNOW...
UM YOU MEAN RISQUÉ?
THIS IS A REGULAR PHOTO ALBUM...
ANYWAY, YOU CAN'T LEAVE THAT HERE. YOU'LL HAVE TO TAKE IT HOME.
THERE. NOW WITH MY SIGNATURE, YOU CAN SELL IT FOR $8 MILLION.
SCRIBBLE SCRIBBLE
LISTEN WHEN SOMEBODY'S TALKING TO YOU!
COULD THAT BE THE INSPECTOR...?!
HMM?
OH.
MS. NAKAMURA!! YOU'RE TOO LOUD!! SOFT TOUCH! SOFT TOUCH! REMEMBER?
S-SORRY! ROGER!
FWAP
FWAP
FWAP

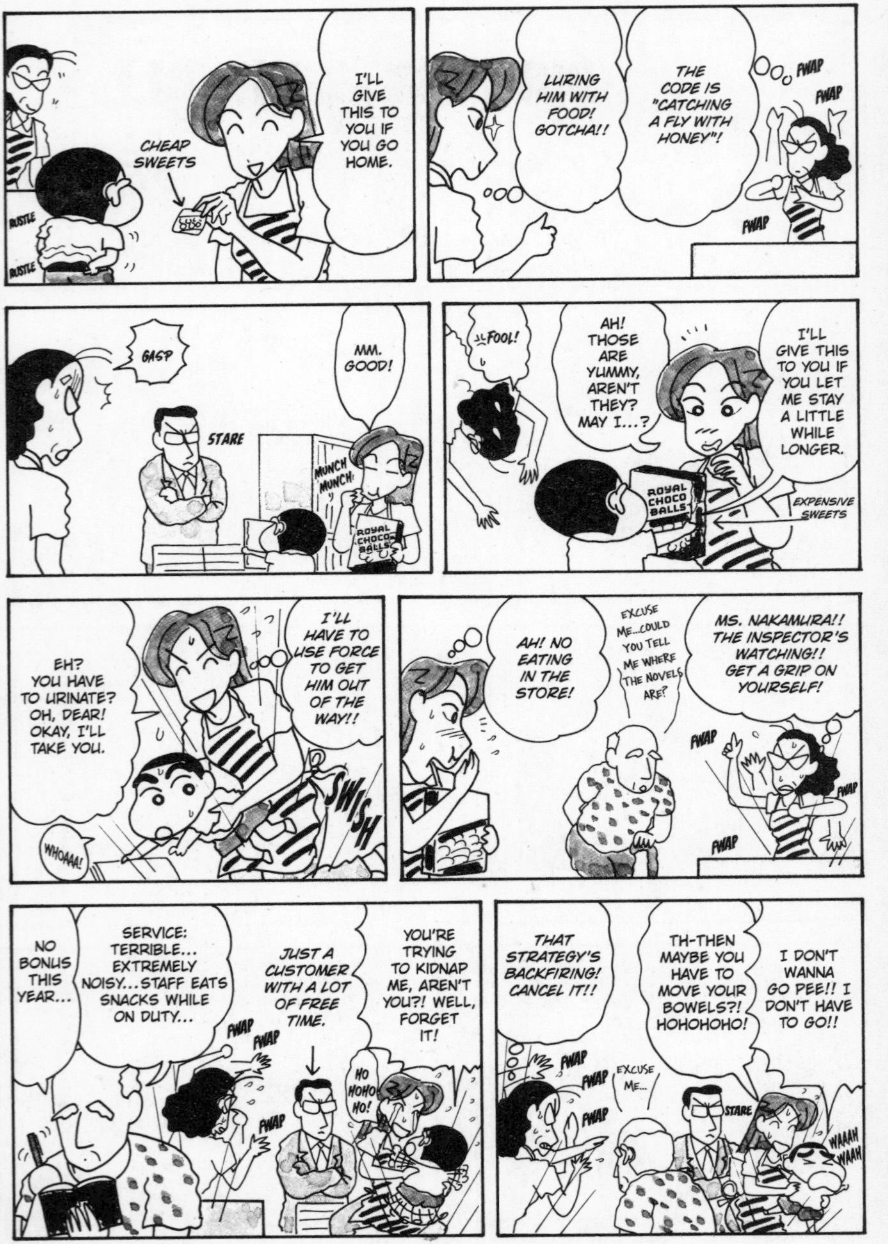
CHEAP SWEETS
RUSTLE
RUSTLE
I'LL GIVE THIS TO YOU IF YOU GO HOME.
LURING HIM WITH FOOD! GOTCHA!!
THE CODE IS "CATCHING A FLY WITH HONEY"!
FWAP
FWAP
FWAP
GASP
STARE
MM. GOOD!
MUNCH MUNCH
ROYAL CHOCO BALLS
FOOL!
AH! THOSE ARE YUMMY, AREN'T THEY? MAY I...?
I'LL GIVE THIS TO YOU IF YOU LET ME STAY A LITTLE WHILE LONGER.
ROYAL CHOCO BALLS
EXPENSIVE SWEETS
EH? YOU HAVE TO URINATE? OH, DEAR! OKAY, I'LL TAKE YOU.
I'LL HAVE TO USE FORCE TO GET HIM OUT OF THE WAY!!
SWISH
WHOAAA!
AH! NO EATING IN THE STORE!
EXCUSE ME...COULD YOU TELL ME WHERE THE NOVELS ARE?
MS. NAKAMURA!! THE INSPECTOR'S WATCHING!! GET A GRIP ON YOURSELF!
FWAP
FWAP
FWAP
NO BONUS THIS YEAR...
SERVICE: TERRIBLE... EXTREMELY NOISY...STAFF EATS SNACKS WHILE ON DUTY...
JUST A CUSTOMER WITH A LOT OF FREE TIME.
YOU'RE TRYING TO KIDNAP ME, AREN'T YOU?! WELL, FORGET IT!
FWAP
FWAP
FWAP
HO HOHO HO!
THAT STRATEGY'S BACKFIRING! CANCEL IT!!
TH-THEN MAYBE YOU HAVE TO MOVE YOUR BOWELS?! HOHOHOHO!
I DON'T WANNA GO PEE!! I DON'T HAVE TO GO!!
FWAP
FWAP
FWAP
EXCUSE ME...
STARE
WAAAH WAAAH

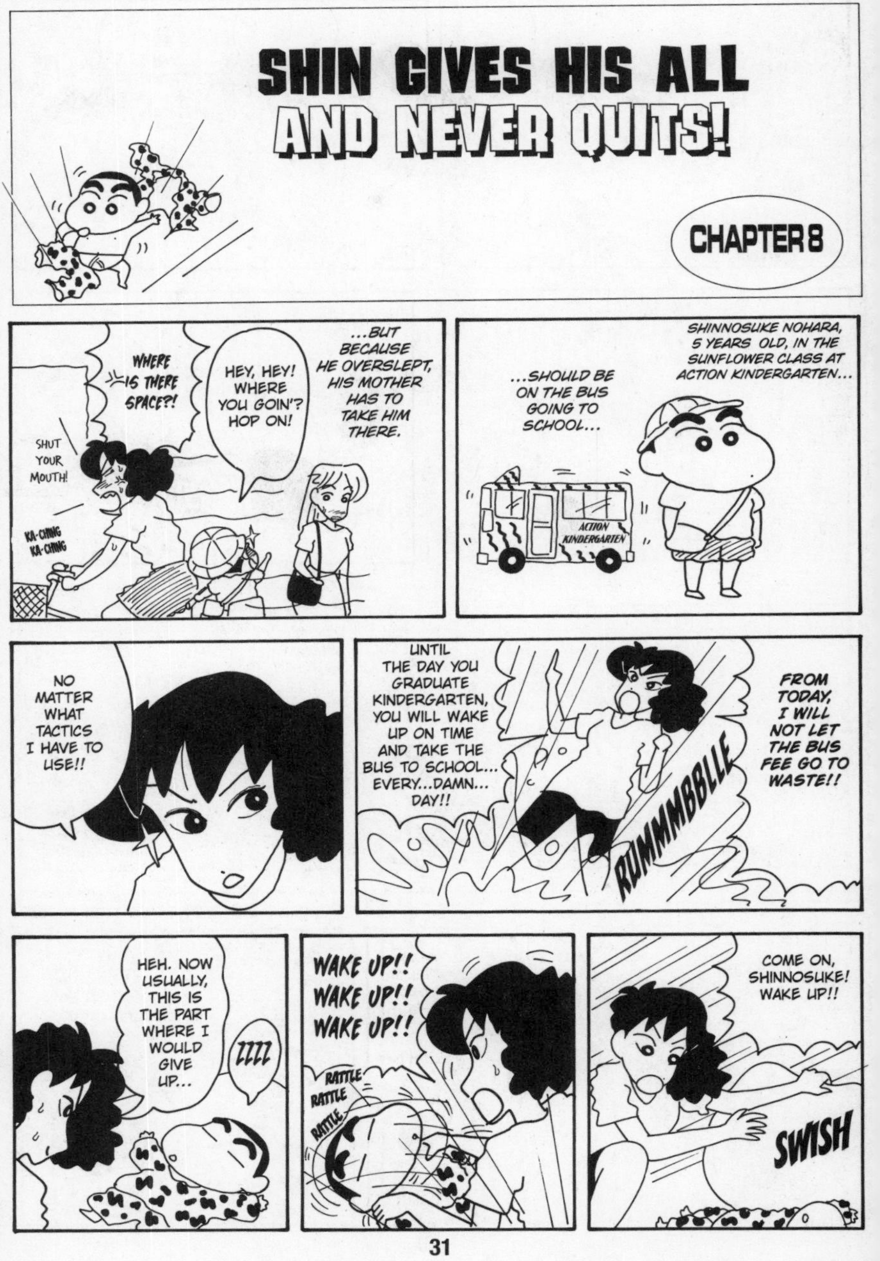
SHIN GIVES HIS ALL AND NEVER QUITS!
CHAPTER 8
SHINNOSUKE NOHARA, 5 YEARS OLD, IN THE SUNFLOWER CLASS AT ACTION KINDERGARTEN...
...SHOULD BE ON THE BUS GOING TO SCHOOL...
ACTION KINDERGARTEN
...BUT BECAUSE HE OVERSLEPT, HIS MOTHER HAS TO TAKE HIM THERE.
HEY, HEY! WHERE YOU GOIN'? HOP ON!
WHERE IS THERE SPACE?!
SHUT YOUR MOUTH!
KA-CHING KA-CHING
FROM TODAY, I WILL NOT LET THE BUS FEE GO TO WASTE!!
UNTIL THE DAY YOU GRADUATE KINDERGARTEN, YOU WILL WAKE UP ON TIME AND TAKE THE BUS TO SCHOOL... EVERY...DAMN... DAY!!
RUMMMBBLLE
NO MATTER WHAT TACTICS I HAVE TO USE!!
COME ON, SHINNOSUKE! WAKE UP!!
SWISH
WAKE UP!!
WAKE UP!!
WAKE UP!!
RATTLE
RATTLE
RATTLE
HEH. NOW USUALLY, THIS IS THE PART WHERE I WOULD GIVE UP...
ZZZZ

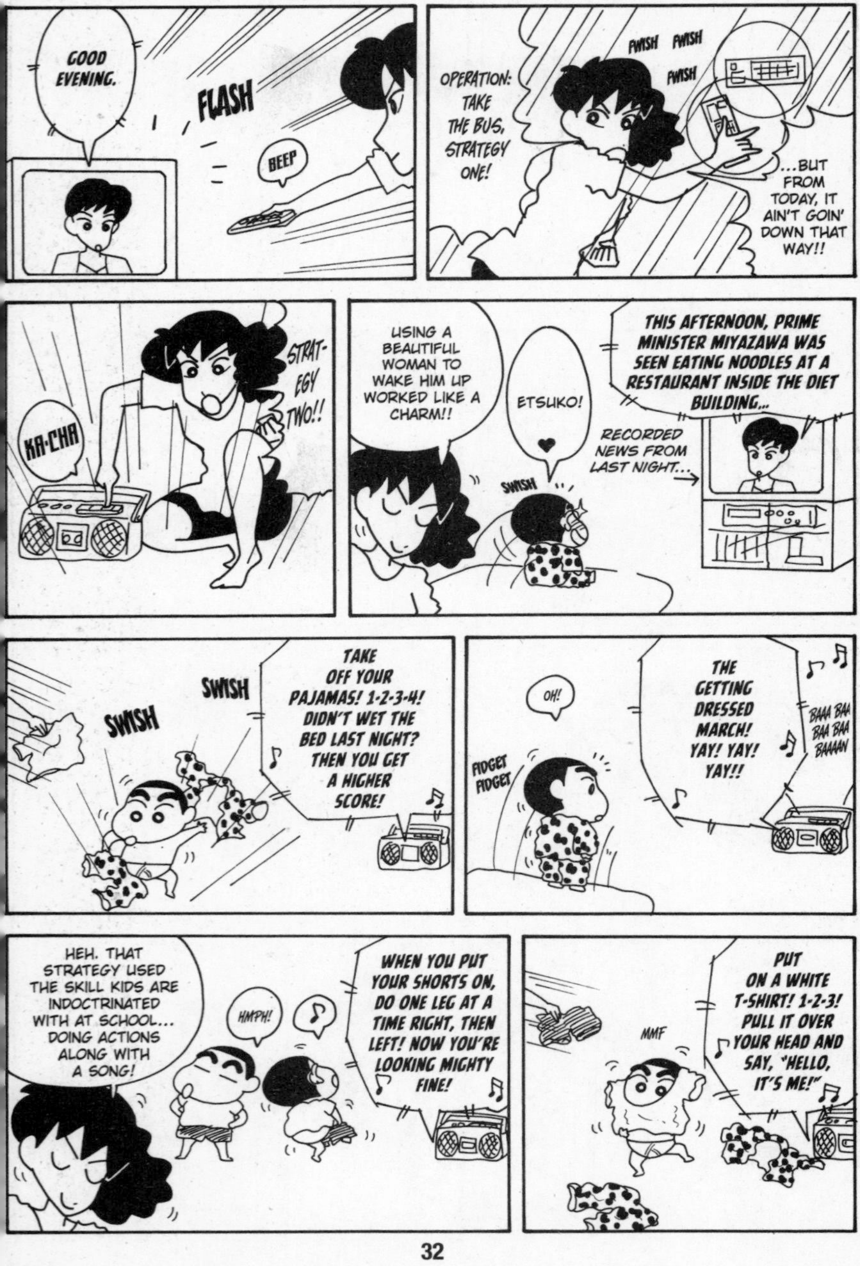
FWISH FWISH
FWISH
OPERATION: TAKE THE BUS, STRATEGY ONE!
...BUT FROM TODAY, IT AIN'T GOIN' DOWN THAT WAY!!
GOOD EVENING.
FLASH
BEEP
THIS AFTERNOON, PRIME MINISTER MIYAZAWA WAS SEEN EATING NOODLES AT A RESTAURANT INSIDE THE DIET BUILDING...
ETSUKO!
USING A BEAUTIFUL WOMAN TO WAKE HIM UP WORKED LIKE A CHARM!!
RECORDED NEWS FROM LAST NIGHT...
SWISH
STRAT-EGY TWO!!
KA-CHA
THE GETTING DRESSED MARCH! YAY! YAY! YAY!!
BAAA BAA BAA BAA BAAAAN
OH!
FIDGET FIDGET
TAKE OFF YOUR PAJAMAS! 1-2-3-4! DIDN'T WET THE BED LAST NIGHT? THEN YOU GET A HIGHER SCORE!
SWISH
SWISH
PUT ON A WHITE T-SHIRT! 1-2-3! PULL IT OVER YOUR HEAD AND SAY, "HELLO, IT'S ME!"
MMF
WHEN YOU PUT YOUR SHORTS ON, DO ONE LEG AT A TIME RIGHT, THEN LEFT! NOW YOU'RE LOOKING MIGHTY FINE!
HMPH!
HEH. THAT STRATEGY USED THE SKILL KIDS ARE INDOCTRINATED WITH AT SCHOOL... DOING ACTIONS ALONG WITH A SONG!

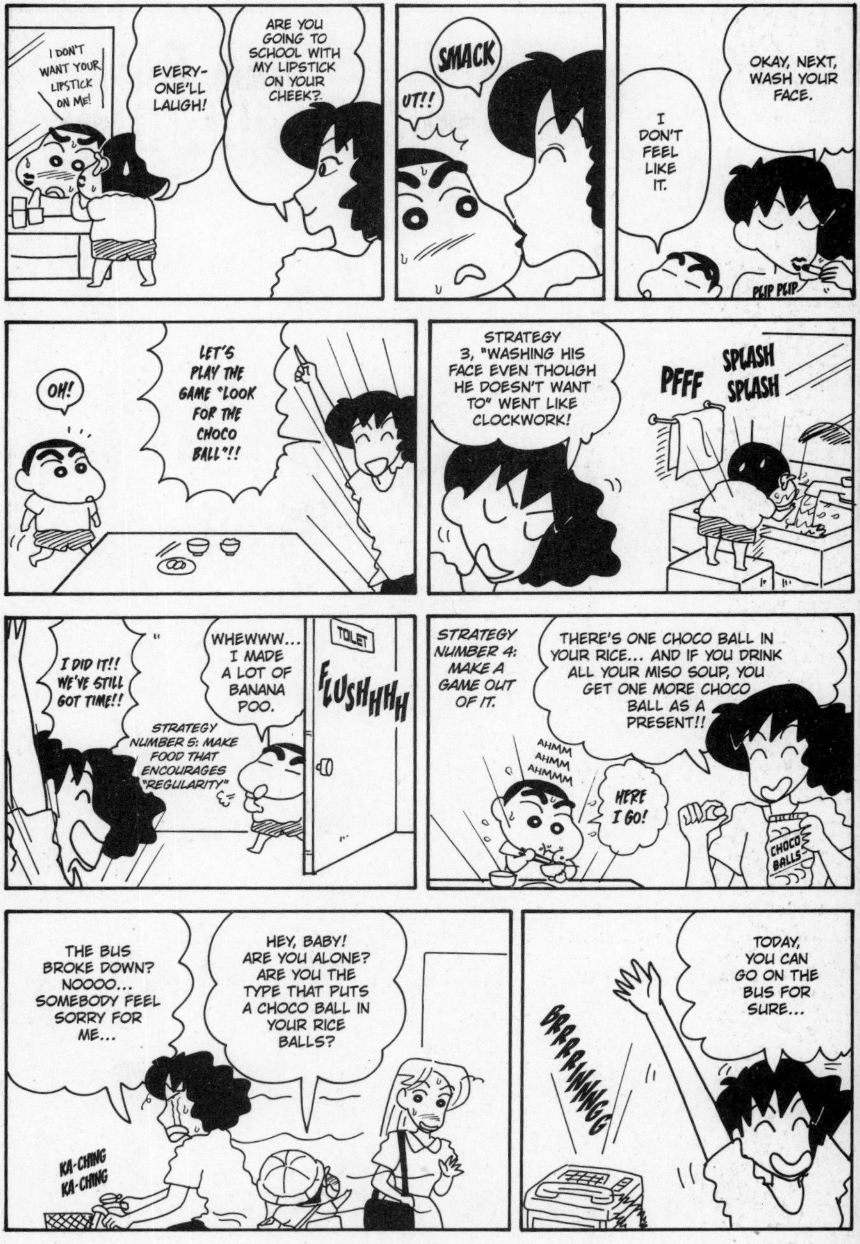
OKAY, NEXT, WASH YOUR FACE.
I DON'T FEEL LIKE IT.
PLIP PLIP
SMACK
UT!!
ARE YOU GOING TO SCHOOL WITH MY LIPSTICK ON YOUR CHEEK?
EVERY-ONE'LL LAUGH!
I DON'T WANT YOUR LIPSTICK ON ME!
STRATEGY 3, "WASHING HIS FACE EVEN THOUGH HE DOESN'T WANT TO" WENT LIKE CLOCKWORK!
PFFF
SPLASH SPLASH
LET'S PLAY THE GAME "LOOK FOR THE CHOCO BALL"!!
OH!
STRATEGY NUMBER 4: MAKE A GAME OUT OF IT.
THERE'S ONE CHOCO BALL IN YOUR RICE... AND IF YOU DRINK ALL YOUR MISO SOUP, YOU GET ONE MORE CHOCO BALL AS A PRESENT!!
HERE I GO!
AHMM AHMM AHMMM
CHOCO BALLS
TOILET
WHEWWW... I MADE A LOT OF BANANA POO.
FLUSHHHH
STRATEGY NUMBER 5: MAKE FOOD THAT ENCOURAGES "REGULARITY"
I DID IT!! WE'VE STILL GOT TIME!!
TODAY, YOU CAN GO ON THE BUS FOR SURE...
BRRRINNNGG
HEY, BABY! ARE YOU ALONE? ARE YOU THE TYPE THAT PUTS A CHOCO BALL IN YOUR RICE BALLS?
THE BUS BROKE DOWN? NOOOO... SOMEBODY FEEL SORRY FOR ME...
KA-CHING KA-CHING

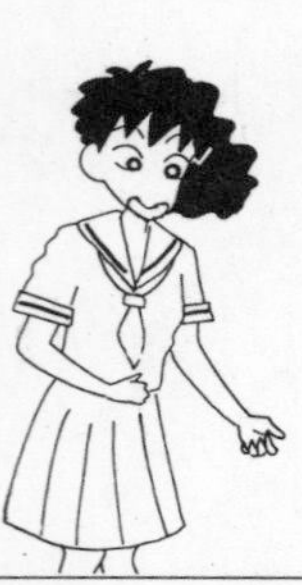

SHIN GIVES HIS ALL AND NEVER QUITS!

CHAPTER 9

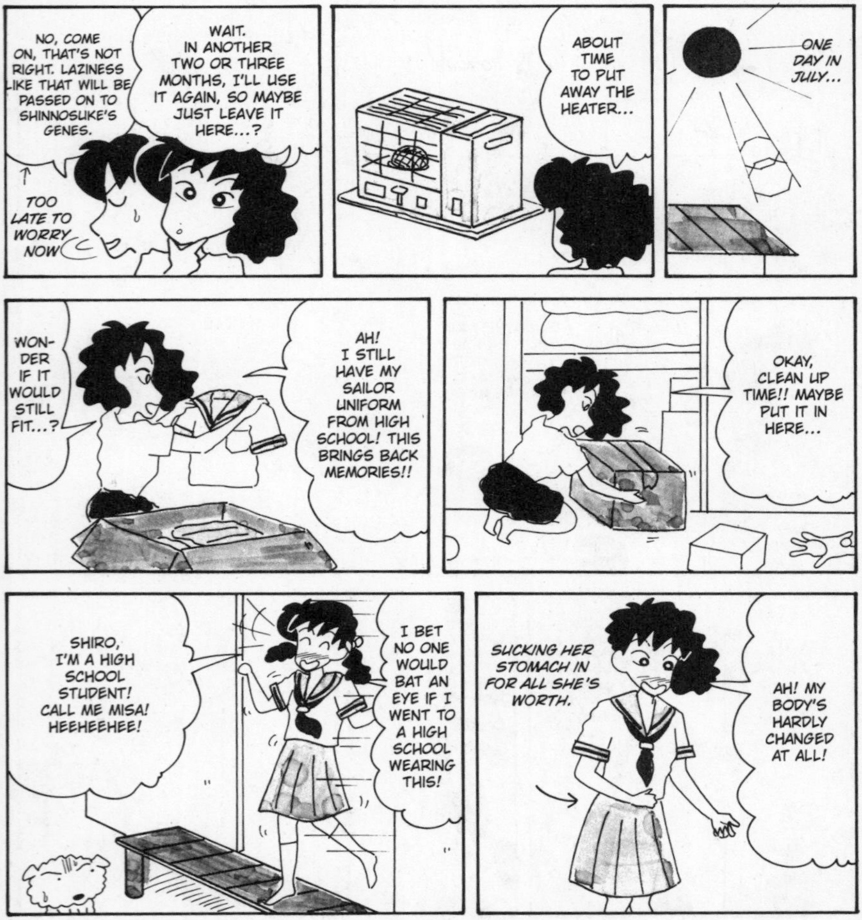
ONE DAY IN JULY...
ABOUT TIME TO PUT AWAY THE HEATER...
WAIT. IN ANOTHER TWO OR THREE MONTHS, I'LL USE IT AGAIN, SO MAYBE JUST LEAVE IT HERE...?
NO, COME ON, THAT'S NOT RIGHT. LAZINESS LIKE THAT WILL BE PASSED ON TO SHINNOSUKE'S GENES.
TOO LATE TO WORRY NOW
OKAY, CLEAN UP TIME!! MAYBE PUT IT IN HERE...
AH! I STILL HAVE MY SAILOR UNIFORM FROM HIGH SCHOOL! THIS BRINGS BACK MEMORIES!!
WON-DER IF IT WOULD STILL FIT...?
AH! MY BODY'S HARDLY CHANGED AT ALL!
SUCKING HER STOMACH IN FOR ALL SHE'S WORTH.
I BET NO ONE WOULD BAT AN EYE IF I WENT TO A HIGH SCHOOL WEARING THIS!
SHIRO, I'M A HIGH SCHOOL STUDENT! CALL ME MISA! HEEHEEHEE!

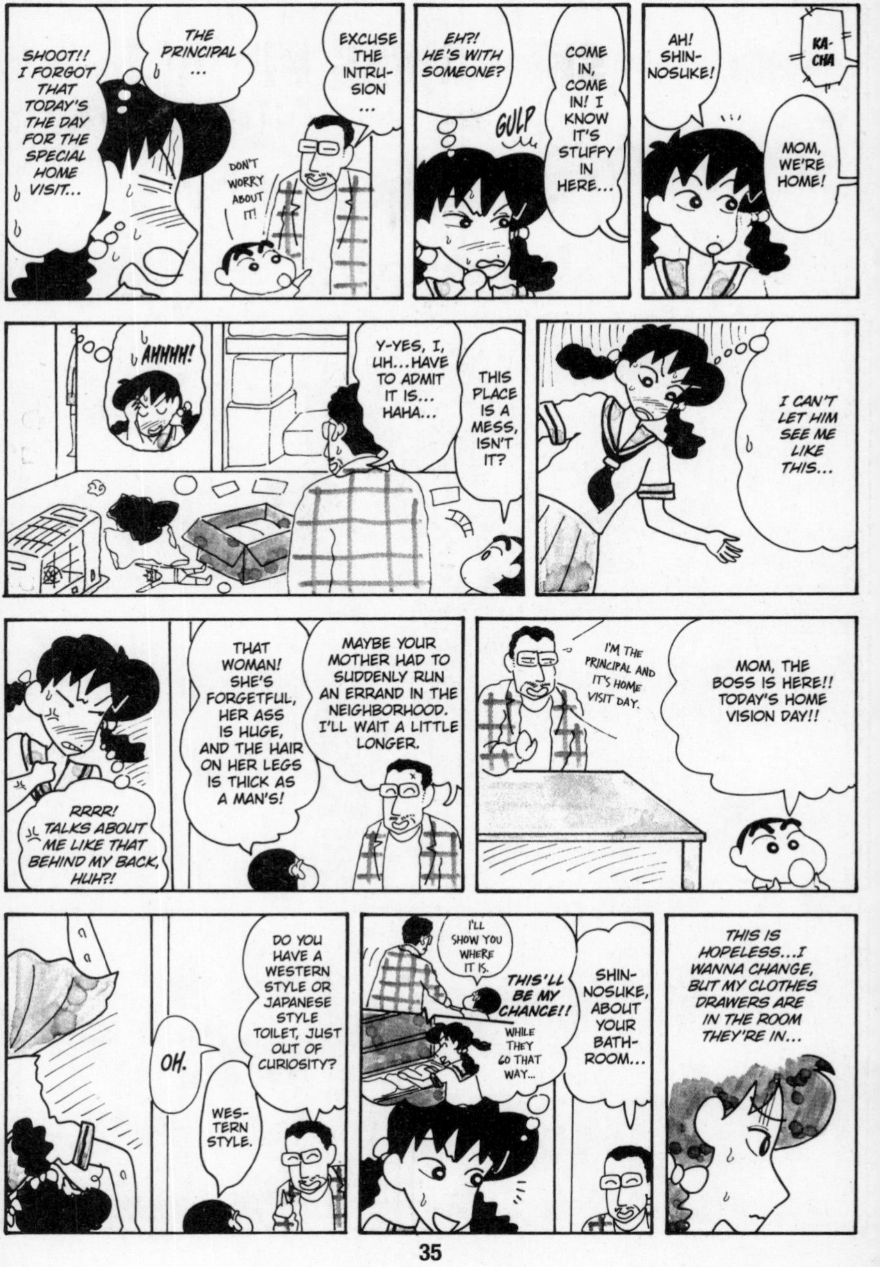
KA-CHA
AH! SHIN-NOSUKE!
MOM, WE'RE HOME!
COME IN, COME IN! I KNOW IT'S STUFFY IN HERE...
EH?! HE'S WITH SOMEONE?
GULP
EXCUSE THE INTRUSION...
THE PRINCIPAL...
SHOOT!! I FORGOT THAT TODAY'S THE DAY FOR THE SPECIAL HOME VISIT...
DON'T WORRY ABOUT IT!
I CAN'T LET HIM SEE ME LIKE THIS...
THIS PLACE IS A MESS, ISN'T IT?
Y-YES, I, UH...HAVE TO ADMIT IT IS... HAHA...
AHHHH!
MOM, THE BOSS IS HERE!! TODAY'S HOME VISION DAY!!
I'M THE PRINCIPAL AND IT'S HOME VISIT DAY.
MAYBE YOUR MOTHER HAD TO SUDDENLY RUN AN ERRAND IN THE NEIGHBORHOOD. I'LL WAIT A LITTLE LONGER.
THAT WOMAN! SHE'S FORGETFUL, HER ASS IS HUGE, AND THE HAIR ON HER LEGS IS THICK AS A MAN'S!
RRRR! TALKS ABOUT ME LIKE THAT BEHIND MY BACK, HUH?!
THIS IS HOPELESS...I WANNA CHANGE, BUT MY CLOTHES DRAWERS ARE IN THE ROOM THEY'RE IN...
SHIN-NOSUKE, ABOUT YOUR BATH-ROOM...
THIS'LL BE MY CHANCE!! WHILE THEY GO THAT WAY...
I'LL SHOW YOU WHERE IT IS.
DO YOU HAVE A WESTERN STYLE OR JAPANESE STYLE TOILET, JUST OUT OF CURIOSITY?
OH.
WES-TERN STYLE.

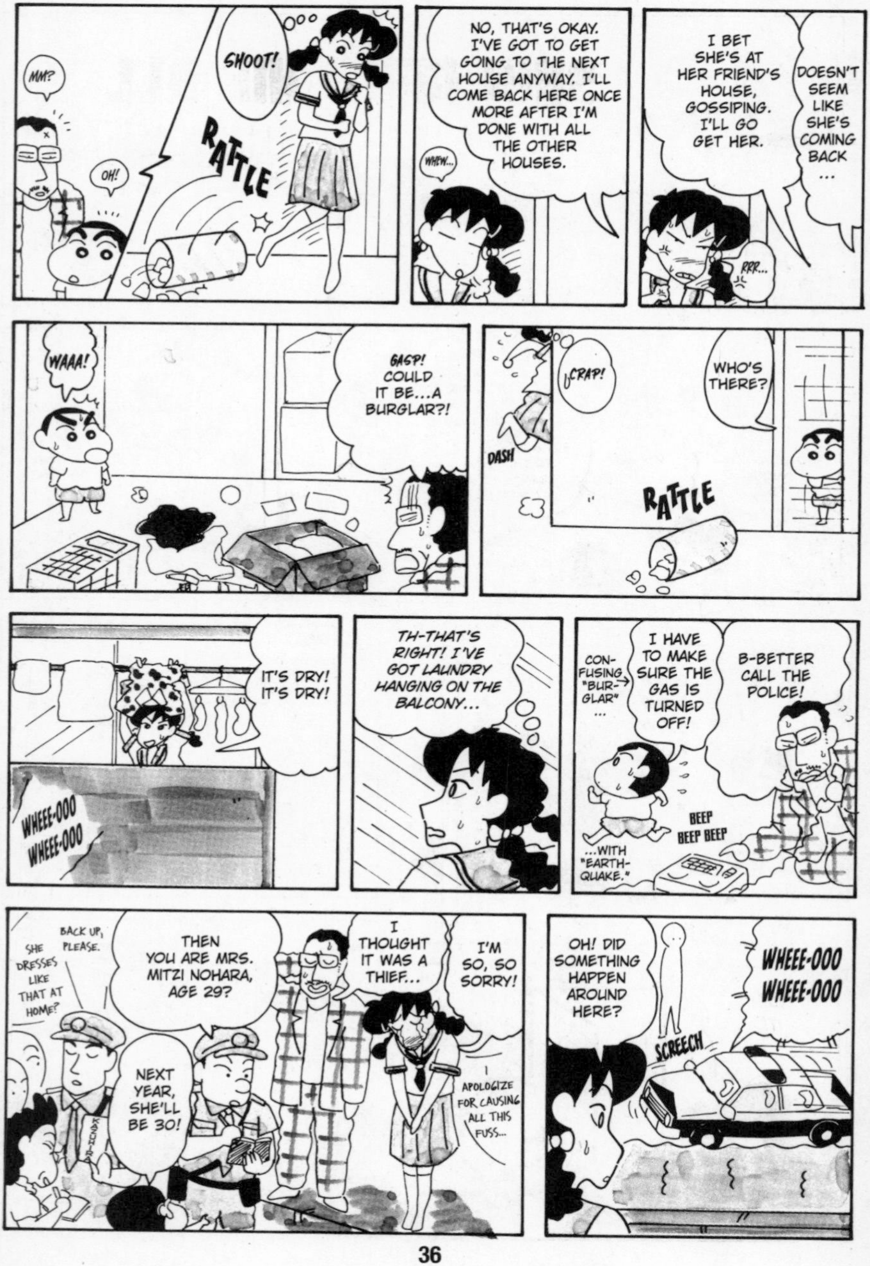
DOESN'T SEEM LIKE SHE'S COMING BACK ...
I BET SHE'S AT HER FRIEND'S HOUSE, GOSSIPING. I'LL GO GET HER.
RRR...
NO, THAT'S OKAY. I'VE GOT TO GET GOING TO THE NEXT HOUSE ANYWAY. I'LL COME BACK HERE ONCE MORE AFTER I'M DONE WITH ALL THE OTHER HOUSES.
WHEW...
SHOOT!
MM?
RATTLE
OH!
WHO'S THERE?
CRAP!
DASH
RATTLE
GASP! COULD IT BE...A BURGLAR?!
WAAA!
B-BETTER CALL THE POLICE!
I HAVE TO MAKE SURE THE GAS IS TURNED OFF!
CON-FUSING "BUR-GLAR" ...
BEEP BEEP BEEP
...WITH "EARTH-QUAKE."
TH-THAT'S RIGHT! I'VE GOT LAUNDRY HANGING ON THE BALCONY...
IT'S DRY! IT'S DRY!
WHEEE-OOO WHEEE-OOO
WHEEE-OOO WHEEE-OOO
OH! DID SOMETHING HAPPEN AROUND HERE?
SCREECH
I'M SO, SO SORRY!
I APOLOGIZE FOR CAUSING ALL THIS FUSS...
I THOUGHT IT WAS A THIEF...
THEN YOU ARE MRS. MITZI NOHARA, AGE 29?
NEXT YEAR, SHE'LL BE 30!
BACK UP, PLEASE.
SHE DRESSES LIKE THAT AT HOME?

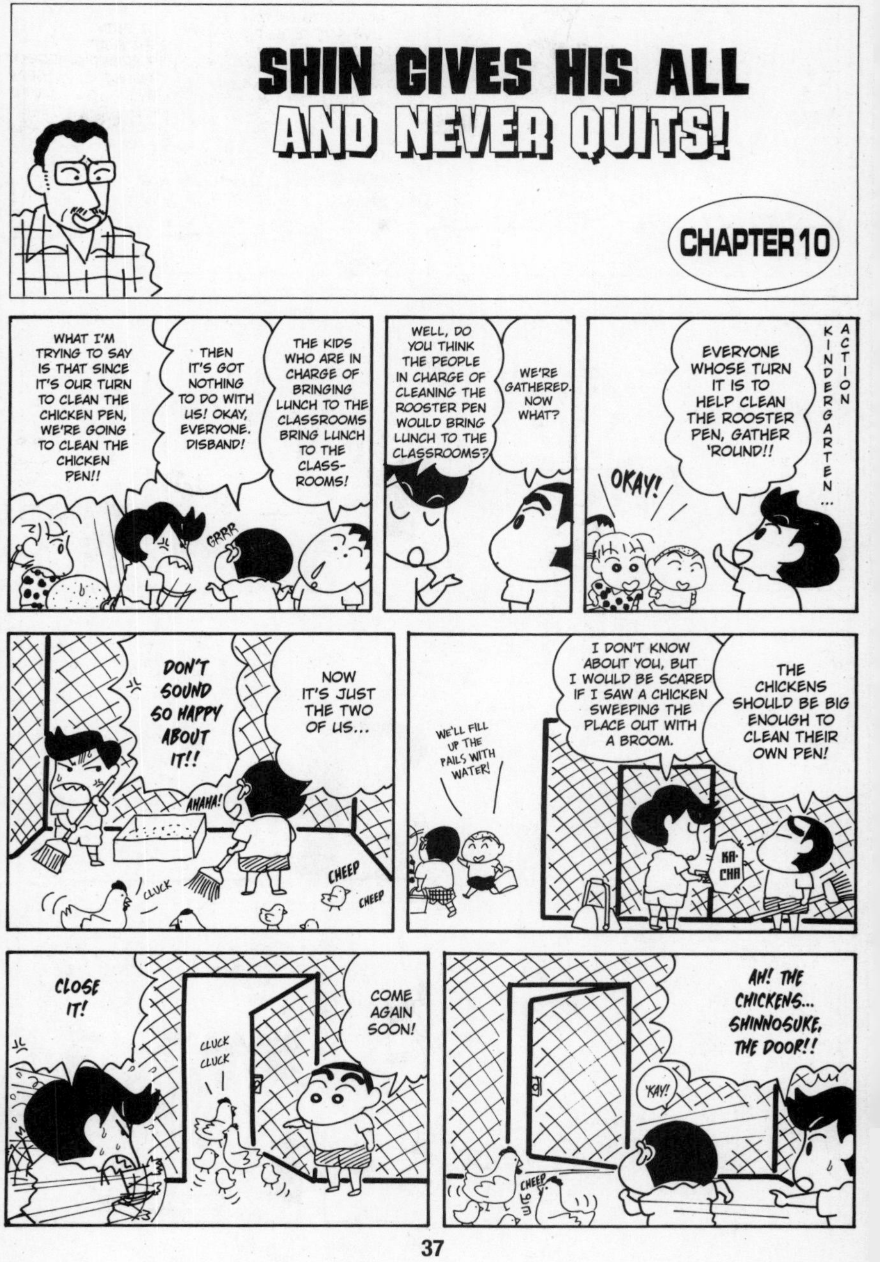
SHIN GIVES HIS ALL AND NEVER QUITS!
CHAPTER 10
KINDERGARTEN ACTION...
EVERYONE WHOSE TURN IT IS TO HELP CLEAN THE ROOSTER PEN, GATHER 'ROUND!!
OKAY!
WE'RE GATHERED. NOW WHAT?
WELL, DO YOU THINK THE PEOPLE IN CHARGE OF CLEANING THE ROOSTER PEN WOULD BRING LUNCH TO THE CLASSROOMS?
THE KIDS WHO ARE IN CHARGE OF BRINGING LUNCH TO THE CLASSROOMS BRING LUNCH TO THE CLASS-ROOMS!
THEN IT'S GOT NOTHING TO DO WITH US! OKAY, EVERYONE. DISBAND!
WHAT I'M TRYING TO SAY IS THAT SINCE IT'S OUR TURN TO CLEAN THE CHICKEN PEN, WE'RE GOING TO CLEAN THE CHICKEN PEN!!
GRRR
THE CHICKENS SHOULD BE BIG ENOUGH TO CLEAN THEIR OWN PEN!
I DON'T KNOW ABOUT YOU, BUT I WOULD BE SCARED IF I SAW A CHICKEN SWEEPING THE PLACE OUT WITH A BROOM.
KA-CHA
WE'LL FILL UP THE PAILS WITH WATER!
NOW IT'S JUST THE TWO OF US...
DON'T SOUND SO HAPPY ABOUT IT!!
AHAHA!
CHEEP
CHEEP
CLUCK
AH! THE CHICKENS... SHINNOSUKE, THE DOOR!!
'KAY!
CHEEP
COME AGAIN SOON!
CLOSE IT!
CLUCK CLUCK

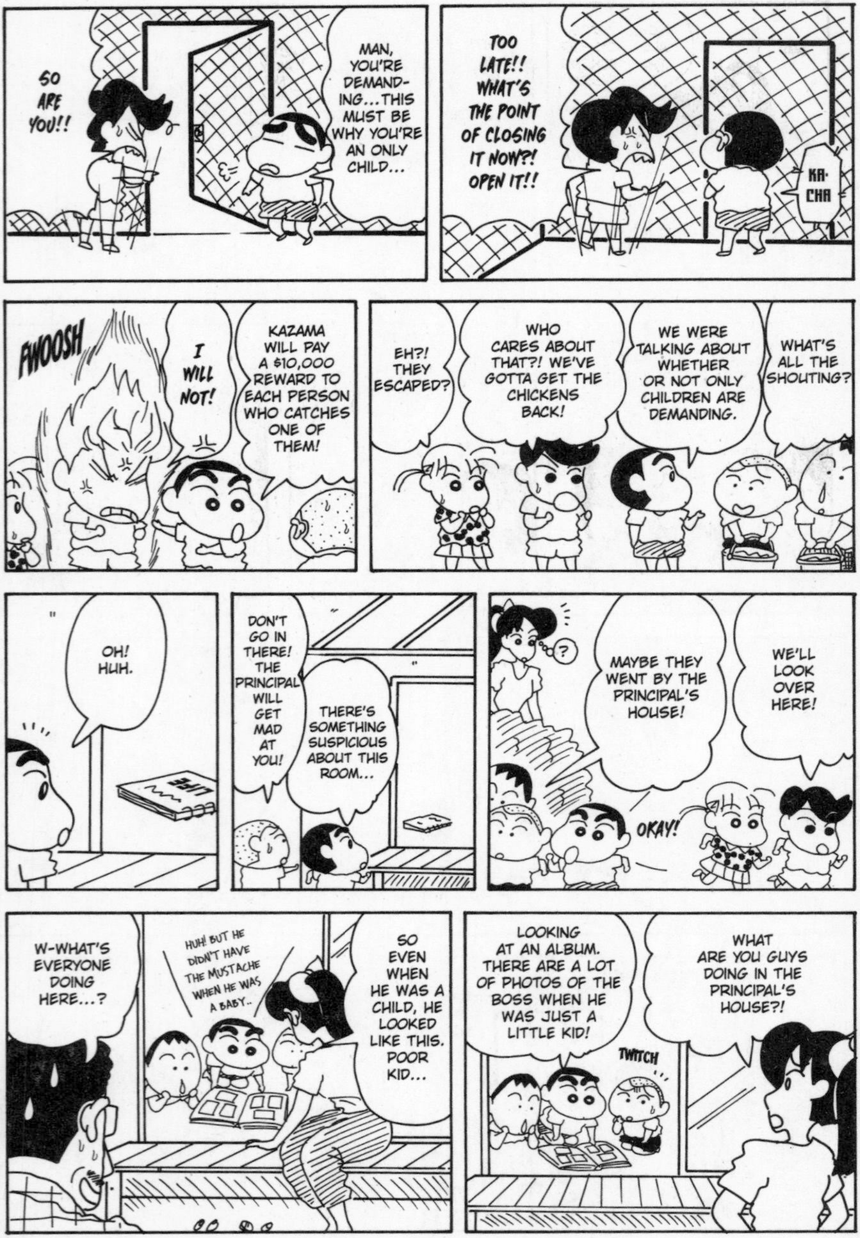
TOO LATE!! WHAT'S THE POINT OF CLOSING IT NOW?! OPEN IT!!
KA-CHA
MAN, YOU'RE DEMANDING... THIS MUST BE WHY YOU'RE AN ONLY CHILD...
SO ARE YOU!!
WHAT'S ALL THE SHOUTING?
WE WERE TALKING ABOUT WHETHER OR NOT ONLY CHILDREN ARE DEMANDING.
WHO CARES ABOUT THAT?! WE'VE GOTTA GET THE CHICKENS BACK!
EH?! THEY ESCAPED?
KAZAMA WILL PAY A $10,000 REWARD TO EACH PERSON WHO CATCHES ONE OF THEM!
I WILL NOT!
FWOOSH
WE'LL LOOK OVER HERE!
MAYBE THEY WENT BY THE PRINCIPAL'S HOUSE!
OKAY!
THERE'S SOMETHING SUSPICIOUS ABOUT THIS ROOM...
DON'T GO IN THERE! THE PRINCIPAL WILL GET MAD AT YOU!
OH! HUH.
LIFE
WHAT ARE YOU GUYS DOING IN THE PRINCIPAL'S HOUSE?!
LOOKING AT AN ALBUM. THERE ARE A LOT OF PHOTOS OF THE BOSS WHEN HE WAS JUST A LITTLE KID!
TWITCH
SO EVEN WHEN HE WAS A CHILD, HE LOOKED LIKE THIS. POOR KID...
HUH! BUT HE DIDN'T HAVE THE MUSTACHE WHEN HE WAS A BABY..
W-WHAT'S EVERYONE DOING HERE...?

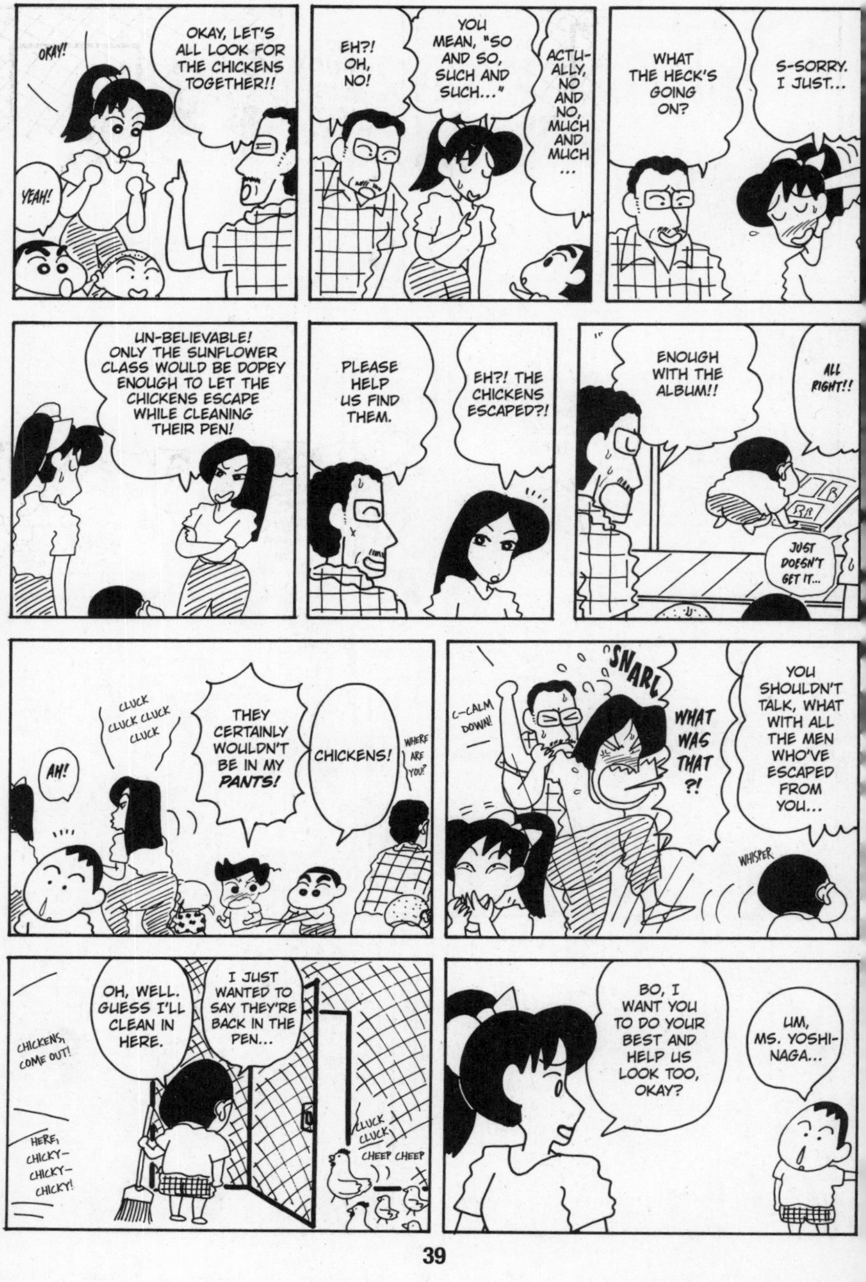
S-SORRY. I JUST...
WHAT THE HECK'S GOING ON?
ACTU-ALLY, NO AND NO, MUCH AND MUCH...
YOU MEAN, "SO AND SO, SUCH AND SUCH..."
EH?! OH, NO!
OKAY, LET'S ALL LOOK FOR THE CHICKENS TOGETHER!!
OKAY!
YEAH!
ALL RIGHT!!
ENOUGH WITH THE ALBUM!!
JUST DOESN'T GET IT...
EH?! THE CHICKENS ESCAPED?!
PLEASE HELP US FIND THEM.
UN-BELIEVABLE! ONLY THE SUNFLOWER CLASS WOULD BE DOPEY ENOUGH TO LET THE CHICKENS ESCAPE WHILE CLEANING THEIR PEN!
YOU SHOULDN'T TALK, WHAT WITH ALL THE MEN WHO'VE ESCAPED FROM YOU...
SNARL
WHAT WAS THAT ?!
C-CALM DOWN!
WHISPER
WHERE ARE YOU?
CHICKENS!
THEY CERTAINLY WOULDN'T BE IN MY *PANTS!*
CLUCK CLUCK CLUCK CLUCK
AH!
UM, MS. YOSHI-NAGA...
BO, I WANT YOU TO DO YOUR BEST AND HELP US LOOK TOO, OKAY?
I JUST WANTED TO SAY THEY'RE BACK IN THE PEN...
OH, WELL. GUESS I'LL CLEAN IN HERE.
CHICKENS, COME OUT!
CLUCK CLUCK
CHEEP CHEEP
HERE, CHICKY-CHICKY-CHICKY!

SHIN GIVES HIS ALL AND NEVER QUITS!

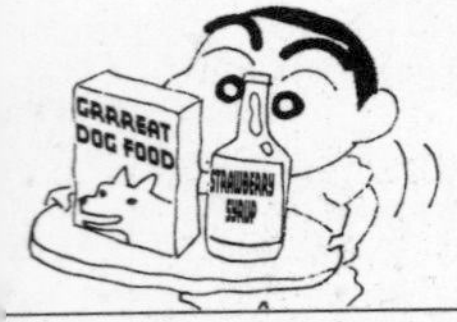
GRRREAT DOG FOOD
STRAWBERRY SYRUP

CHAPTER 11

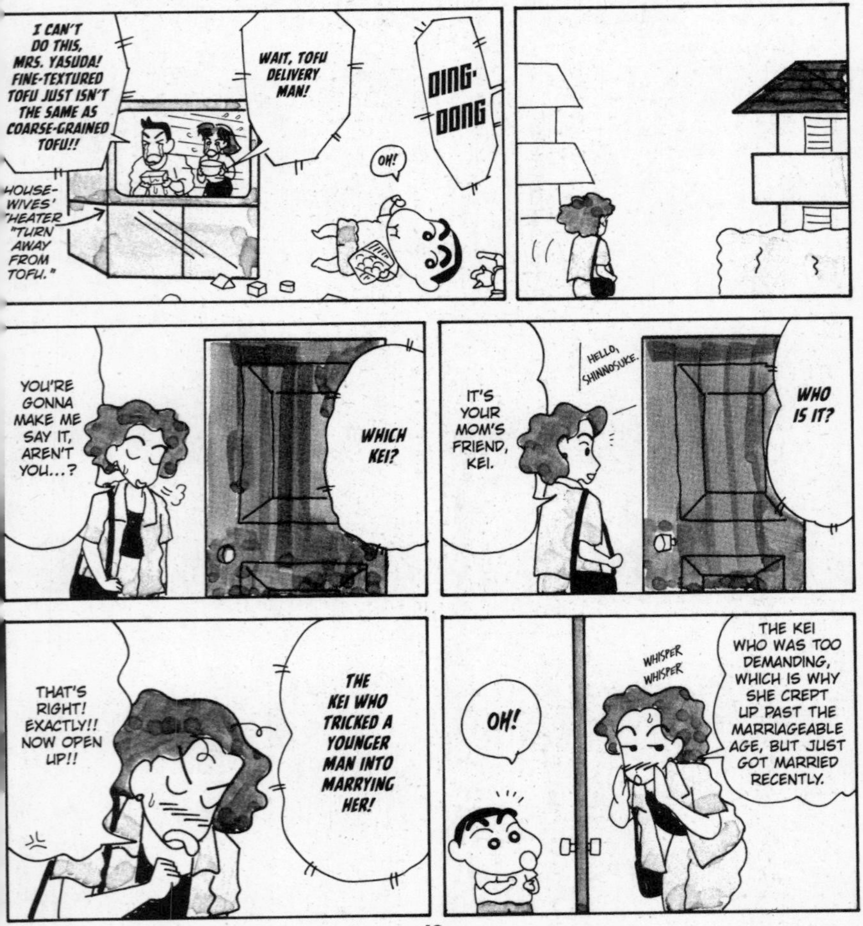
DING-DONG
WAIT, TOFU DELIVERY MAN!
I CAN'T DO THIS, MRS. YASUDA! FINE-TEXTURED TOFU JUST ISN'T THE SAME AS COARSE-GRAINED TOFU!!
OH!
HOUSE-WIVES' "HEATER "TURN AWAY FROM TOFU."
WHO IS IT?
HELLO, SHINNOSUKE.
IT'S YOUR MOM'S FRIEND, KEI.
WHICH KEI?
YOU'RE GONNA MAKE ME SAY IT, AREN'T YOU...?
THE KEI WHO WAS TOO DEMANDING, WHICH IS WHY SHE CREPT UP PAST THE MARRIAGEABLE AGE, BUT JUST GOT MARRIED RECENTLY.
WHISPER WHISPER
OH!
THE KEI WHO TRICKED A YOUNGER MAN INTO MARRYING HER!
THAT'S RIGHT! EXACTLY!! NOW OPEN UP!!

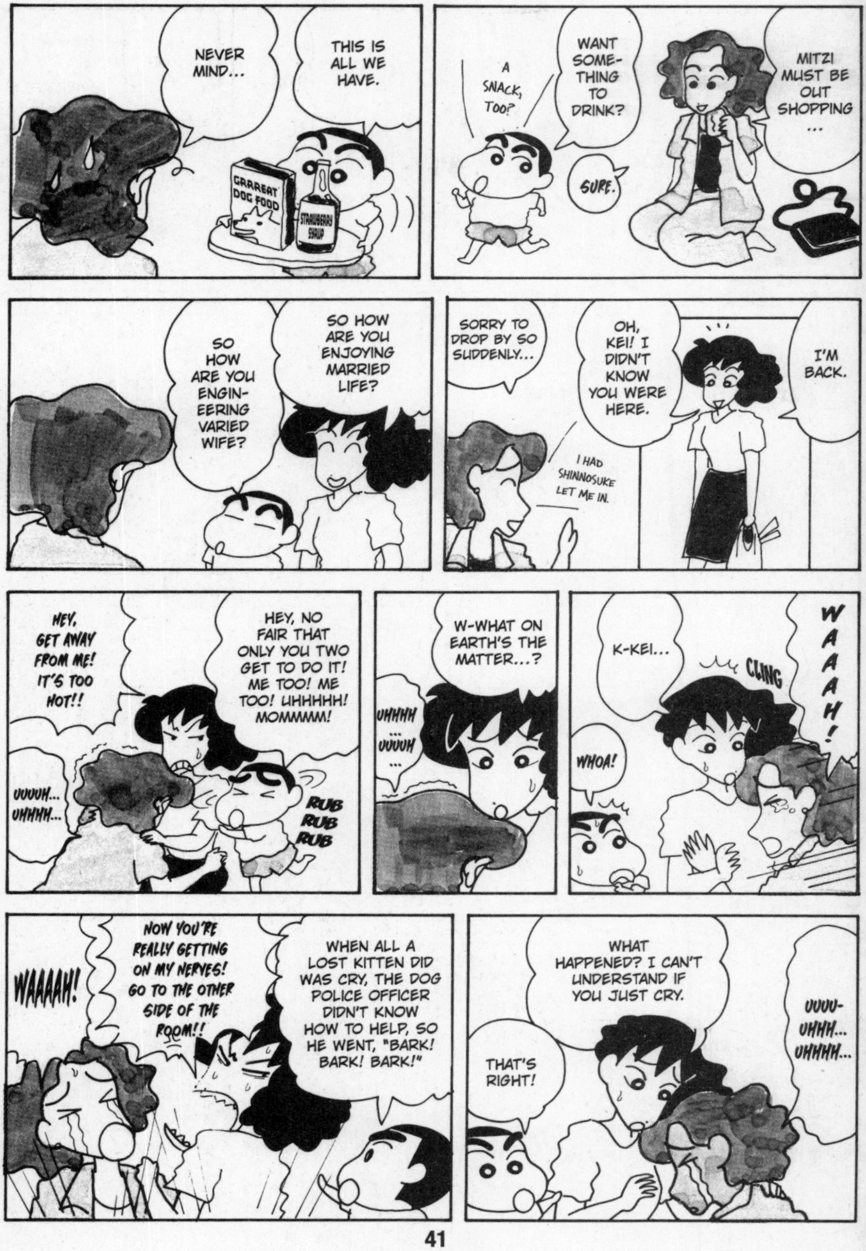
MITZI MUST BE OUT SHOPPING ...
WANT SOMETHING TO DRINK?
A SNACK, TOO?
SURE.
THIS IS ALL WE HAVE.
GRRREAT DOG FOOD
STRAWBERRY SYRUP
NEVER MIND...
I'M BACK.
OH, KEI! I DIDN'T KNOW YOU WERE HERE.
SORRY TO DROP BY SO SUDDENLY...
I HAD SHINNOSUKE LET ME IN.
SO HOW ARE YOU ENJOYING MARRIED LIFE?
SO HOW ARE YOU ENGINEERING VARIED WIFE?
WAAAAH!
CLING
K-KEI...
WHOA!
W-WHAT ON EARTH'S THE MATTER...?
UHHHH ... UUUUH ...
HEY, NO FAIR THAT ONLY YOU TWO GET TO DO IT! ME TOO! ME TOO! UHHHHH! MOMMMMM!
HEY, GET AWAY FROM ME! IT'S TOO HOT!!
UUUUH... UHHHH...
RUB RUB RUB
UUUU-UHHH... UHHHH...
WHAT HAPPENED? I CAN'T UNDERSTAND IF YOU JUST CRY.
THAT'S RIGHT!
WHEN ALL A LOST KITTEN DID WAS CRY, THE DOG POLICE OFFICER DIDN'T KNOW HOW TO HELP, SO HE WENT, "BARK! BARK! BARK!"
NOW YOU'RE REALLY GETTING ON MY NERVES! GO TO THE OTHER SIDE OF THE ROOM!!
WAAAAH!

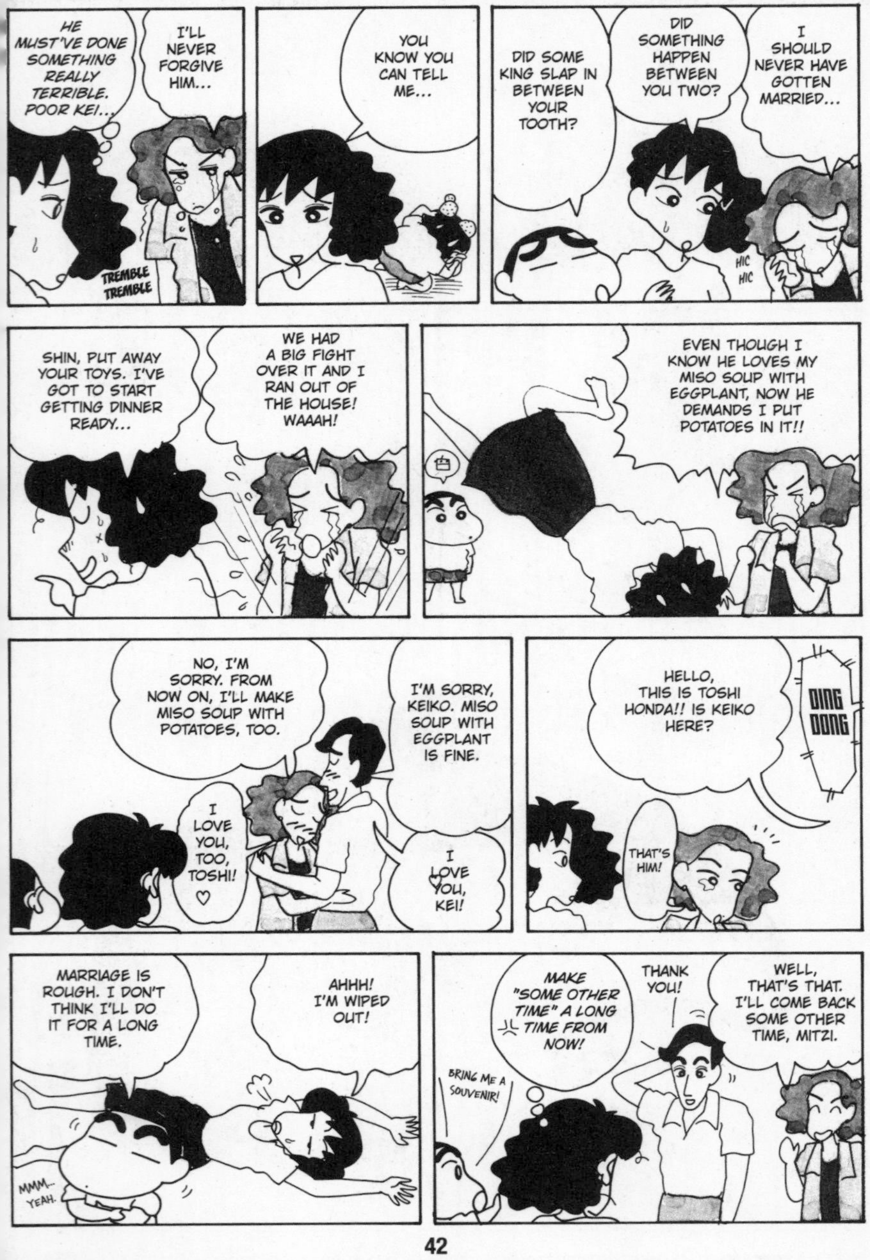
I SHOULD NEVER HAVE GOTTEN MARRIED...
DID SOMETHING HAPPEN BETWEEN YOU TWO?
DID SOME KING SLAP IN BETWEEN YOUR TOOTH?
HIC HIC
YOU KNOW YOU CAN TELL ME...
I'LL NEVER FORGIVE HIM...
HE MUST'VE DONE SOMETHING REALLY TERRIBLE. POOR KEI...
TREMBLE TREMBLE
EVEN THOUGH I KNOW HE LOVES MY MISO SOUP WITH EGGPLANT, NOW HE DEMANDS I PUT POTATOES IN IT!!
WE HAD A BIG FIGHT OVER IT AND I RAN OUT OF THE HOUSE! WAAAH!
SHIN, PUT AWAY YOUR TOYS. I'VE GOT TO START GETTING DINNER READY...
DING DONG
HELLO, THIS IS TOSHI HONDA!! IS KEIKO HERE?
THAT'S HIM!
I'M SORRY, KEIKO. MISO SOUP WITH EGGPLANT IS FINE.
NO, I'M SORRY. FROM NOW ON, I'LL MAKE MISO SOUP WITH POTATOES, TOO.
I LOVE YOU, KEI!
I LOVE YOU, TOO, TOSHI! ♡
WELL, THAT'S THAT. I'LL COME BACK SOME OTHER TIME, MITZI.
THANK YOU!
MAKE "SOME OTHER TIME" A LONG TIME FROM NOW!
BRING ME A SOUVENIR!
AHHH! I'M WIPED OUT!
MARRIAGE IS ROUGH. I DON'T THINK I'LL DO IT FOR A LONG TIME.
MMM.. YEAH.

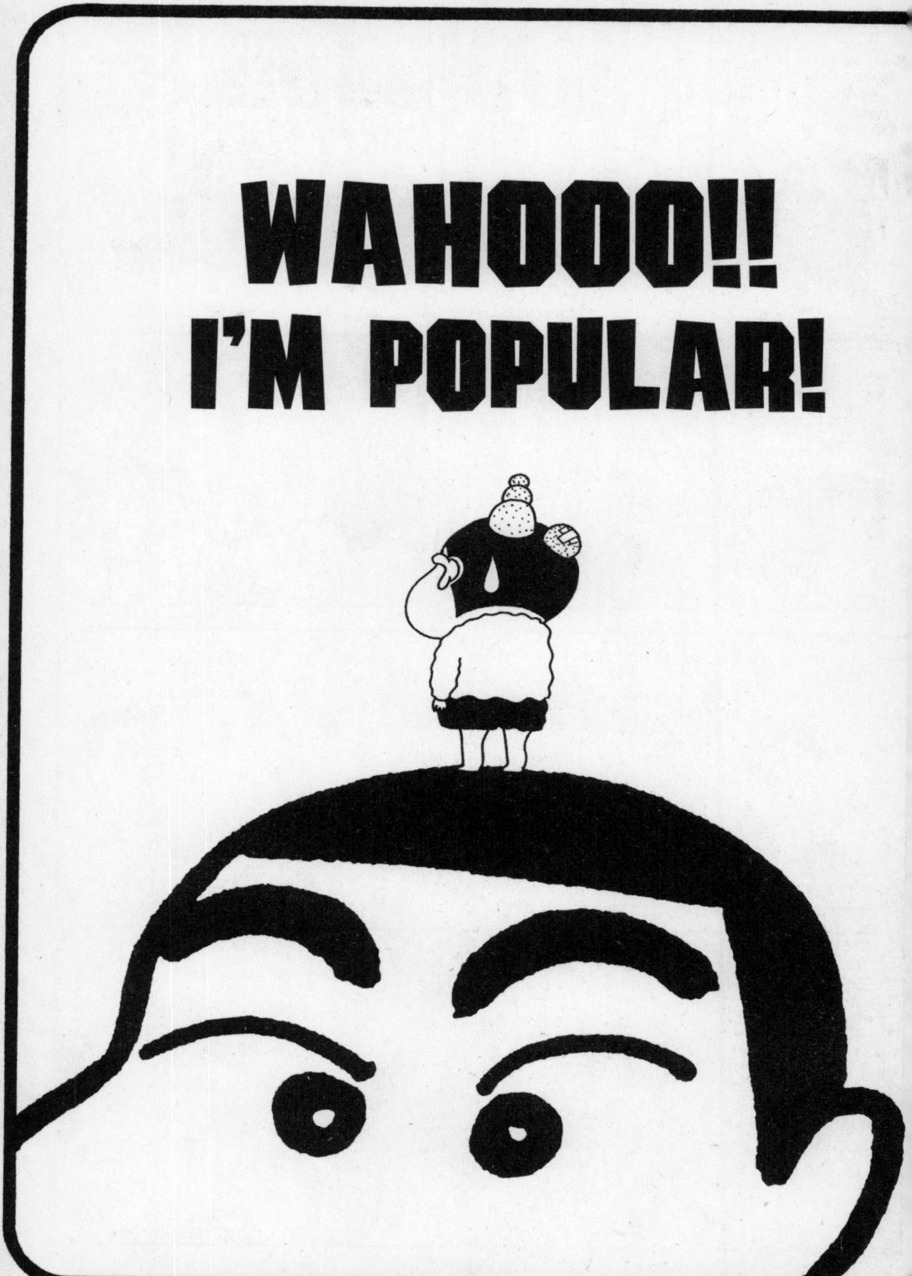
WAHOOO!!
I'M POPULAR!

WAHOOO!! I'M POPULAR!

CHAPTER 1

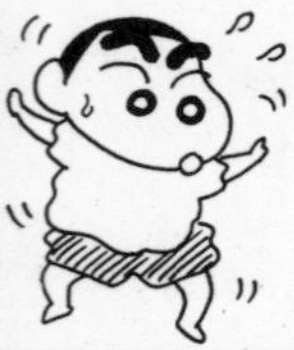

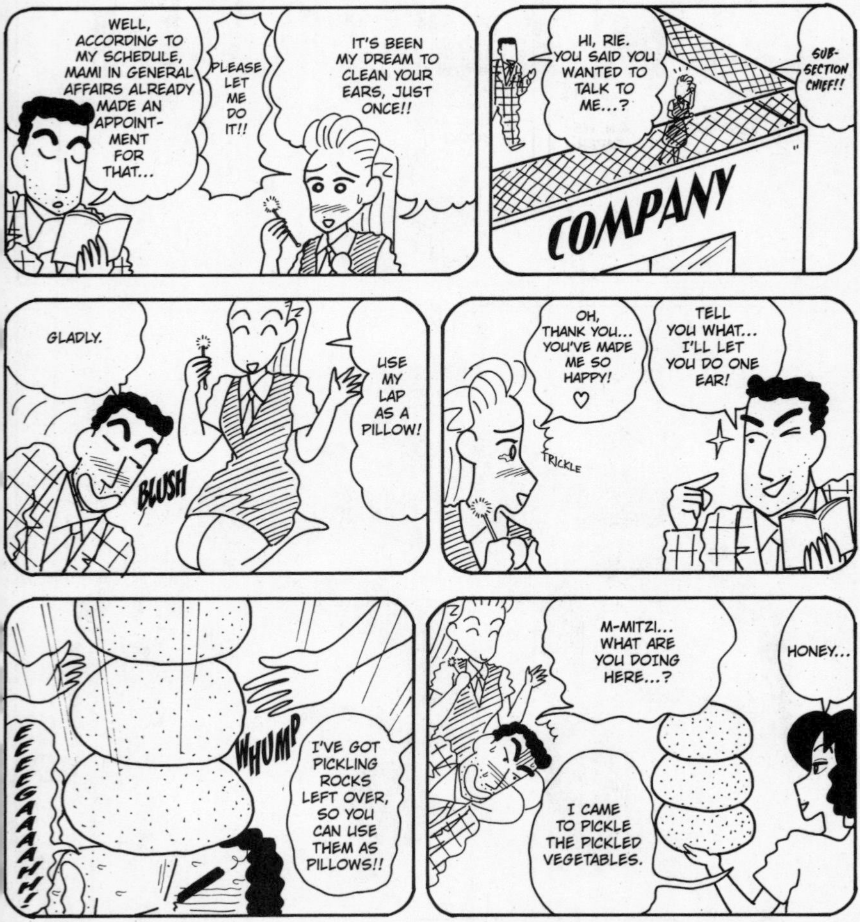
SUB-SECTION CHIEF!!
HI, RIE. YOU SAID YOU WANTED TO TALK TO ME...?
COMPANY
IT'S BEEN MY DREAM TO CLEAN YOUR EARS, JUST ONCE!!
PLEASE LET ME DO IT!!
WELL, ACCORDING TO MY SCHEDULE, MAMI IN GENERAL AFFAIRS ALREADY MADE AN APPOINTMENT FOR THAT...
TELL YOU WHAT... I'LL LET YOU DO ONE EAR!
OH, THANK YOU... YOU'VE MADE ME SO HAPPY! ♡
TRICKLE
USE MY LAP AS A PILLOW!
GLADLY.
BLUSH
HONEY...
M-MITZI... WHAT ARE YOU DOING HERE...?
I CAME TO PICKLE THE PICKLED VEGETABLES.
I'VE GOT PICKLING ROCKS LEFT OVER, SO YOU CAN USE THEM AS PILLOWS!!
WHUMP
EEEEGAAAAAHH!

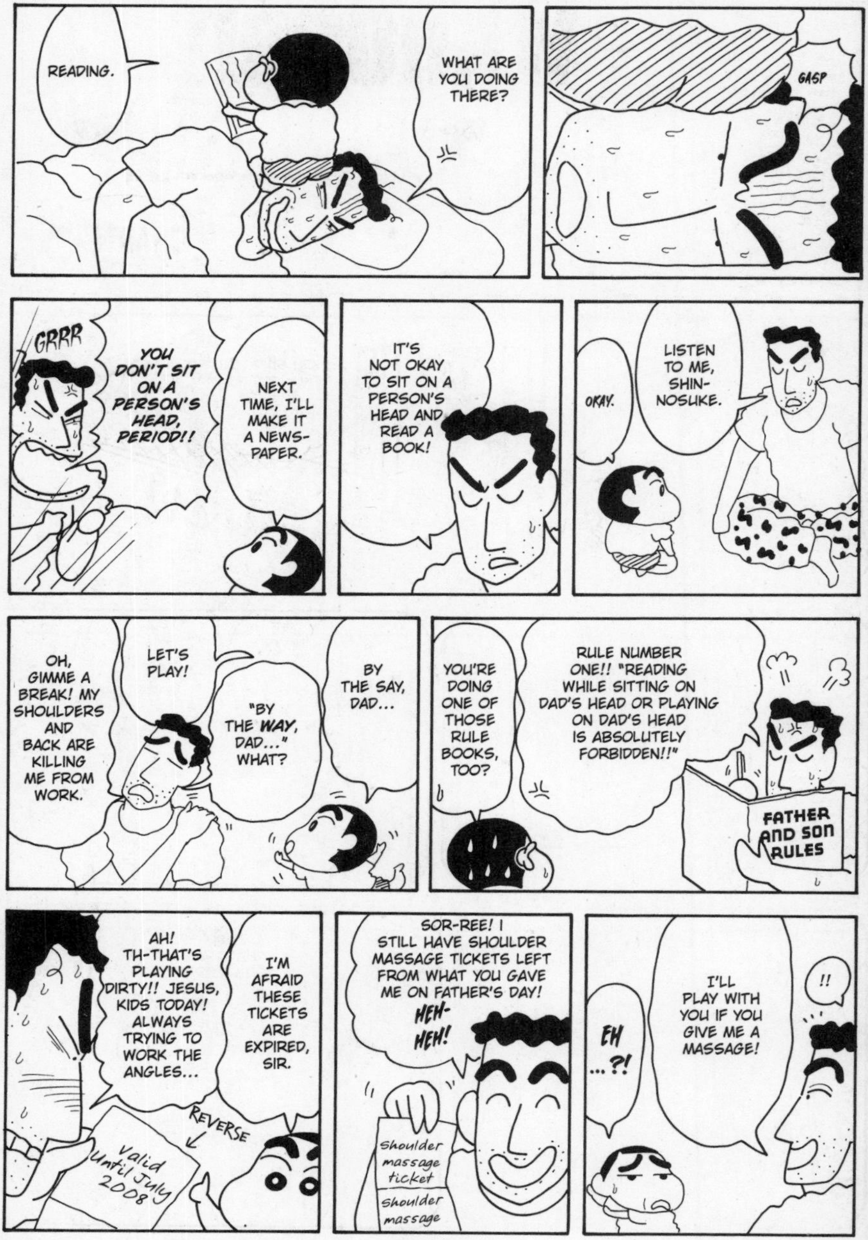
GASP
WHAT ARE YOU DOING THERE?
READING.
LISTEN TO ME, SHINNOSUKE.
OKAY.
IT'S NOT OKAY TO SIT ON A PERSON'S HEAD AND READ A BOOK!
NEXT TIME, I'LL MAKE IT A NEWSPAPER.
GRRR
YOU DON'T SIT ON A PERSON'S HEAD, PERIOD!!
RULE NUMBER ONE!! "READING WHILE SITTING ON DAD'S HEAD OR PLAYING ON DAD'S HEAD IS ABSOLUTELY FORBIDDEN!!"
FATHER AND SON RULES
YOU'RE DOING ONE OF THOSE RULE BOOKS, TOO?
BY THE SAY, DAD...
"BY THE WAY, DAD..." WHAT?
LET'S PLAY!
OH, GIMME A BREAK! MY SHOULDERS AND BACK ARE KILLING ME FROM WORK.
!!
I'LL PLAY WITH YOU IF YOU GIVE ME A MASSAGE!
EH ...?!
SOR-REE! I STILL HAVE SHOULDER MASSAGE TICKETS LEFT FROM WHAT YOU GAVE ME ON FATHER'S DAY!
HEH-HEH!
Shoulder massage ticket
Shoulder massage
I'M AFRAID THESE TICKETS ARE EXPIRED, SIR.
AH! TH-THAT'S PLAYING DIRTY!! JESUS, KIDS TODAY! ALWAYS TRYING TO WORK THE ANGLES...
REVERSE
Valid Until July 2008

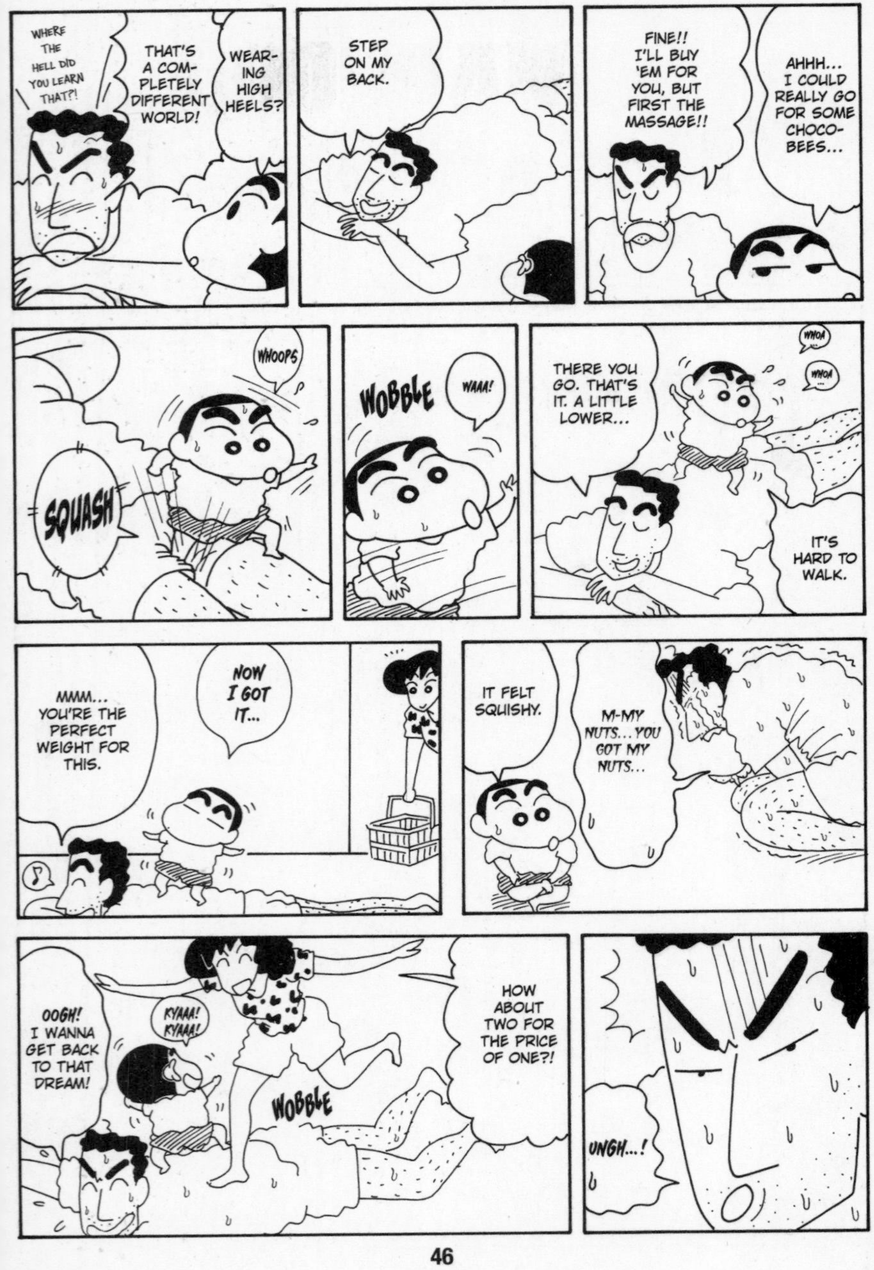
AHHH... I COULD REALLY GO FOR SOME CHOCO-BEES...
FINE!! I'LL BUY 'EM FOR YOU, BUT FIRST THE MASSAGE!!
STEP ON MY BACK.
WEAR-ING HIGH HEELS?
THAT'S A COM-PLETELY DIFFERENT WORLD!
WHERE THE HELL DID YOU LEARN THAT?!
WHOA
WHOA
THERE YOU GO. THAT'S IT. A LITTLE LOWER...
IT'S HARD TO WALK.
WAAA!
WOBBLE
WHOOPS
SQUASH
M-MY NUTS... YOU GOT MY NUTS...
IT FELT SQUISHY.
NOW I GOT IT...
MMM... YOU'RE THE PERFECT WEIGHT FOR THIS.
UNGH...!
HOW ABOUT TWO FOR THE PRICE OF ONE?!
KYAAA! KYAAA!
OOGH! I WANNA GET BACK TO THAT DREAM!
WOBBLE

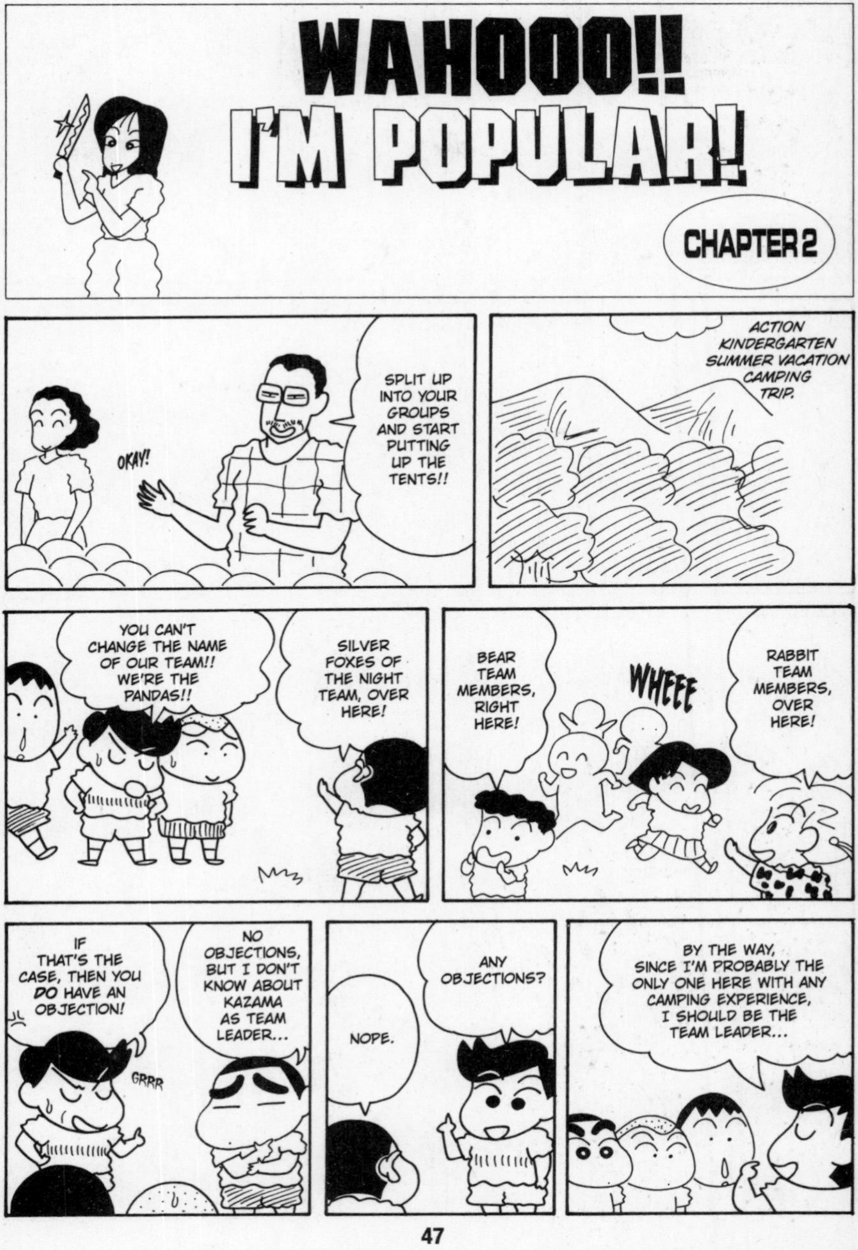
WAHOOO!! I'M POPULAR!
CHAPTER 2
ACTION KINDERGARTEN SUMMER VACATION CAMPING TRIP.
SPLIT UP INTO YOUR GROUPS AND START PUTTING UP THE TENTS!!
OKAY!
RABBIT TEAM MEMBERS, OVER HERE!
WHEEE
BEAR TEAM MEMBERS, RIGHT HERE!
SILVER FOXES OF THE NIGHT TEAM, OVER HERE!
YOU CAN'T CHANGE THE NAME OF OUR TEAM!! WE'RE THE PANDAS!!
BY THE WAY, SINCE I'M PROBABLY THE ONLY ONE HERE WITH ANY CAMPING EXPERIENCE, I SHOULD BE THE TEAM LEADER...
ANY OBJECTIONS?
NOPE.
NO OBJECTIONS, BUT I DON'T KNOW ABOUT KAZAMA AS TEAM LEADER...
IF THAT'S THE CASE, THEN YOU DO HAVE AN OBJECTION!
GRRR

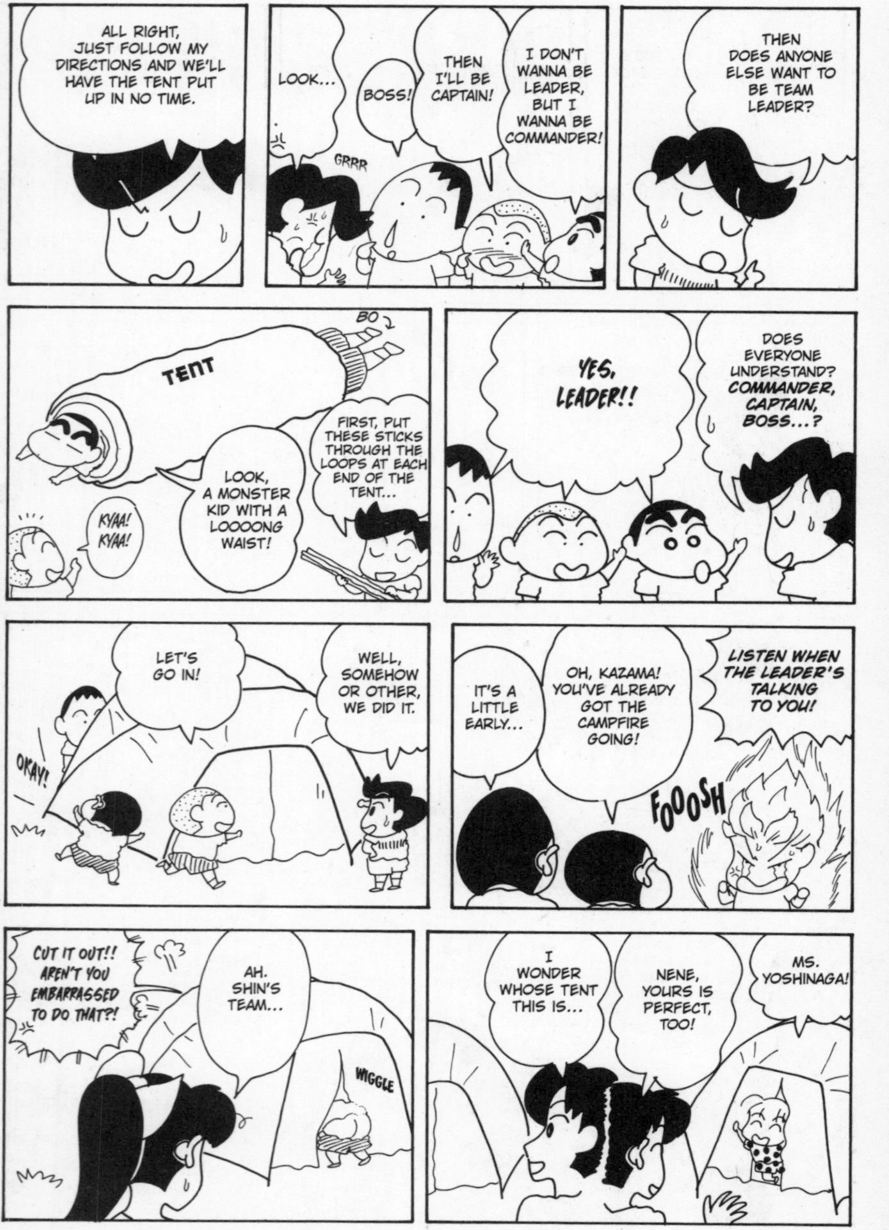
ALL RIGHT, JUST FOLLOW MY DIRECTIONS AND WE'LL HAVE THE TENT PUT UP IN NO TIME.
I DON'T WANNA BE LEADER, BUT I WANNA BE COMMANDER!
THEN I'LL BE CAPTAIN!
BOSS!
LOOK...
GRRR
THEN DOES ANYONE ELSE WANT TO BE TEAM LEADER?
TENT
BO
FIRST, PUT THESE STICKS THROUGH THE LOOPS AT EACH END OF THE TENT...
LOOK, A MONSTER KID WITH A LOOOONG WAIST!
KYAA! KYAA!
DOES EVERYONE UNDERSTAND? COMMANDER, CAPTAIN, BOSS...?
YES, LEADER!!
WELL, SOMEHOW OR OTHER, WE DID IT.
LET'S GO IN!
OKAY!
LISTEN WHEN THE LEADER'S TALKING TO YOU!
FOOOSH
OH, KAZAMA! YOU'VE ALREADY GOT THE CAMPFIRE GOING!
IT'S A LITTLE EARLY...
AH. SHIN'S TEAM...
WIGGLE
CUT IT OUT!! AREN'T YOU EMBARRASSED TO DO THAT?!
MS. YOSHINAGA!
NENE, YOURS IS PERFECT, TOO!
I WONDER WHOSE TENT THIS IS...

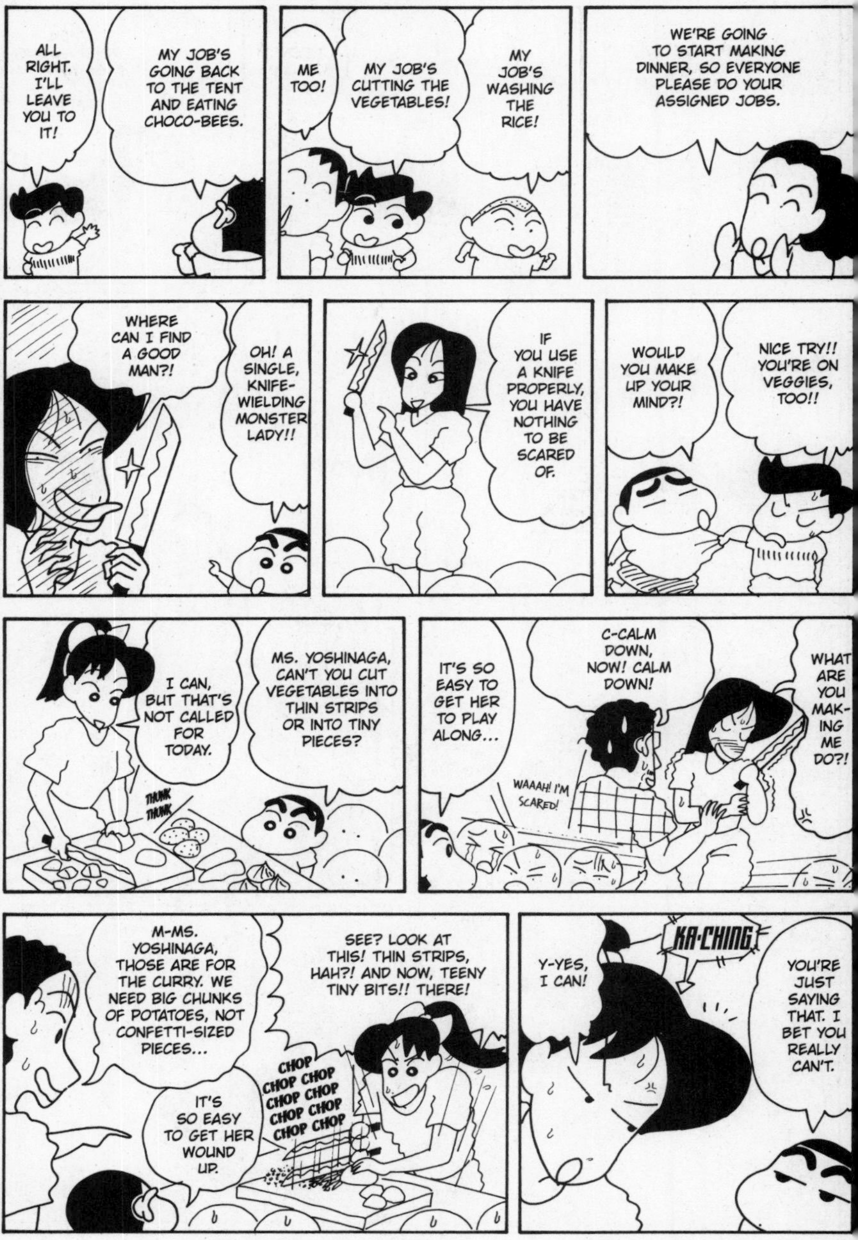
WE'RE GOING TO START MAKING DINNER, SO EVERYONE PLEASE DO YOUR ASSIGNED JOBS.
MY JOB'S WASHING THE RICE!
MY JOB'S CUTTING THE VEGETABLES!
ME TOO!
MY JOB'S GOING BACK TO THE TENT AND EATING CHOCO-BEES.
ALL RIGHT. I'LL LEAVE YOU TO IT!
NICE TRY!! YOU'RE ON VEGGIES, TOO!!
WOULD YOU MAKE UP YOUR MIND?!
IF YOU USE A KNIFE PROPERLY, YOU HAVE NOTHING TO BE SCARED OF.
OH! A SINGLE, KNIFE-WIELDING MONSTER LADY!!
WHERE CAN I FIND A GOOD MAN?!
WHAT ARE YOU MAK-ING ME DO?!
C-CALM DOWN, NOW! CALM DOWN!
IT'S SO EASY TO GET HER TO PLAY ALONG...
WAAAH! I'M SCARED!
MS. YOSHINAGA, CAN'T YOU CUT VEGETABLES INTO THIN STRIPS OR INTO TINY PIECES?
I CAN, BUT THAT'S NOT CALLED FOR TODAY.
THUNK THUNK
YOU'RE JUST SAYING THAT. I BET YOU REALLY CAN'T.
KA-CHING
Y-YES, I CAN!
SEE? LOOK AT THIS! THIN STRIPS, HAH?! AND NOW, TEENY TINY BITS!! THERE!
M-MS. YOSHINAGA, THOSE ARE FOR THE CURRY. WE NEED BIG CHUNKS OF POTATOES, NOT CONFETTI-SIZED PIECES...
CHOP CHOP CHOP CHOP CHOP CHOP CHOP CHOP CHOP CHOP
IT'S SO EASY TO GET HER WOUND UP.

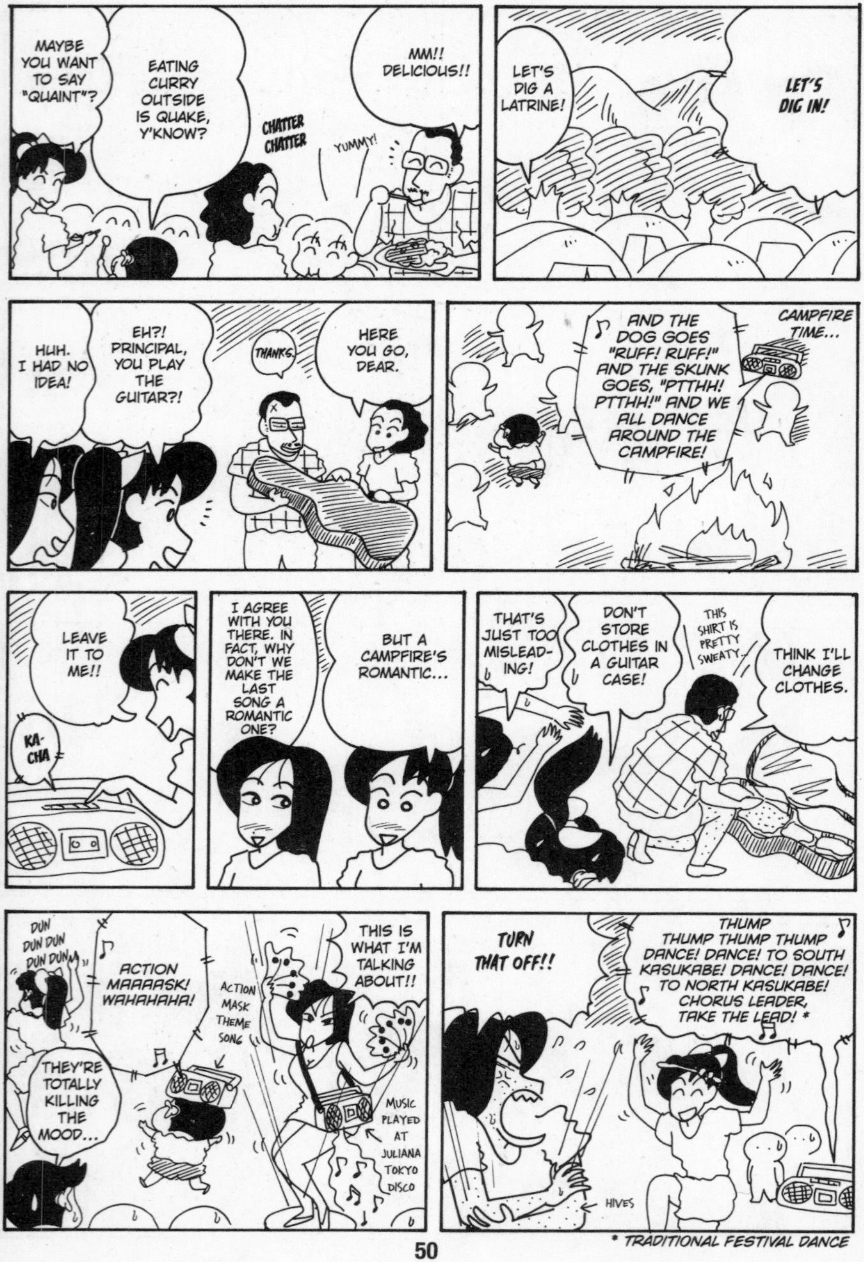
LET'S DIG IN!
LET'S DIG A LATRINE!
MM!! DELICIOUS!!
YUMMY!
CHATTER CHATTER
EATING CURRY OUTSIDE IS QUAKE, Y'KNOW?
MAYBE YOU WANT TO SAY "QUAINT"?
CAMPFIRE TIME...
AND THE DOG GOES "RUFF! RUFF!" AND THE SKUNK GOES, "PTTHH! PTTHH!" AND WE ALL DANCE AROUND THE CAMPFIRE!
HERE YOU GO, DEAR.
THANKS.
EH?! PRINCIPAL, YOU PLAY THE GUITAR?!
HUH. I HAD NO IDEA!
THINK I'LL CHANGE CLOTHES.
THIS SHIRT IS PRETTY SWEATY...
DON'T STORE CLOTHES IN A GUITAR CASE!
THAT'S JUST TOO MISLEAD-ING!
BUT A CAMPFIRE'S ROMANTIC...
I AGREE WITH YOU THERE. IN FACT, WHY DON'T WE MAKE THE LAST SONG A ROMANTIC ONE?
LEAVE IT TO ME!!
KA-CHA
THUMP THUMP THUMP THUMP DANCE! DANCE! TO SOUTH KASUKABE! DANCE! DANCE! TO NORTH KASUKABE! CHORUS LEADER, TAKE THE LEAD! *
TURN THAT OFF!!
HIVES
THIS IS WHAT I'M TALKING ABOUT!!
ACTION MASK THEME SONG
MUSIC PLAYED AT JULIANA TOKYO DISCO
ACTION MAAAASK! WAHAHAHA!
DUN DUN DUN DUN DUN DUN
THEY'RE TOTALLY KILLING THE MOOD...

* TRADITIONAL FESTIVAL DANCE

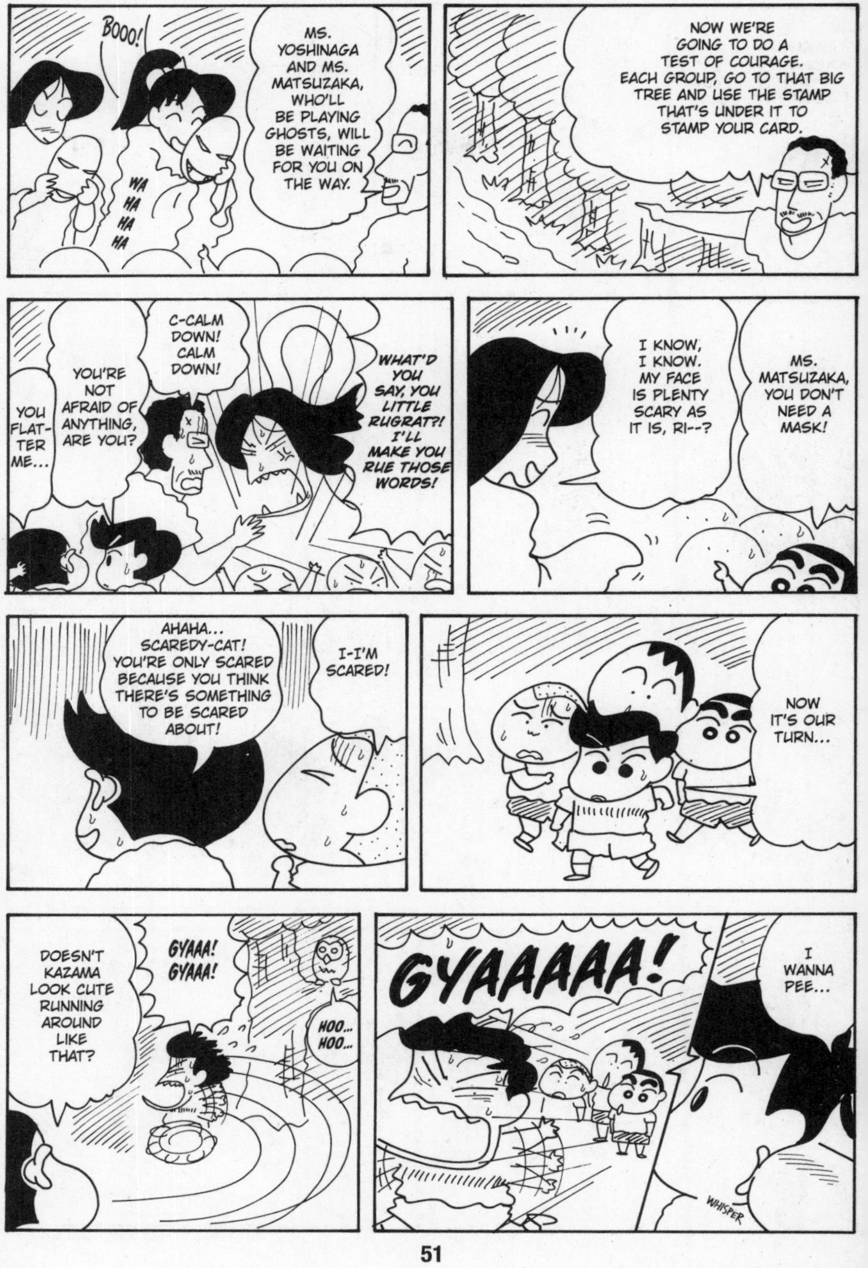
NOW WE'RE GOING TO DO A TEST OF COURAGE. EACH GROUP, GO TO THAT BIG TREE AND USE THE STAMP THAT'S UNDER IT TO STAMP YOUR CARD.
MS. YOSHINAGA AND MS. MATSUZAKA, WHO'LL BE PLAYING GHOSTS, WILL BE WAITING FOR YOU ON THE WAY.
BOOO!
WA HA HA HA
MS. MATSUZAKA, YOU DON'T NEED A MASK!
I KNOW, I KNOW. MY FACE IS PLENTY SCARY AS IT IS, RI--?
WHAT'D YOU SAY, YOU LITTLE RUGRAT?! I'LL MAKE YOU RUE THOSE WORDS!
C-CALM DOWN! CALM DOWN!
YOU'RE NOT AFRAID OF ANYTHING, ARE YOU?
YOU FLAT-TER ME...
NOW IT'S OUR TURN...
I-I'M SCARED!
AHAHA... SCAREDY-CAT! YOU'RE ONLY SCARED BECAUSE YOU THINK THERE'S SOMETHING TO BE SCARED ABOUT!
I WANNA PEE...
GYAAAAAA!
WHISPER
HOO... HOO...
GYAAA! GYAAA!
DOESN'T KAZAMA LOOK CUTE RUNNING AROUND LIKE THAT?

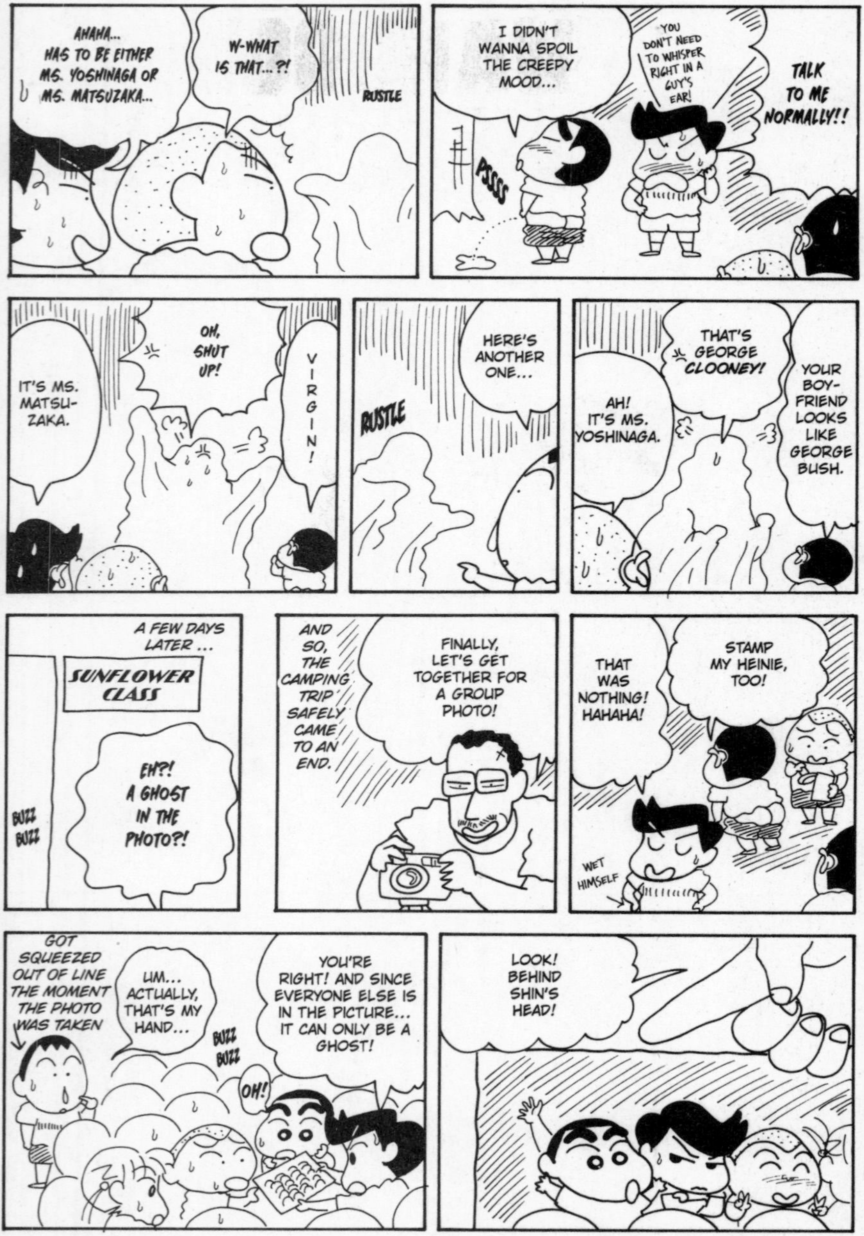
YOU DON'T NEED TO WHISPER RIGHT IN A GUY'S EAR!
TALK TO ME NORMALLY!!
I DIDN'T WANNA SPOIL THE CREEPY MOOD...
PSSSS
RUSTLE
W-WHAT IS THAT...?!
AHAHA... HAS TO BE EITHER MS. YOSHINAGA OR MS. MATSUZAKA...
AH! IT'S MS. YOSHINAGA.
YOUR BOY-FRIEND LOOKS LIKE GEORGE BUSH.
THAT'S GEORGE CLOONEY!
HERE'S ANOTHER ONE...
RUSTLE
IT'S MS. MATSU-ZAKA.
VIRGIN!
OH, SHUT UP!
STAMP MY HEINIE, TOO!
THAT WAS NOTHING! HAHAHA!
WET HIMSELF
FINALLY, LET'S GET TOGETHER FOR A GROUP PHOTO!
AND SO, THE CAMPING TRIP SAFELY CAME TO AN END.
A FEW DAYS LATER...
SUNFLOWER CLASS
EH?! A GHOST IN THE PHOTO?!
BUZZ BUZZ
LOOK! BEHIND SHIN'S HEAD!
OH!
YOU'RE RIGHT! AND SINCE EVERYONE ELSE IS IN THE PICTURE... IT CAN ONLY BE A GHOST!
BUZZ BUZZ
UM... ACTUALLY, THAT'S MY HAND...
GOT SQUEEZED OUT OF LINE THE MOMENT THE PHOTO WAS TAKEN

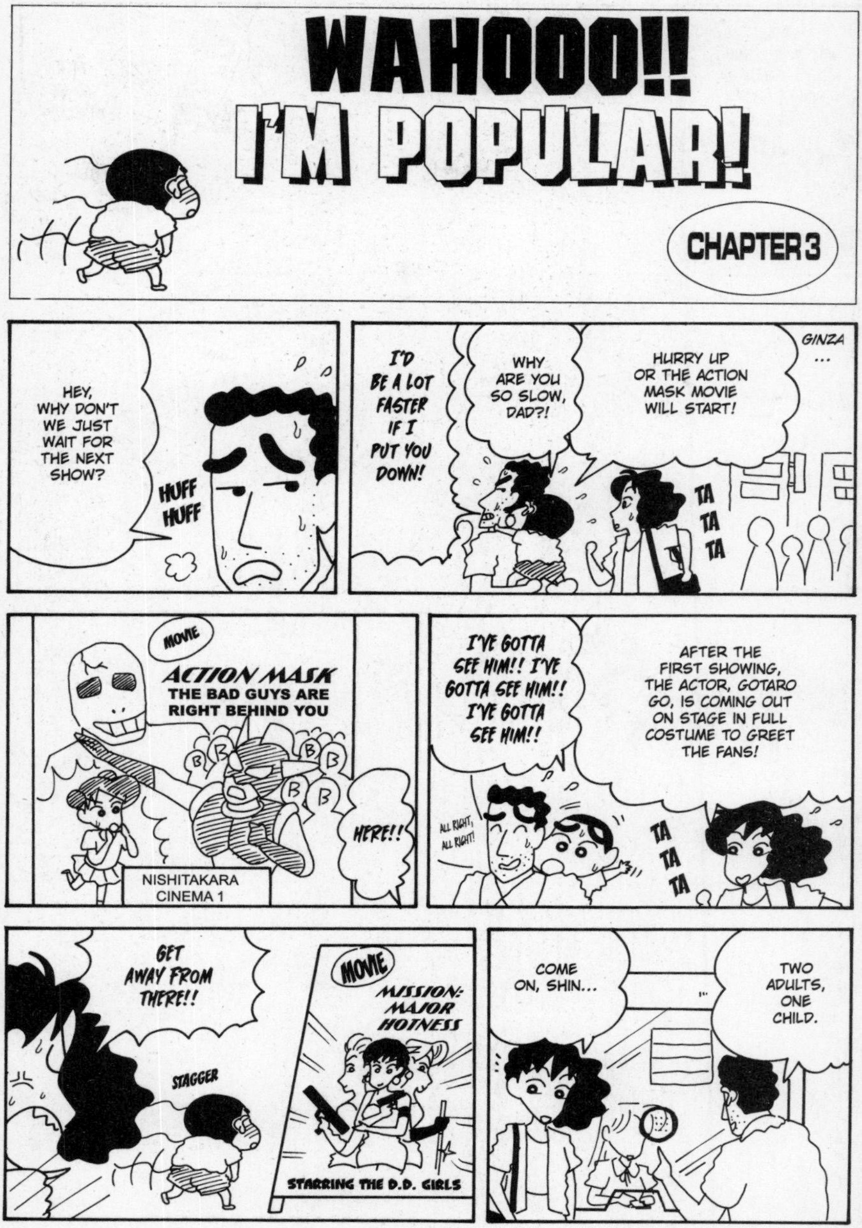
WAHOOO!! I'M POPULAR!
CHAPTER 3
GINZA ...
HURRY UP OR THE ACTION MASK MOVIE WILL START!
WHY ARE YOU SO SLOW, DAD?!
I'D BE A LOT FASTER IF I PUT YOU DOWN!
TA TA TA
HEY, WHY DON'T WE JUST WAIT FOR THE NEXT SHOW?
HUFF HUFF
AFTER THE FIRST SHOWING, THE ACTOR, GOTARO GO, IS COMING OUT ON STAGE IN FULL COSTUME TO GREET THE FANS!
I'VE GOTTA SEE HIM!! I'VE GOTTA SEE HIM!! I'VE GOTTA SEE HIM!!
ALL RIGHT, ALL RIGHT!
TA TA TA
MOVIE
ACTION MASK
THE BAD GUYS ARE RIGHT BEHIND YOU
HERE!!
NISHITAKARA CINEMA 1
TWO ADULTS, ONE CHILD.
COME ON, SHIN...
MOVIE
MISSION: MAJOR HOTNESS
STARRING THE D.D. GIRLS
GET AWAY FROM THERE!!
STAGGER

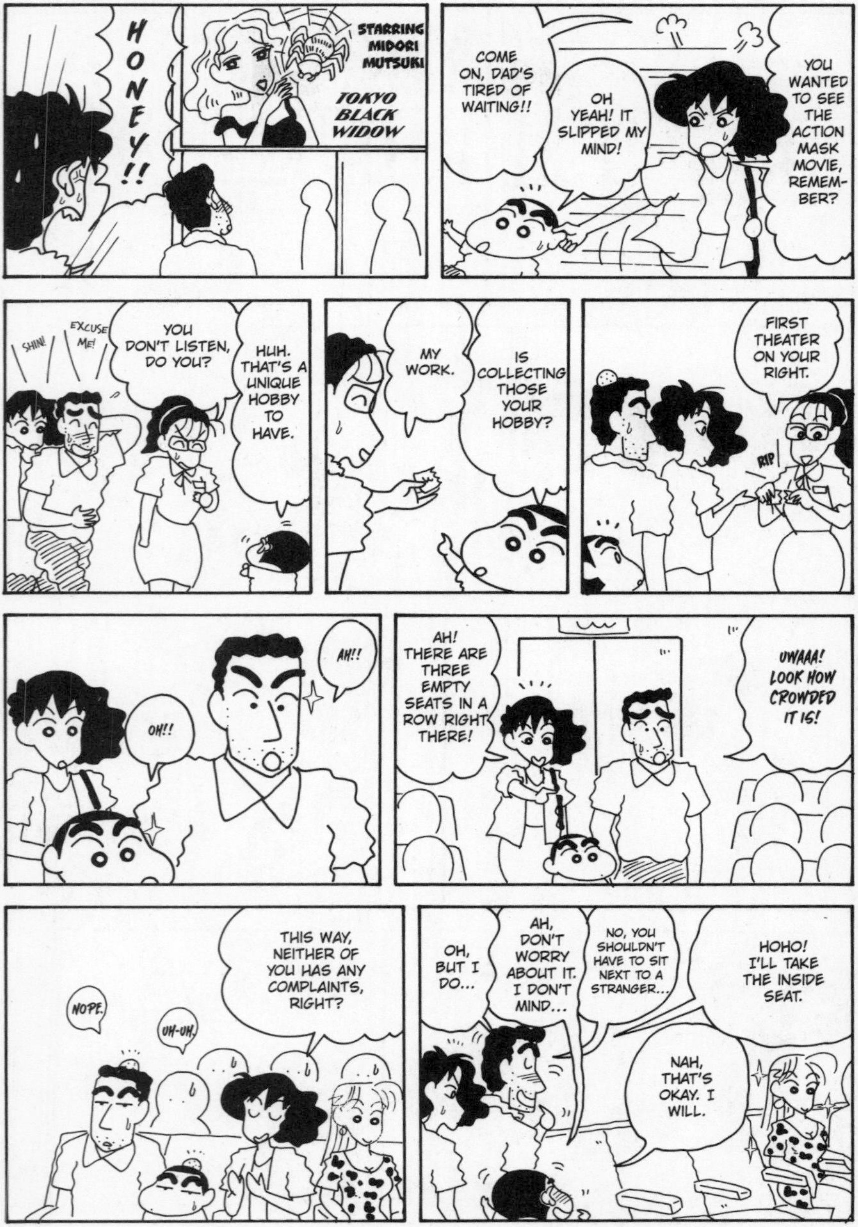
YOU WANTED TO SEE THE ACTION MASK MOVIE, REMEMBER?
OH YEAH! IT SLIPPED MY MIND!
COME ON, DAD'S TIRED OF WAITING!!
STARRING MIDORI MUTSUKI
TOKYO BLACK WIDOW
HONEY!!
FIRST THEATER ON YOUR RIGHT.
RIP
IS COLLECTING THOSE YOUR HOBBY?
MY WORK.
HUH. THAT'S A UNIQUE HOBBY TO HAVE.
YOU DON'T LISTEN, DO YOU?
EXCUSE ME!
SHIN!
UWAAA! LOOK HOW CROWDED IT IS!
AH! THERE ARE THREE EMPTY SEATS IN A ROW RIGHT THERE!
AH!!
OH!!
HOHO! I'LL TAKE THE INSIDE SEAT.
NAH, THAT'S OKAY. I WILL.
NO, YOU SHOULDN'T HAVE TO SIT NEXT TO A STRANGER...
AH, DON'T WORRY ABOUT IT. I DON'T MIND...
OH, BUT I DO...
THIS WAY, NEITHER OF YOU HAS ANY COMPLAINTS, RIGHT?
UH-UH.
NOPE.

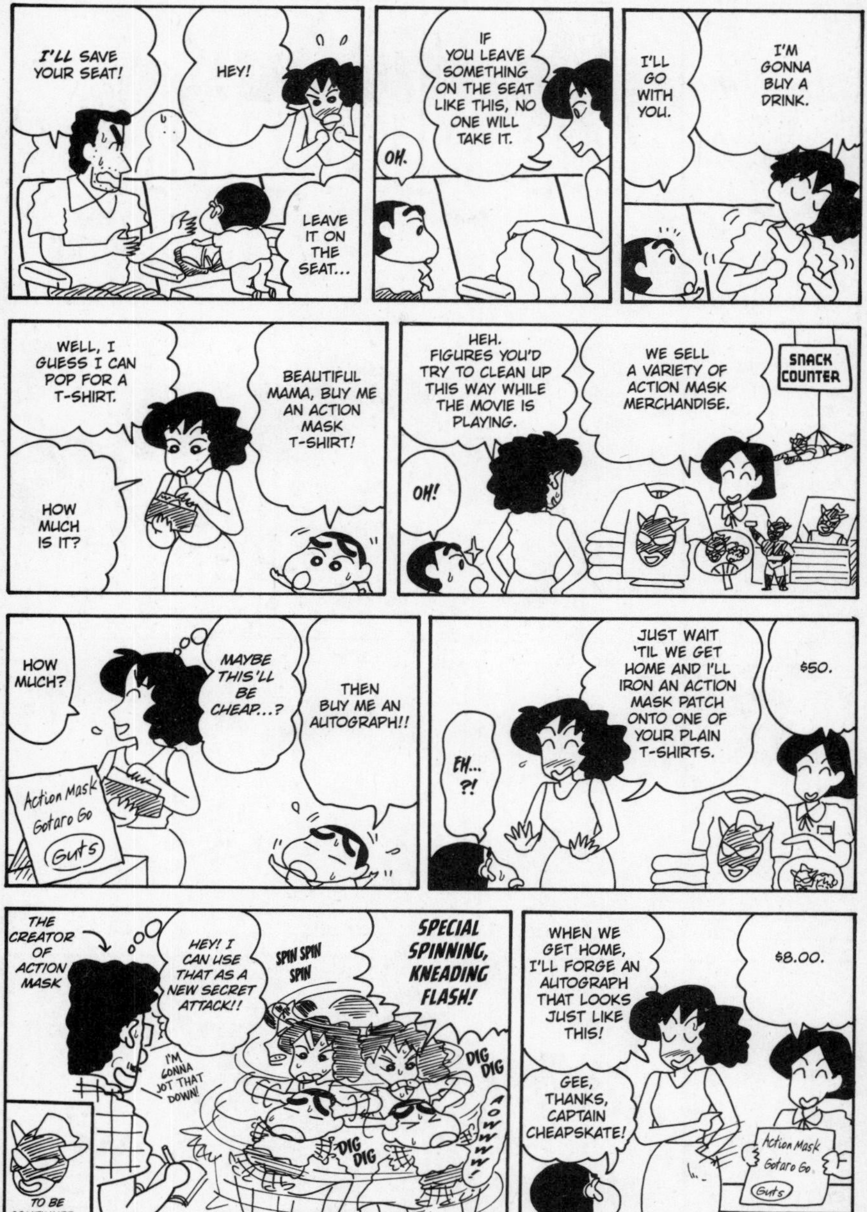
I'M GONNA BUY A DRINK.
I'LL GO WITH YOU.
IF YOU LEAVE SOMETHING ON THE SEAT LIKE THIS, NO ONE WILL TAKE IT.
OH.
HEY!
I'LL SAVE YOUR SEAT!
LEAVE IT ON THE SEAT...
SNACK COUNTER
WE SELL A VARIETY OF ACTION MASK MERCHANDISE.
HEH. FIGURES YOU'D TRY TO CLEAN UP THIS WAY WHILE THE MOVIE IS PLAYING.
OH!
BEAUTIFUL MAMA, BUY ME AN ACTION MASK T-SHIRT!
WELL, I GUESS I CAN POP FOR A T-SHIRT.
HOW MUCH IS IT?
$50.
JUST WAIT 'TIL WE GET HOME AND I'LL IRON AN ACTION MASK PATCH ONTO ONE OF YOUR PLAIN T-SHIRTS.
EH...?!
THEN BUY ME AN AUTOGRAPH!!
MAYBE THIS'LL BE CHEAP...?
HOW MUCH?
Action Mask Gotaro Go Guts
$8.00.
WHEN WE GET HOME, I'LL FORGE AN AUTOGRAPH THAT LOOKS JUST LIKE THIS!
GEE, THANKS, CAPTAIN CHEAPSKATE!
Action Mask Gotaro Go Guts
SPECIAL SPINNING, KNEADING FLASH!
SPIN SPIN SPIN
HEY! I CAN USE THAT AS A NEW SECRET ATTACK!!
THE CREATOR OF ACTION MASK
DIG DIG
AOWWWWW!
I'M GONNA JOT THAT DOWN!
DIG DIG
TO BE CONTINUED...

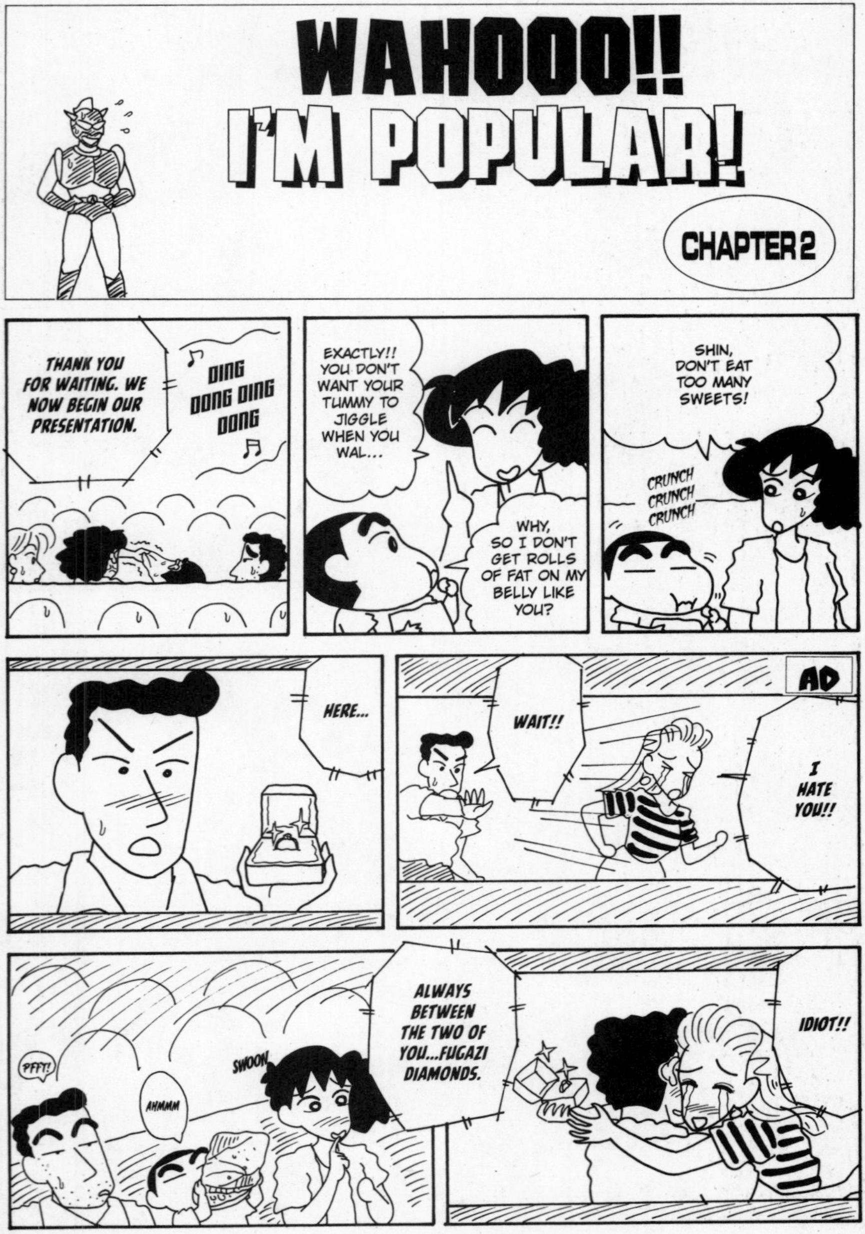
WAHOOO!! I'M POPULAR!
CHAPTER 2
SHIN, DON'T EAT TOO MANY SWEETS!
CRUNCH CRUNCH CRUNCH
EXACTLY!! YOU DON'T WANT YOUR TUMMY TO JIGGLE WHEN YOU WAL...
WHY, SO I DON'T GET ROLLS OF FAT ON MY BELLY LIKE YOU?
DING DONG DING DONG
THANK YOU FOR WAITING. WE NOW BEGIN OUR PRESENTATION.
AD
I HATE YOU!!
WAIT!!
HERE...
IDIOT!!
ALWAYS BETWEEN THE TWO OF YOU...FUGAZI DIAMONDS.
SWOON
AHMMM
PFFT!

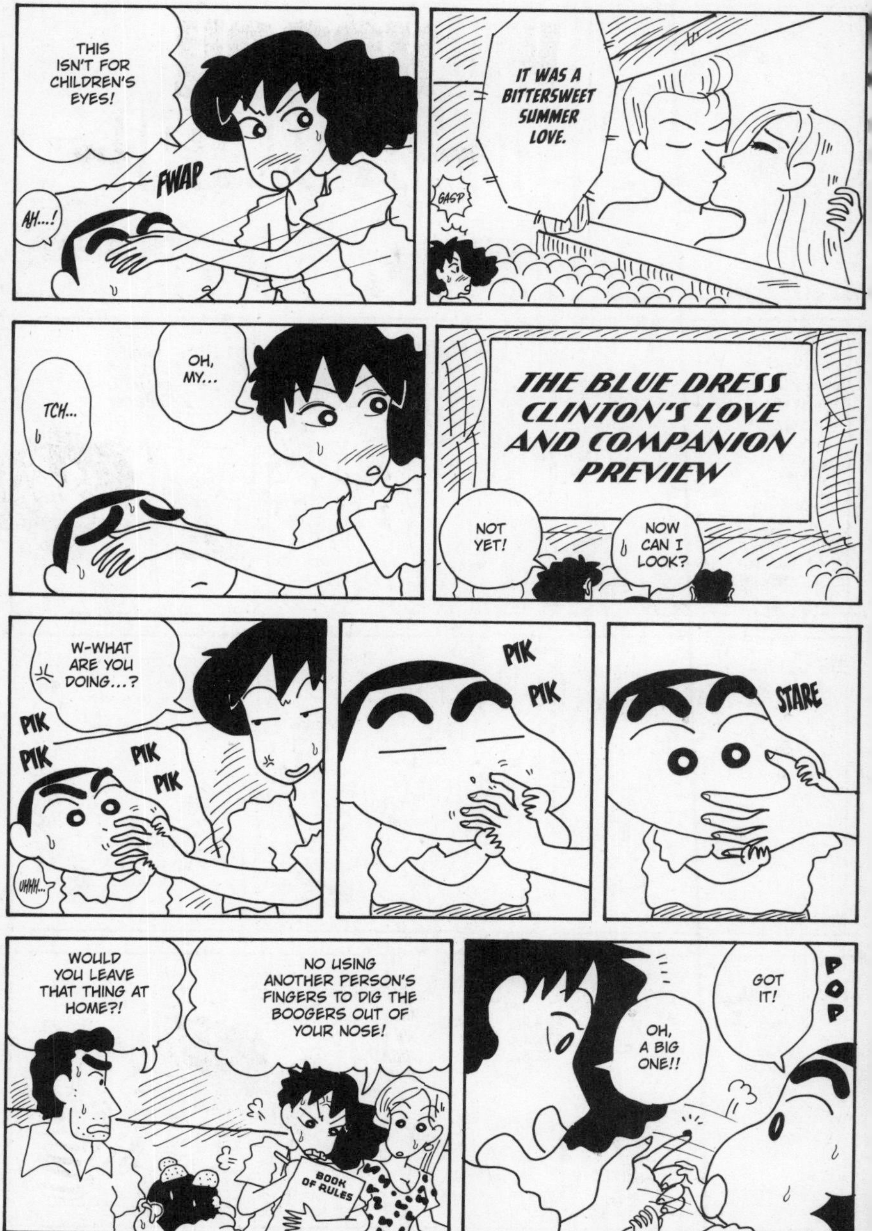
IT WAS A BITTERSWEET SUMMER LOVE.
GASP
THIS ISN'T FOR CHILDREN'S EYES!
FWAP
AH...!
THE BLUE DRESS CLINTON'S LOVE AND COMPANION PREVIEW
NOW CAN I LOOK?
NOT YET!
OH, MY...
TCH...
STARE
PIK
PIK
W-WHAT ARE YOU DOING...?
PIK
PIK
PIK
PIK
UHHH...!
POP
GOT IT!
OH, A BIG ONE!!
NO USING ANOTHER PERSON'S FINGERS TO DIG THE BOOGERS OUT OF YOUR NOSE!
WOULD YOU LEAVE THAT THING AT HOME?!
BOOK OF RULES

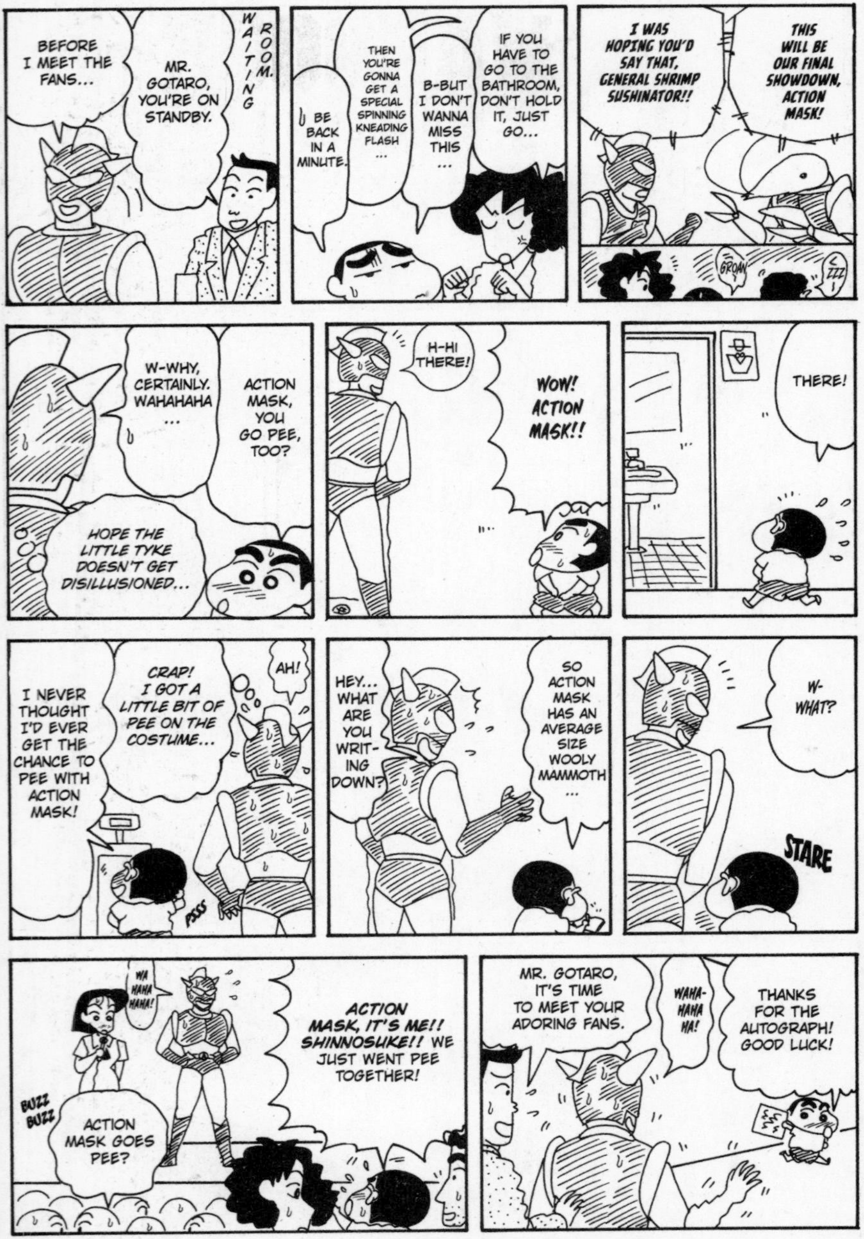

THIS WILL BE OUR FINAL SHOWDOWN, ACTION MASK!
I WAS HOPING YOU'D SAY THAT, GENERAL SHRIMP SUSHINATOR!!
ZZZ
GROAN
IF YOU HAVE TO GO TO THE BATHROOM, DON'T HOLD IT, JUST GO...
B-BUT I DON'T WANNA MISS THIS ...
THEN YOU'RE GONNA GET A SPECIAL SPINNING KNEADING FLASH ...
BE BACK IN A MINUTE.
WAITING ROOM.
MR. GOTARO, YOU'RE ON STANDBY.
BEFORE I MEET THE FANS...
THERE!
H-HI THERE!
WOW! ACTION MASK!!
ACTION MASK, YOU GO PEE, TOO?
W-WHY, CERTAINLY. WAHAHAHA ...
HOPE THE LITTLE TYKE DOESN'T GET DISILLUSIONED...
W-WHAT?
STARE
SO ACTION MASK HAS AN AVERAGE SIZE WOOLY MAMMOTH ...
HEY... WHAT ARE YOU WRITING DOWN?
AH!
CRAP! I GOT A LITTLE BIT OF PEE ON THE COSTUME...
I NEVER THOUGHT I'D EVER GET THE CHANCE TO PEE WITH ACTION MASK!
PSSS
THANKS FOR THE AUTOGRAPH! GOOD LUCK!
WAHAHAHA HA!
MR. GOTARO, IT'S TIME TO MEET YOUR ADORING FANS.
ACTION MASK, IT'S ME!! SHINNOSUKE!! WE JUST WENT PEE TOGETHER!
WA HAHA HAHA!
BUZZ BUZZ
ACTION MASK GOES PEE?

WAHOOO!! I'M POPULAR!

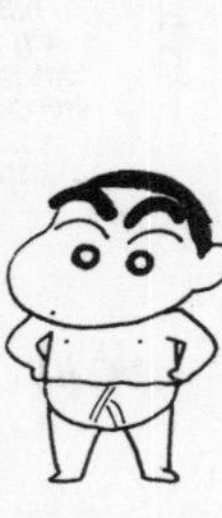

CHAPTER 5

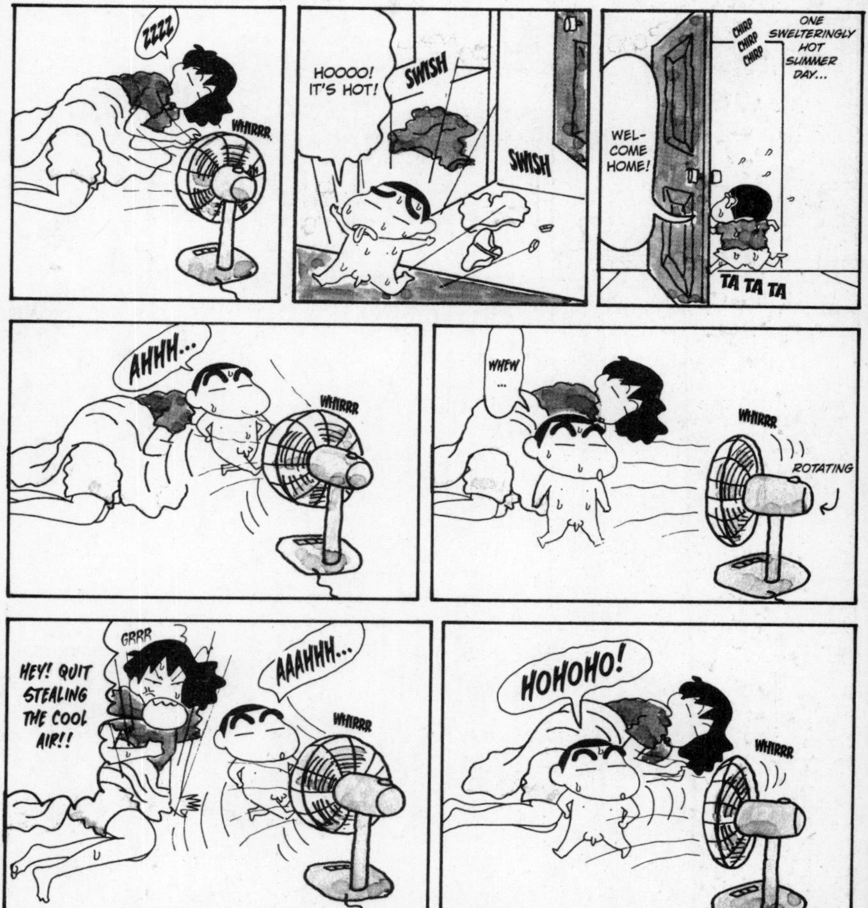

ONE SWELTERINGLY HOT SUMMER DAY...
CHIRP CHIRP CHIRP
WEL-COME HOME!
TA TA TA
HOOOO! IT'S HOT!
SWISH
SWISH
ZZZZ
WHIRRR
WHEW...
WHIRRR
ROTATING
AHHH...
WHIRRR
HOHOHO!
WHIRRR
GRRR
HEY! QUIT STEALING THE COOL AIR!!
AAAHHH...
WHIRRR

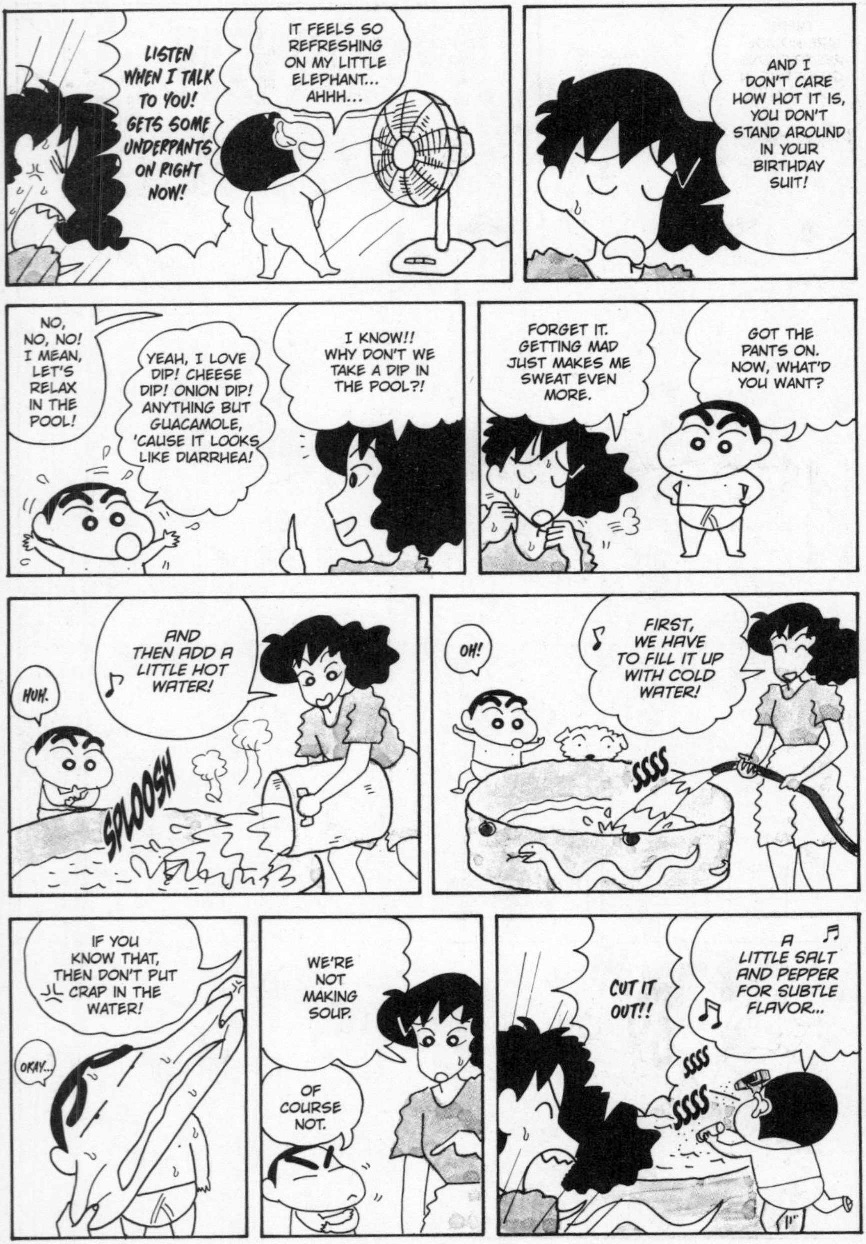
AND I DON'T CARE HOW HOT IT IS, YOU DON'T STAND AROUND IN YOUR BIRTHDAY SUIT!
IT FEELS SO REFRESHING ON MY LITTLE ELEPHANT... AHHH...
LISTEN WHEN I TALK TO YOU! GETS SOME UNDERPANTS ON RIGHT NOW!
GOT THE PANTS ON. NOW, WHAT'D YOU WANT?
FORGET IT. GETTING MAD JUST MAKES ME SWEAT EVEN MORE.
I KNOW!! WHY DON'T WE TAKE A DIP IN THE POOL?!
YEAH, I LOVE DIP! CHEESE DIP! ONION DIP! ANYTHING BUT GUACAMOLE, 'CAUSE IT LOOKS LIKE DIARRHEA!
NO, NO, NO! I MEAN, LET'S RELAX IN THE POOL!
FIRST, WE HAVE TO FILL IT UP WITH COLD WATER!
OH!
SSSS
AND THEN ADD A LITTLE HOT WATER!
HUH.
SPLOOSH
A LITTLE SALT AND PEPPER FOR SUBTLE FLAVOR...
SSSS
SSSS
CUT IT OUT!!
WE'RE NOT MAKING SOUP.
OF COURSE NOT.
IF YOU KNOW THAT, THEN DON'T PUT CRAP IN THE WATER!
OKAY...

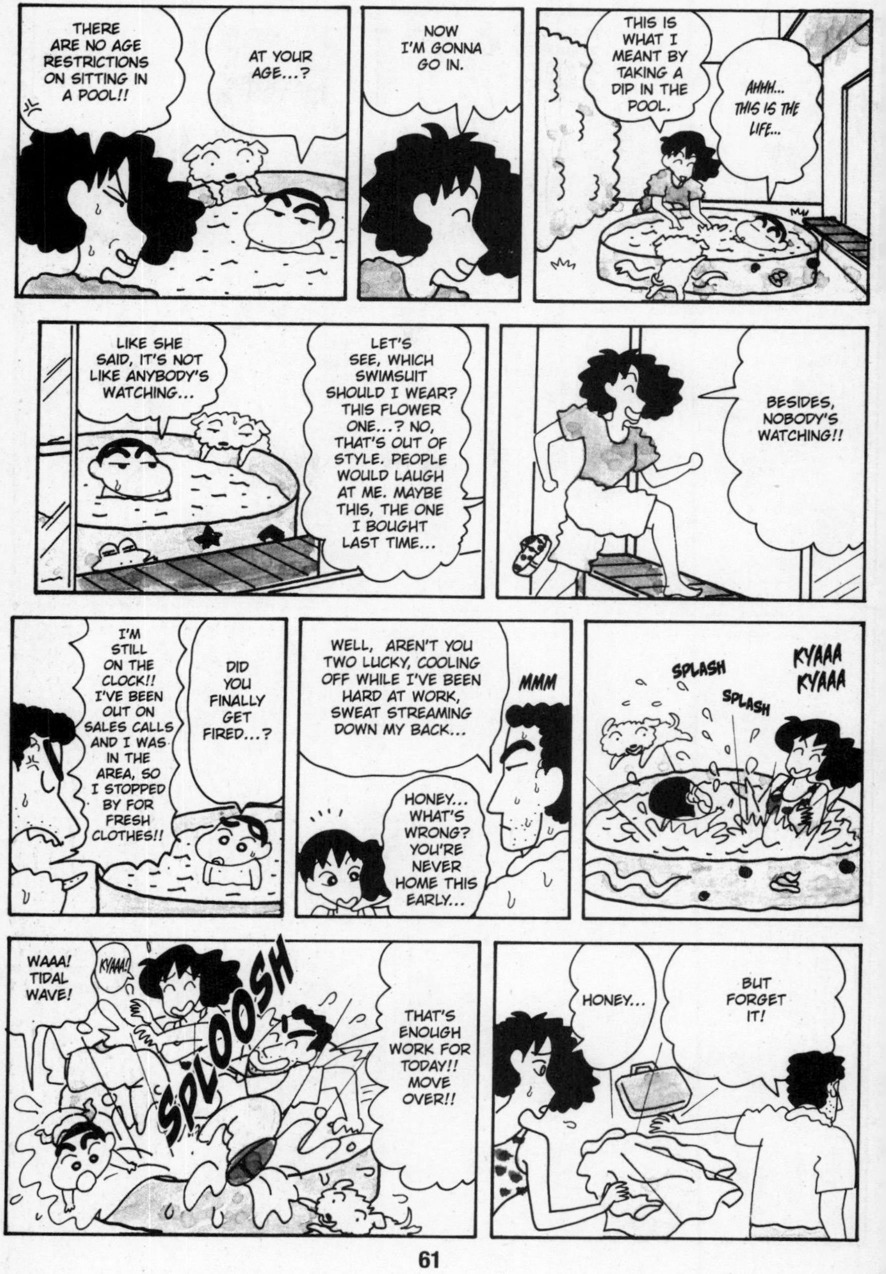
AHHH... THIS IS THE LIFE...
THIS IS WHAT I MEANT BY TAKING A DIP IN THE POOL.
NOW I'M GONNA GO IN.
AT YOUR AGE...?
THERE ARE NO AGE RESTRICTIONS ON SITTING IN A POOL!!
BESIDES, NOBODY'S WATCHING!!
LET'S SEE, WHICH SWIMSUIT SHOULD I WEAR? THIS FLOWER ONE...? NO, THAT'S OUT OF STYLE. PEOPLE WOULD LAUGH AT ME. MAYBE THIS, THE ONE I BOUGHT LAST TIME...
LIKE SHE SAID, IT'S NOT LIKE ANYBODY'S WATCHING...
KYAAA KYAAA
SPLASH
SPLASH
MMM
WELL, AREN'T YOU TWO LUCKY, COOLING OFF WHILE I'VE BEEN HARD AT WORK, SWEAT STREAMING DOWN MY BACK...
HONEY... WHAT'S WRONG? YOU'RE NEVER HOME THIS EARLY...
DID YOU FINALLY GET FIRED...?
I'M STILL ON THE CLOCK!! I'VE BEEN OUT ON SALES CALLS AND I WAS IN THE AREA, SO I STOPPED BY FOR FRESH CLOTHES!!
BUT FORGET IT!
HONEY...
THAT'S ENOUGH WORK FOR TODAY!! MOVE OVER!!
SPLOOSH
KYAAA!
WAAA! TIDAL WAVE!

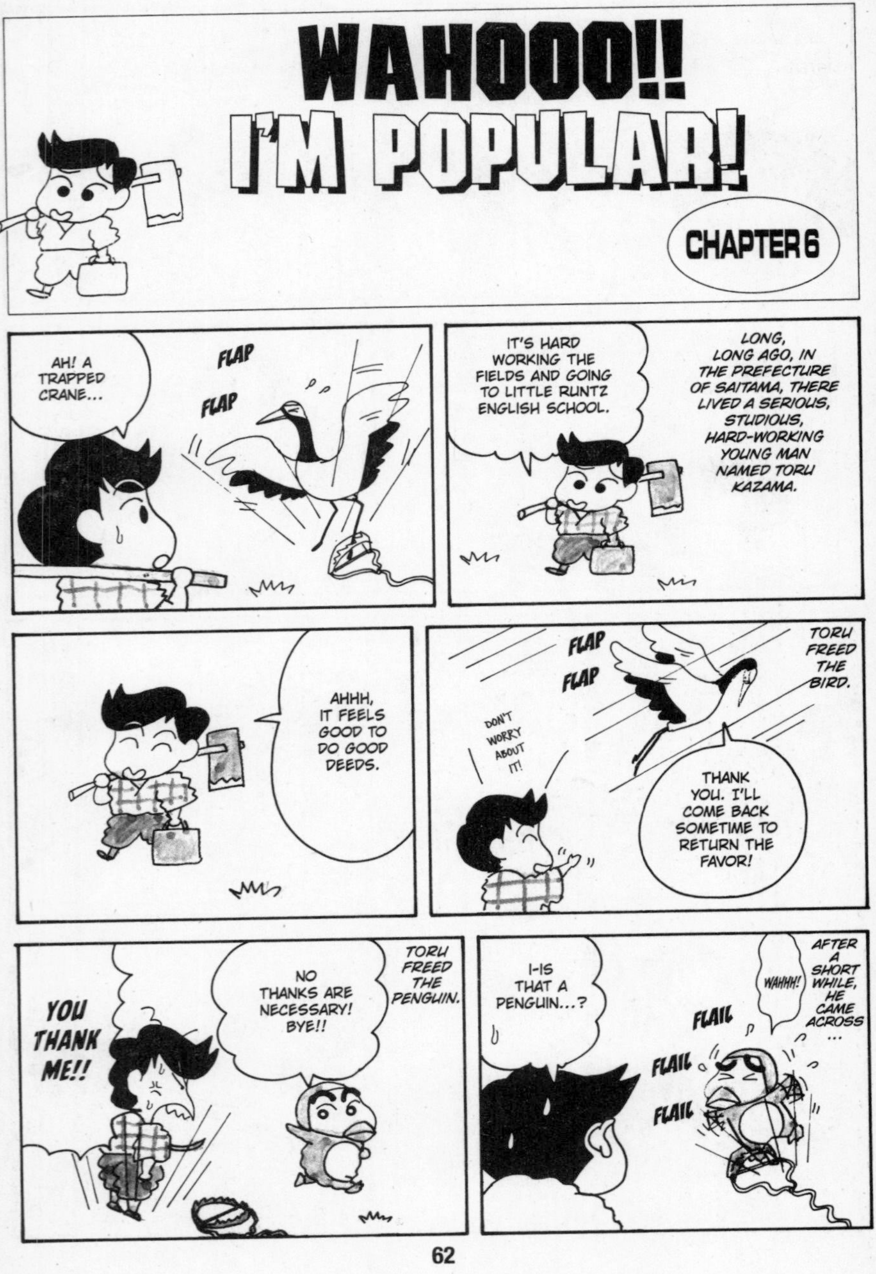
WAHOOO!! I'M POPULAR!
CHAPTER 6
LONG, LONG AGO, IN THE PREFECTURE OF SAITAMA, THERE LIVED A SERIOUS, STUDIOUS, HARD-WORKING YOUNG MAN NAMED TORU KAZAMA.
IT'S HARD WORKING THE FIELDS AND GOING TO LITTLE RUNTZ ENGLISH SCHOOL.
AH! A TRAPPED CRANE...
FLAP
FLAP
TORU FREED THE BIRD.
FLAP
FLAP
DON'T WORRY ABOUT IT!
THANK YOU. I'LL COME BACK SOMETIME TO RETURN THE FAVOR!
AHHH, IT FEELS GOOD TO DO GOOD DEEDS.
AFTER A SHORT WHILE, HE CAME ACROSS...
WAHHH!
I-IS THAT A PENGUIN...?
FLAIL
FLAIL
FLAIL
TORU FREED THE PENGUIN.
NO THANKS ARE NECESSARY! BYE!!
YOU THANK ME!!

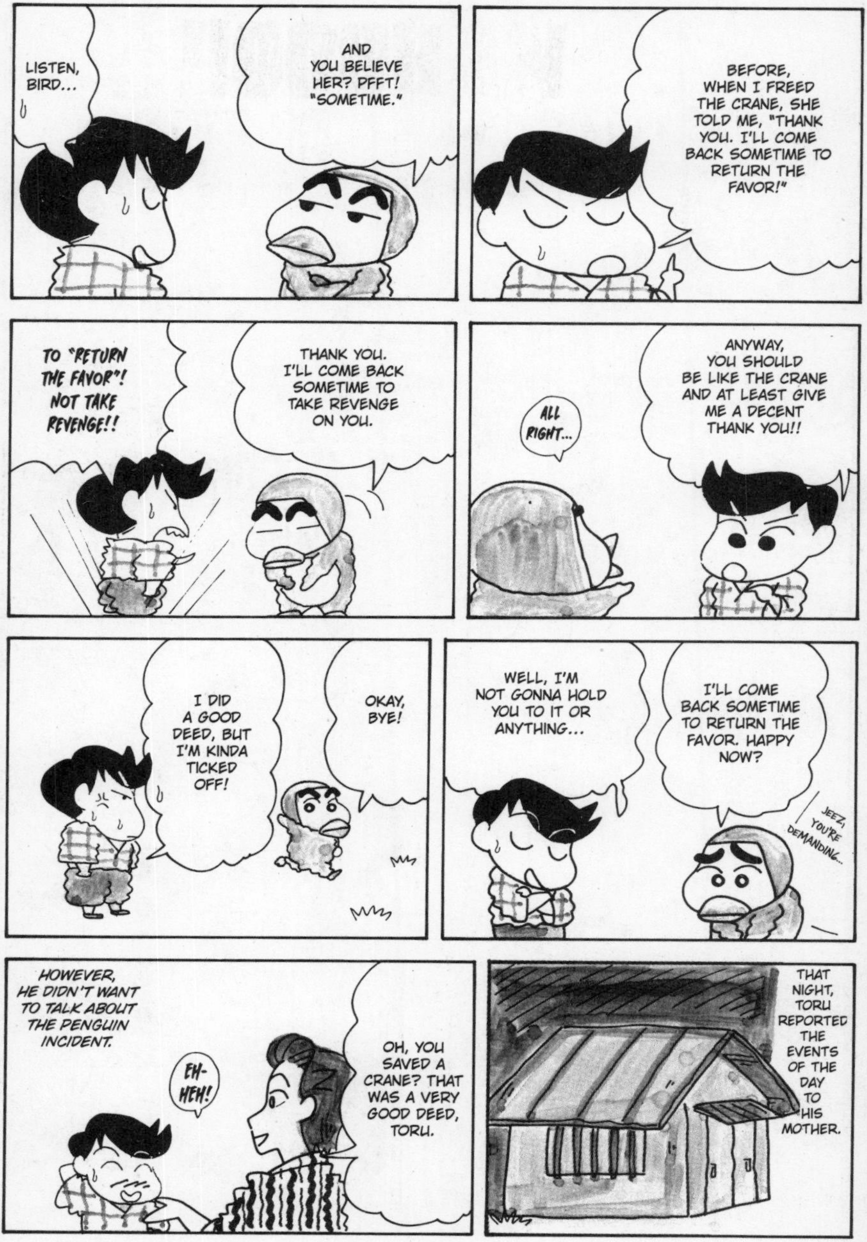
BEFORE, WHEN I FREED THE CRANE, SHE TOLD ME, "THANK YOU. I'LL COME BACK SOMETIME TO RETURN THE FAVOR!"
AND YOU BELIEVE HER? PFFT! "SOMETIME."
LISTEN, BIRD...
ANYWAY, YOU SHOULD BE LIKE THE CRANE AND AT LEAST GIVE ME A DECENT THANK YOU!!
ALL RIGHT...
THANK YOU. I'LL COME BACK SOMETIME TO TAKE REVENGE ON YOU.
TO "RETURN THE FAVOR"! NOT TAKE REVENGE!!
I'LL COME BACK SOMETIME TO RETURN THE FAVOR. HAPPY NOW?
JEEZ, YOU'RE DEMANDING...
WELL, I'M NOT GONNA HOLD YOU TO IT OR ANYTHING...
OKAY, BYE!
I DID A GOOD DEED, BUT I'M KINDA TICKED OFF!
THAT NIGHT, TORU REPORTED THE EVENTS OF THE DAY TO HIS MOTHER.
OH, YOU SAVED A CRANE? THAT WAS A VERY GOOD DEED, TORU.
EH-HEH!
HOWEVER, HE DIDN'T WANT TO TALK ABOUT THE PENGUIN INCIDENT.

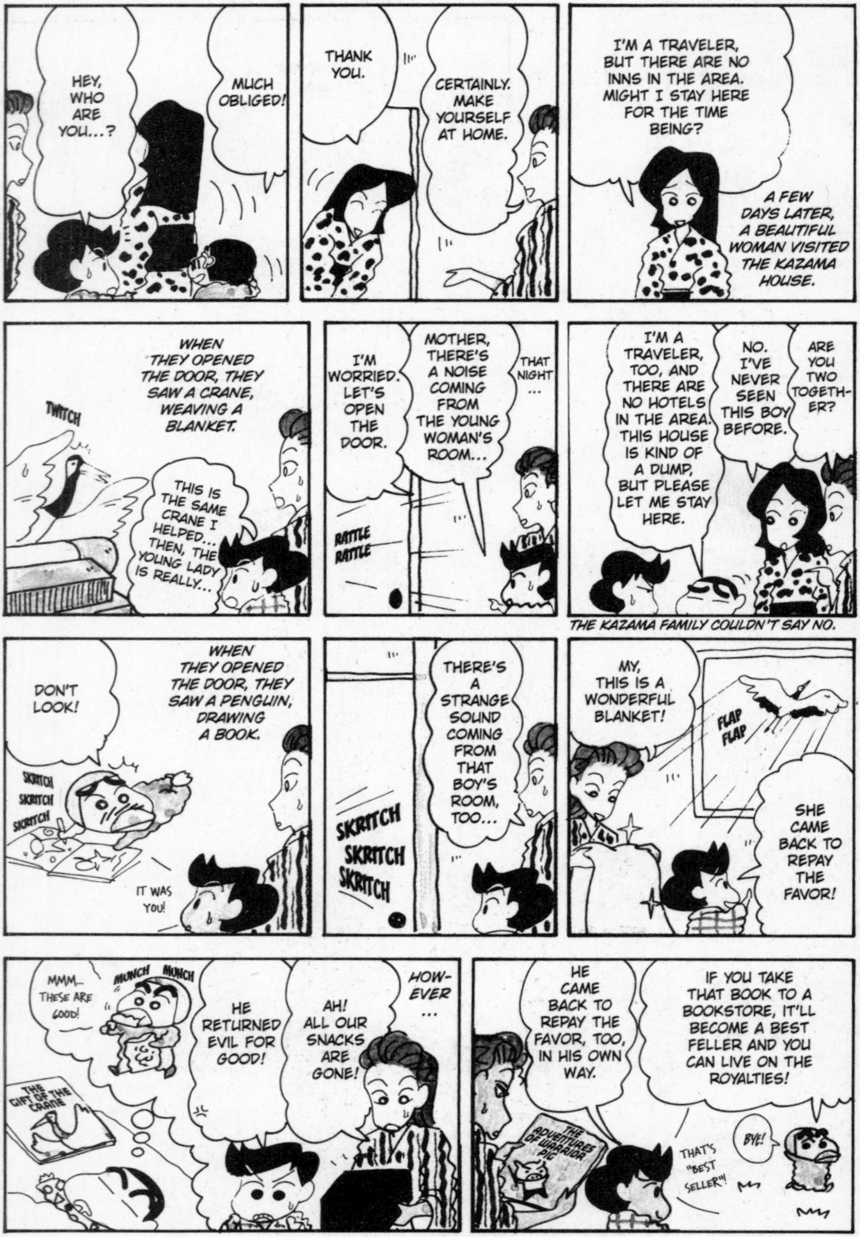
I'M A TRAVELER, BUT THERE ARE NO INNS IN THE AREA. MIGHT I STAY HERE FOR THE TIME BEING?
A FEW DAYS LATER, A BEAUTIFUL WOMAN VISITED THE KAZAMA HOUSE.
CERTAINLY. MAKE YOURSELF AT HOME.
THANK YOU.
MUCH OBLIGED!
HEY, WHO ARE YOU...?
ARE YOU TWO TOGETHER?
NO. I'VE NEVER SEEN THIS BOY BEFORE.
I'M A TRAVELER, TOO, AND THERE ARE NO HOTELS IN THE AREA. THIS HOUSE IS KIND OF A DUMP, BUT PLEASE LET ME STAY HERE.
THE KAZAMA FAMILY COULDN'T SAY NO.
THAT NIGHT ...
MOTHER, THERE'S A NOISE COMING FROM THE YOUNG WOMAN'S ROOM...
I'M WORRIED. LET'S OPEN THE DOOR.
RATTLE RATTLE
WHEN THEY OPENED THE DOOR, THEY SAW A CRANE, WEAVING A BLANKET.
TWITCH
THIS IS THE SAME CRANE I HELPED... THEN, THE YOUNG LADY IS REALLY...
MY, THIS IS A WONDERFUL BLANKET!
FLAP FLAP
SHE CAME BACK TO REPAY THE FAVOR!
THERE'S A STRANGE SOUND COMING FROM THAT BOY'S ROOM, TOO...
SKRITCH SKRITCH SKRITCH
WHEN THEY OPENED THE DOOR, THEY SAW A PENGUIN, DRAWING A BOOK.
DON'T LOOK!
SKRITCH SKRITCH SKRITCH
IT WAS YOU!
IF YOU TAKE THAT BOOK TO A BOOKSTORE, IT'LL BECOME A BEST FELLER AND YOU CAN LIVE ON THE ROYALTIES!
HE CAME BACK TO REPAY THE FAVOR, TOO, IN HIS OWN WAY.
BYE!
THE ADVENTURES OF WARRIOR PIG
THAT'S "BEST SELLER"!
HOW-EVER ...
AH! ALL OUR SNACKS ARE GONE!
HE RETURNED EVIL FOR GOOD!
MUNCH MUNCH
MMM... THESE ARE GOOD!
THE GIFT OF THE CRANE

WAHOOO!! I'M POPULAR!

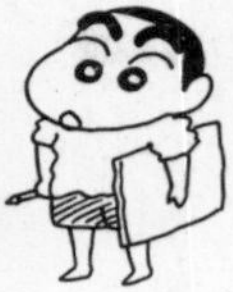

CHAPTER 7

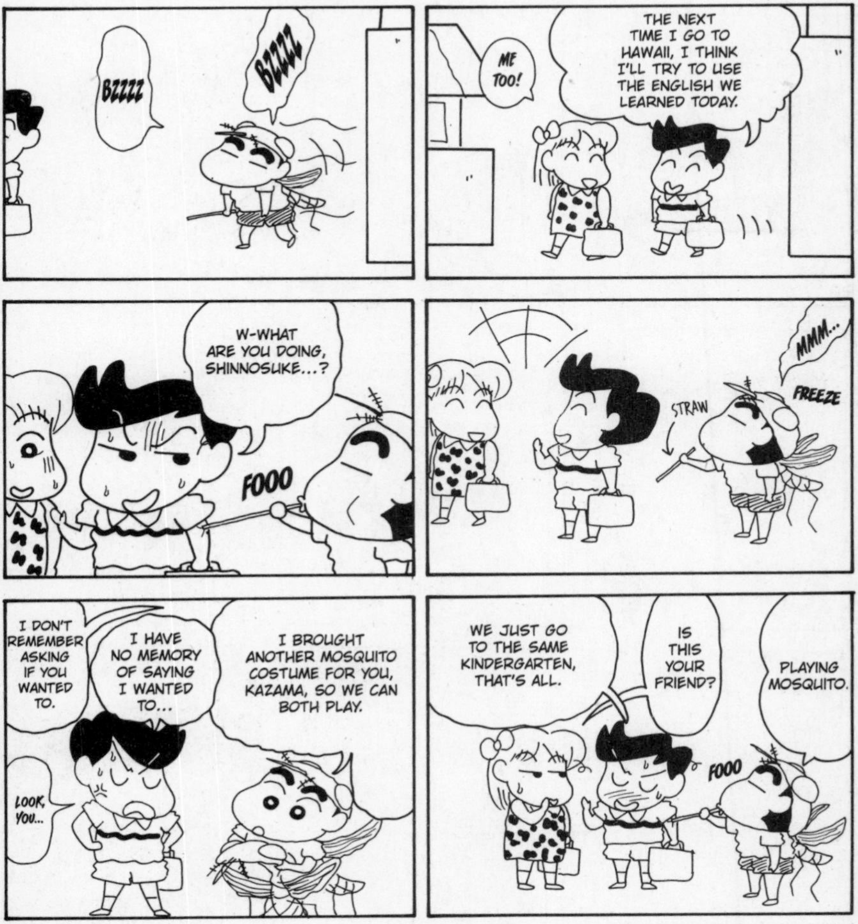
THE NEXT TIME I GO TO HAWAII, I THINK I'LL TRY TO USE THE ENGLISH WE LEARNED TODAY.
ME TOO!
BZZZZ
BZZZZ
MMM...
FREEZE
STRAW
W-WHAT ARE YOU DOING, SHINNOSUKE...?
FOOO
PLAYING MOSQUITO.
IS THIS YOUR FRIEND?
WE JUST GO TO THE SAME KINDERGARTEN, THAT'S ALL.
FOOO
I BROUGHT ANOTHER MOSQUITO COSTUME FOR YOU, KAZAMA, SO WE CAN BOTH PLAY.
I HAVE NO MEMORY OF SAYING I WANTED TO...
I DON'T REMEMBER ASKING IF YOU WANTED TO.
LOOK, YOU...

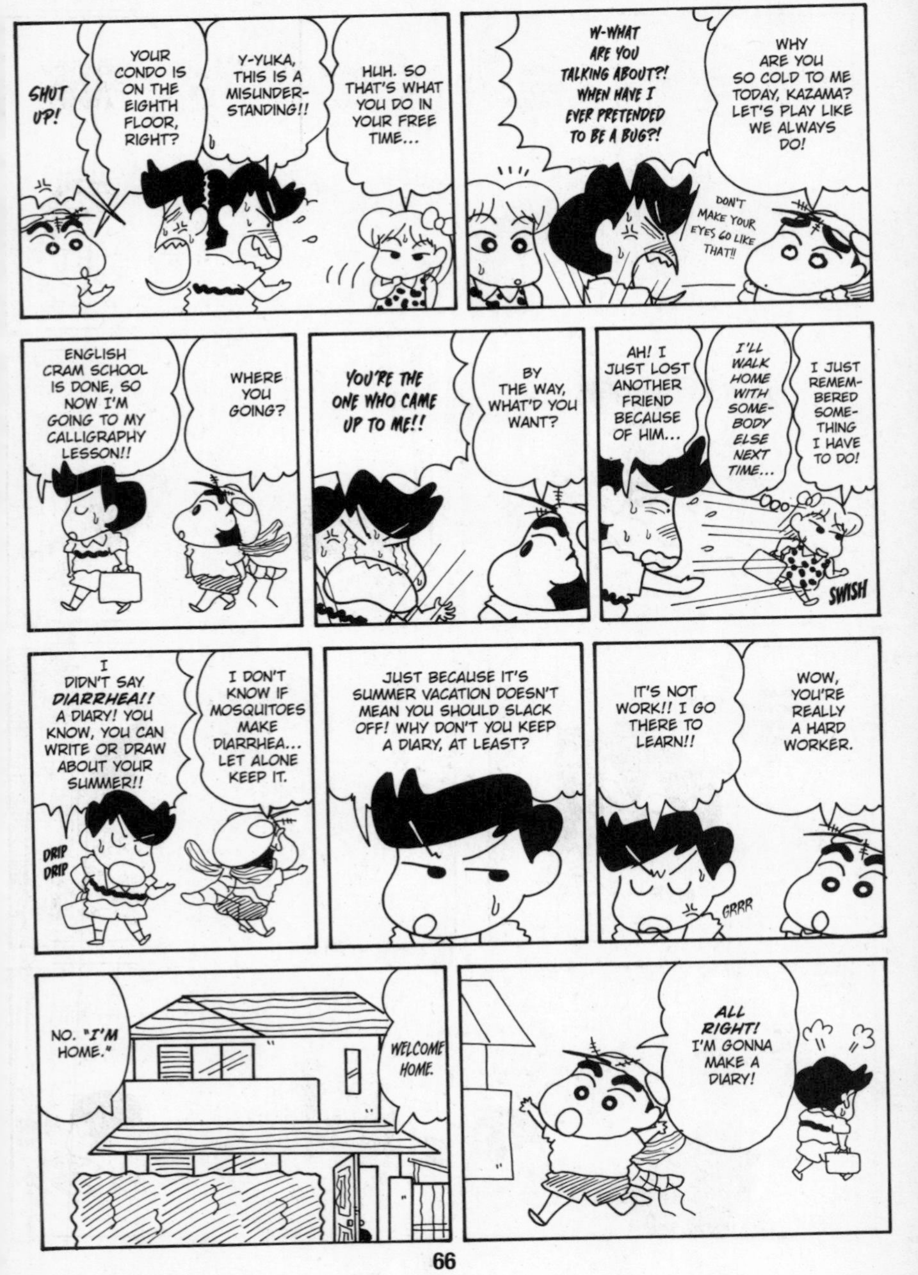
WHY ARE YOU SO COLD TO ME TODAY, KAZAMA? LET'S PLAY LIKE WE ALWAYS DO!
W-WHAT ARE YOU TALKING ABOUT?! WHEN HAVE I EVER PRETENDED TO BE A BUG?!
DON'T MAKE YOUR EYES GO LIKE THAT!!
HUH. SO THAT'S WHAT YOU DO IN YOUR FREE TIME...
Y-YUKA, THIS IS A MISUNDER-STANDING!!
YOUR CONDO IS ON THE EIGHTH FLOOR, RIGHT?
SHUT UP!
I JUST REMEM-BERED SOME-THING I HAVE TO DO!
I'LL WALK HOME WITH SOME-BODY ELSE NEXT TIME...
AH! I JUST LOST ANOTHER FRIEND BECAUSE OF HIM...
SWISH
BY THE WAY, WHAT'D YOU WANT?
YOU'RE THE ONE WHO CAME UP TO ME!!
WHERE YOU GOING?
ENGLISH CRAM SCHOOL IS DONE, SO NOW I'M GOING TO MY CALLIGRAPHY LESSON!!
WOW, YOU'RE REALLY A HARD WORKER.
IT'S NOT WORK!! I GO THERE TO LEARN!!
GRRR
JUST BECAUSE IT'S SUMMER VACATION DOESN'T MEAN YOU SHOULD SLACK OFF! WHY DON'T YOU KEEP A DIARY, AT LEAST?
I DON'T KNOW IF MOSQUITOES MAKE DIARRHEA... LET ALONE KEEP IT.
I DIDN'T SAY DIARRHEA!! A DIARY! YOU KNOW, YOU CAN WRITE OR DRAW ABOUT YOUR SUMMER!!
DRIP DRIP
ALL RIGHT! I'M GONNA MAKE A DIARY!
WELCOME HOME.
NO. "I'M HOME."

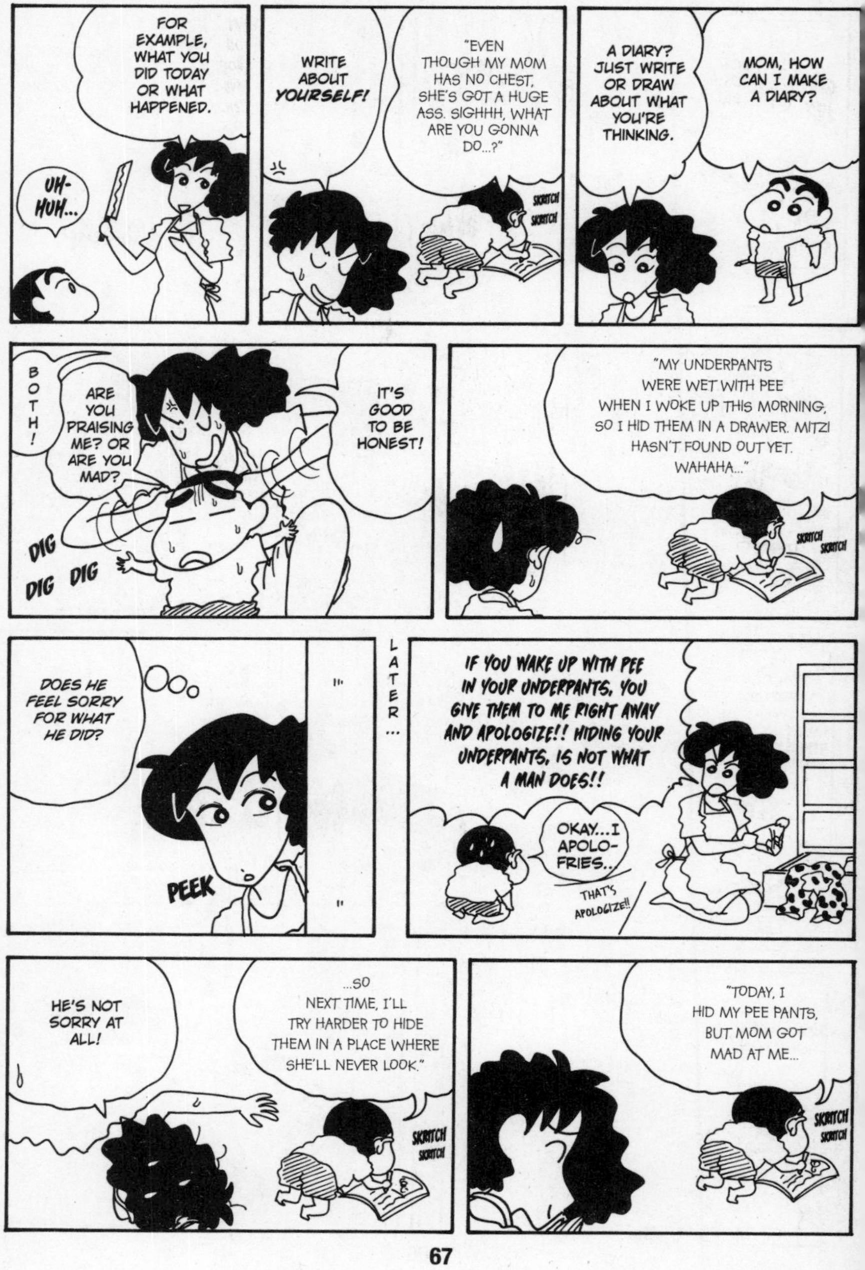
MOM, HOW CAN I MAKE A DIARY?
A DIARY? JUST WRITE OR DRAW ABOUT WHAT YOU'RE THINKING.
"EVEN THOUGH MY MOM HAS NO CHEST, SHE'S GOT A HUGE ASS. SIGHHH, WHAT ARE YOU GONNA DO...?"
SKRITCH SKRITCH
WRITE ABOUT *YOURSELF!*
FOR EXAMPLE, WHAT YOU DID TODAY OR WHAT HAPPENED.
UH-HUH...
"MY UNDERPANTS WERE WET WITH PEE WHEN I WOKE UP THIS MORNING, SO I HID THEM IN A DRAWER. MITZI HASN'T FOUND OUT YET. WAHAHA..."
SKRITCH SKRITCH
IT'S GOOD TO BE HONEST!
ARE YOU PRAISING ME? OR ARE YOU MAD?
BOTH!
DIG DIG DIG
IF YOU WAKE UP WITH PEE IN YOUR UNDERPANTS, YOU GIVE THEM TO ME RIGHT AWAY AND APOLOGIZE!! HIDING YOUR UNDERPANTS, IS NOT WHAT A MAN DOES!!
OKAY...I APOLO-FRIES...
THAT'S APOLOGIZE!!
LATER...
DOES HE FEEL SORRY FOR WHAT HE DID?
PEEK
"TODAY, I HID MY PEE PANTS, BUT MOM GOT MAD AT ME...
SKRITCH SKRITCH
...SO NEXT TIME, I'LL TRY HARDER TO HIDE THEM IN A PLACE WHERE SHE'LL NEVER LOOK."
SKRITCH SKRITCH
HE'S NOT SORRY AT ALL!

WAHOOO!! I'M POPULAR!

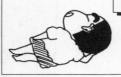

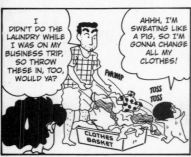

CHAPTER 8

DRIP DRIP
JUST A LITTLE MORE LAUNDRY TO GO...
AHHH, I'M SWEATING LIKE A PIG, SO I'M GONNA CHANGE ALL MY CLOTHES!
TOSS TOSS
FWUMP
I DIDN'T DO THE LAUNDRY WHILE I WAS ON MY BUSINESS TRIP, SO THROW THESE IN, TOO, WOULD YA?
CLOTHES BASKET
THERE'S NO END...
RATTLE RATTLE
RATTLE
HONEY, WOULD YOU PICK UP AFTER YOURSELF? HONESTLY! NEWSPAPERS, GOLF ITEMS ON THE FLOOR...
GOLF
AHHHH... DAD'S SUCH A SLOB! THAT'S WHY HE GETS ATHLETE'S FOOT!
YOU, TOO!!
I DON'T HAVE ATHLETE'S FOOT.
I MEANT THE SLOB PART!
MITZI, I'M STARVING. MAKE COLD NOODLES FOR LUNCH.
MOM, IT'S HOT! FILL UP THE POOL!
AND MY WORK SHIRT IS ALL WRINKLED, SO IF YOU COULD IRON IT...?
MOM, YOU'RE ALL WRINKLED, TOO, SO IF YOU COULD IRON YOURSELF...?
SNAP

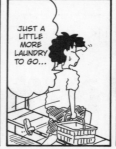

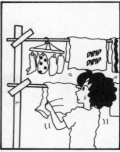

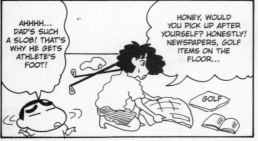

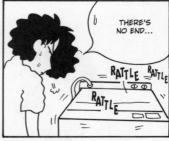

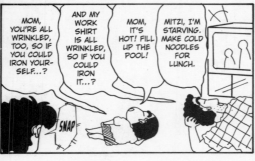

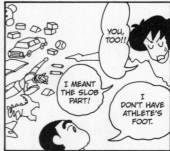

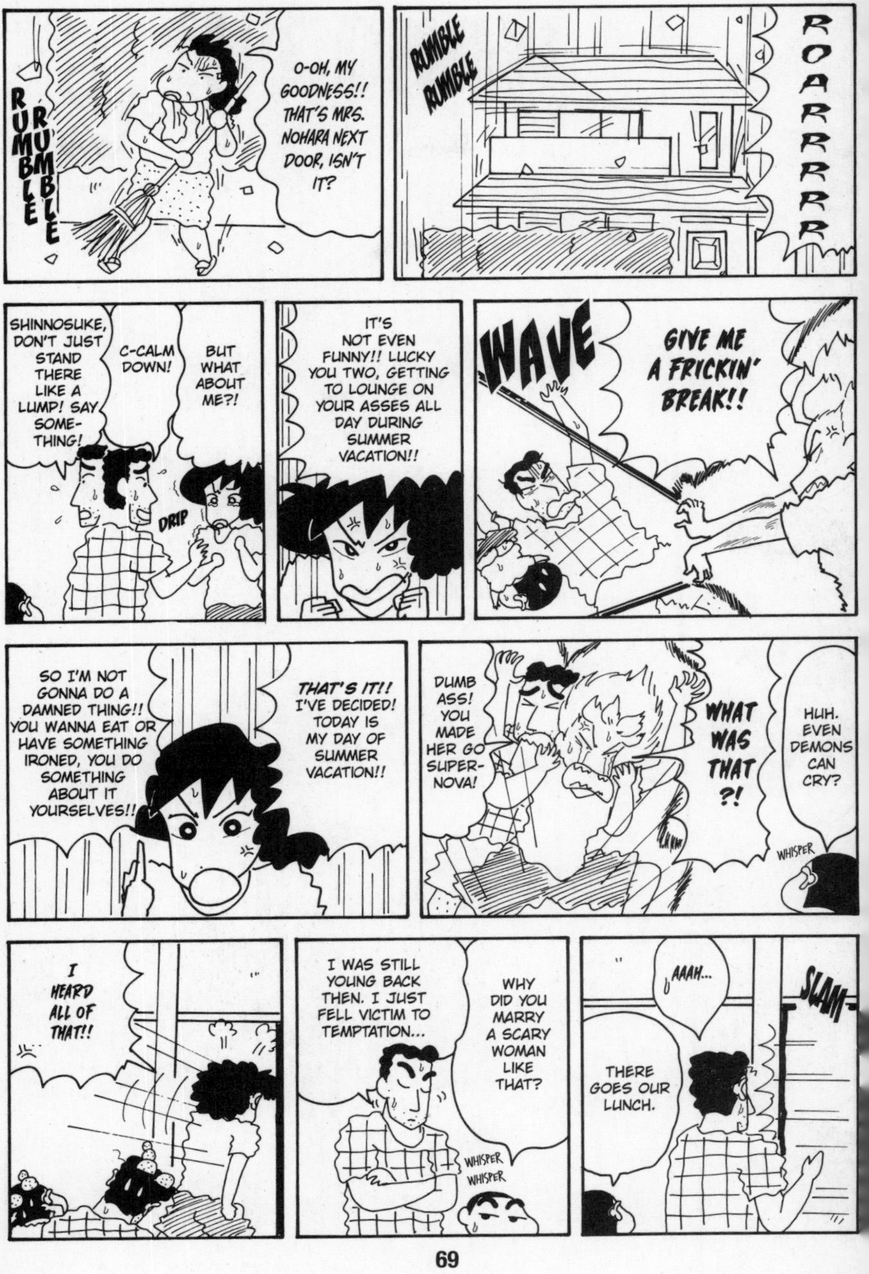
RUMBLE RUMBLE
ROARRRRR
RUMBLE RUMBLE
O-OH, MY GOODNESS!! THAT'S MRS. NOHARA NEXT DOOR, ISN'T IT?
WAVE
GIVE ME A FRICKIN' BREAK!!
IT'S NOT EVEN FUNNY!! LUCKY YOU TWO, GETTING TO LOUNGE ON YOUR ASSES ALL DAY DURING SUMMER VACATION!!
BUT WHAT ABOUT ME?!
C-CALM DOWN!
SHINNOSUKE, DON'T JUST STAND THERE LIKE A LUMP! SAY SOME-THING!
DRIP
HUH. EVEN DEMONS CAN CRY?
WHISPER
WHAT WAS THAT?!
DUMB ASS! YOU MADE HER GO SUPER-NOVA!
THAT'S IT!! I'VE DECIDED! TODAY IS MY DAY OF SUMMER VACATION!!
SO I'M NOT GONNA DO A DAMNED THING!! YOU WANNA EAT OR HAVE SOMETHING IRONED, YOU DO SOMETHING ABOUT IT YOURSELVES!!
AAAH...
SLAM
THERE GOES OUR LUNCH.
WHY DID YOU MARRY A SCARY WOMAN LIKE THAT?
WHISPER WHISPER
I WAS STILL YOUNG BACK THEN. I JUST FELL VICTIM TO TEMPTATION...
I HEARD ALL OF THAT!!

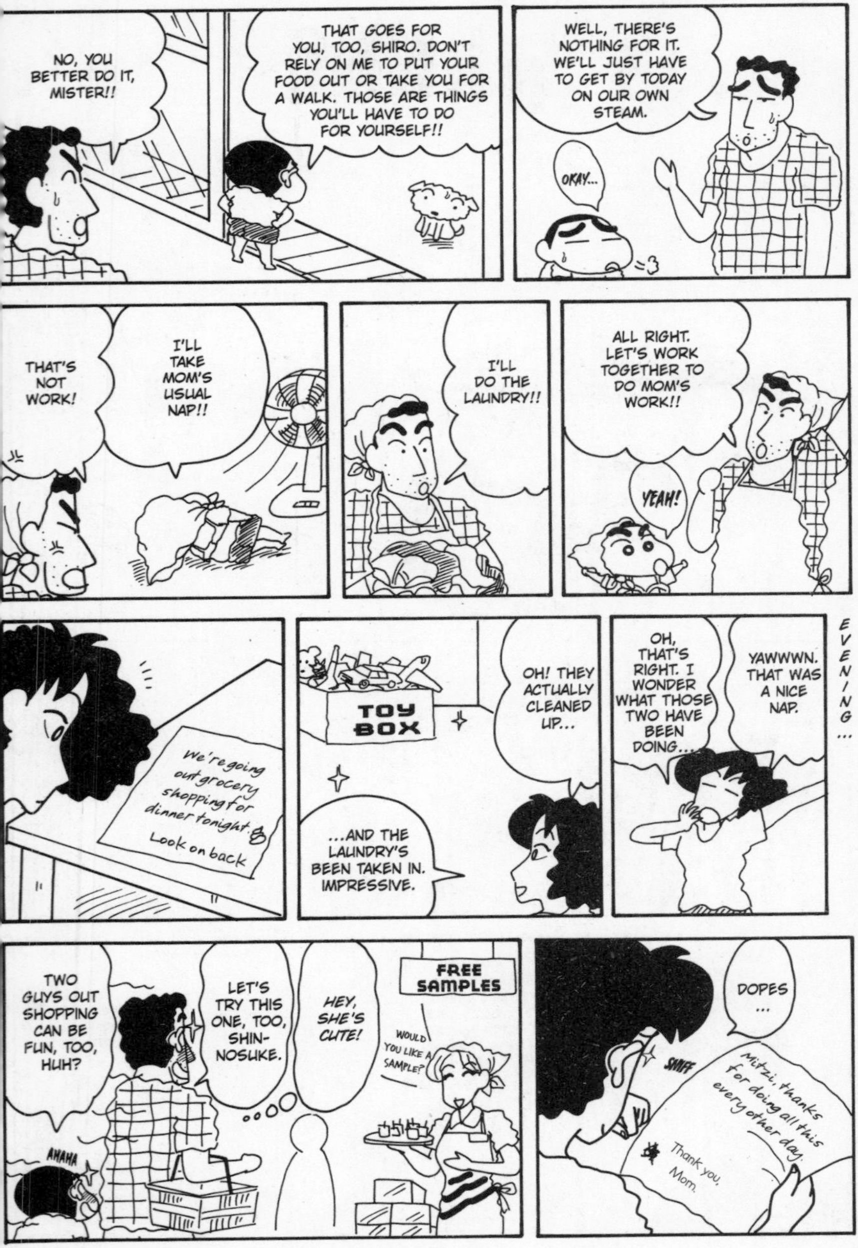
WELL, THERE'S NOTHING FOR IT. WE'LL JUST HAVE TO GET BY TODAY ON OUR OWN STEAM.
OKAY...
THAT GOES FOR YOU, TOO, SHIRO. DON'T RELY ON ME TO PUT YOUR FOOD OUT OR TAKE YOU FOR A WALK. THOSE ARE THINGS YOU'LL HAVE TO DO FOR YOURSELF!!
NO, YOU BETTER DO IT, MISTER!!
ALL RIGHT. LET'S WORK TOGETHER TO DO MOM'S WORK!!
YEAH!
I'LL DO THE LAUNDRY!!
I'LL TAKE MOM'S USUAL NAP!!
THAT'S NOT WORK!
EVENING...
YAWWWN. THAT WAS A NICE NAP.
OH, THAT'S RIGHT. I WONDER WHAT THOSE TWO HAVE BEEN DOING...
OH! THEY ACTUALLY CLEANED UP...
TOY BOX
...AND THE LAUNDRY'S BEEN TAKEN IN. IMPRESSIVE.
We're going out grocery shopping for dinner tonight.
Look on back
DOPES ...
SNIFF
Mitzi, thanks for doing all this every other day.
Thank you, Mom.
FREE SAMPLES
HEY, SHE'S CUTE!
WOULD YOU LIKE A SAMPLE?
LET'S TRY THIS ONE, TOO, SHINNOSUKE.
TWO GUYS OUT SHOPPING CAN BE FUN, TOO, HUH?
AHAHA

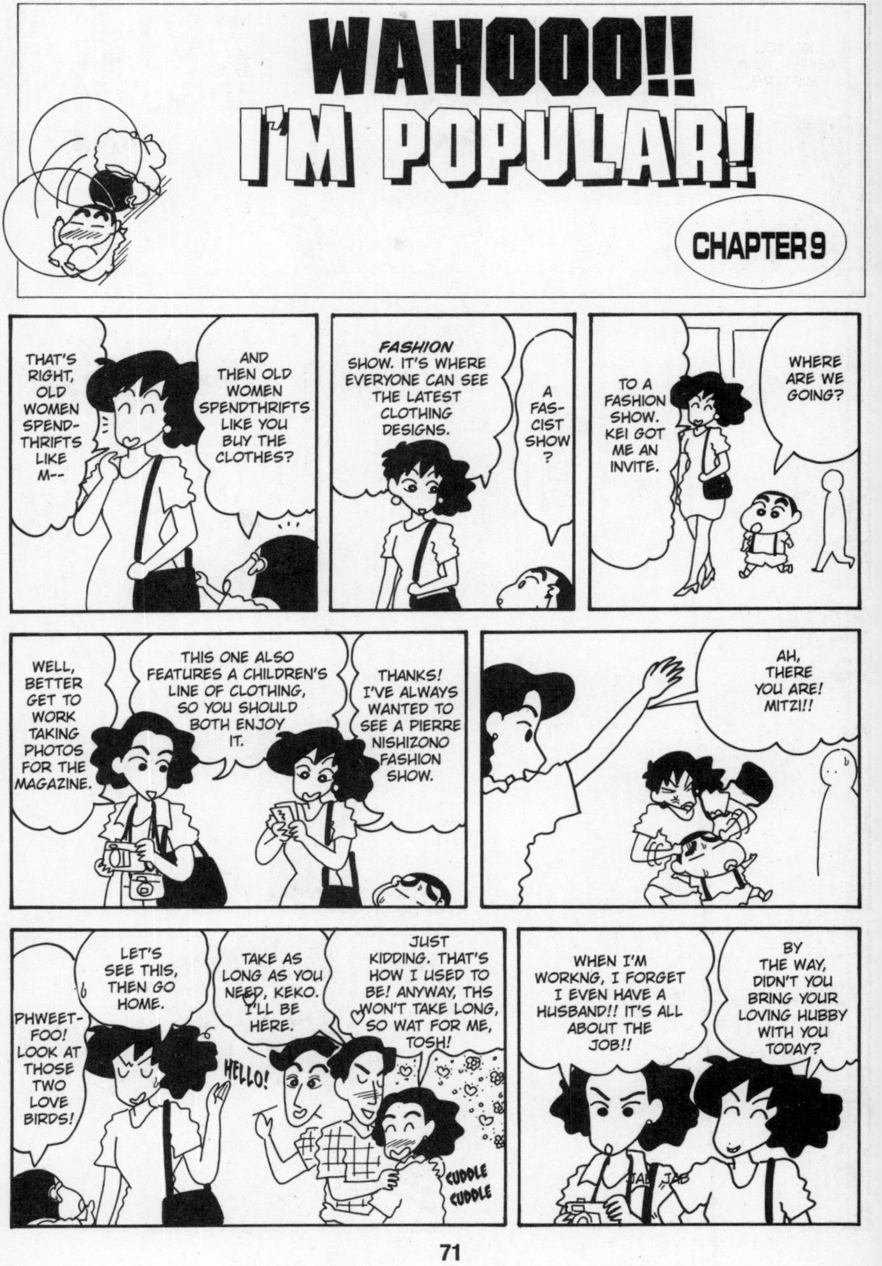
WAHOOO!! I'M POPULAR!
CHAPTER 9
WHERE ARE WE GOING?
TO A FASHION SHOW. KEI GOT ME AN INVITE.
A FAS-CIST SHOW?
FASHION SHOW. IT'S WHERE EVERYONE CAN SEE THE LATEST CLOTHING DESIGNS.
AND THEN OLD WOMEN SPENDTHRIFTS LIKE YOU BUY THE CLOTHES?
THAT'S RIGHT, OLD WOMEN SPEND-THRIFTS LIKE M--
AH, THERE YOU ARE! MITZI!!
THIS ONE ALSO FEATURES A CHILDREN'S LINE OF CLOTHING, SO YOU SHOULD BOTH ENJOY IT.
THANKS! I'VE ALWAYS WANTED TO SEE A PIERRE NISHIZONO FASHION SHOW.
WELL, BETTER GET TO WORK TAKING PHOTOS FOR THE MAGAZINE.
BY THE WAY, DIDN'T YOU BRING YOUR LOVING HUBBY WITH YOU TODAY?
WHEN I'M WORKNG, I FORGET I EVEN HAVE A HUSBAND!! IT'S ALL ABOUT THE JOB!!
JAB JAB
JUST KIDDING. THAT'S HOW I USED TO BE! ANYWAY, THS WON'T TAKE LONG, SO WAT FOR ME, TOSH!
CUDDLE CUDDLE
TAKE AS LONG AS YOU NEED, KEKO. I'LL BE HERE.
HELLO!
LET'S SEE THIS, THEN GO HOME.
PHWEET-FOO! LOOK AT THOSE TWO LOVE BIRDS!

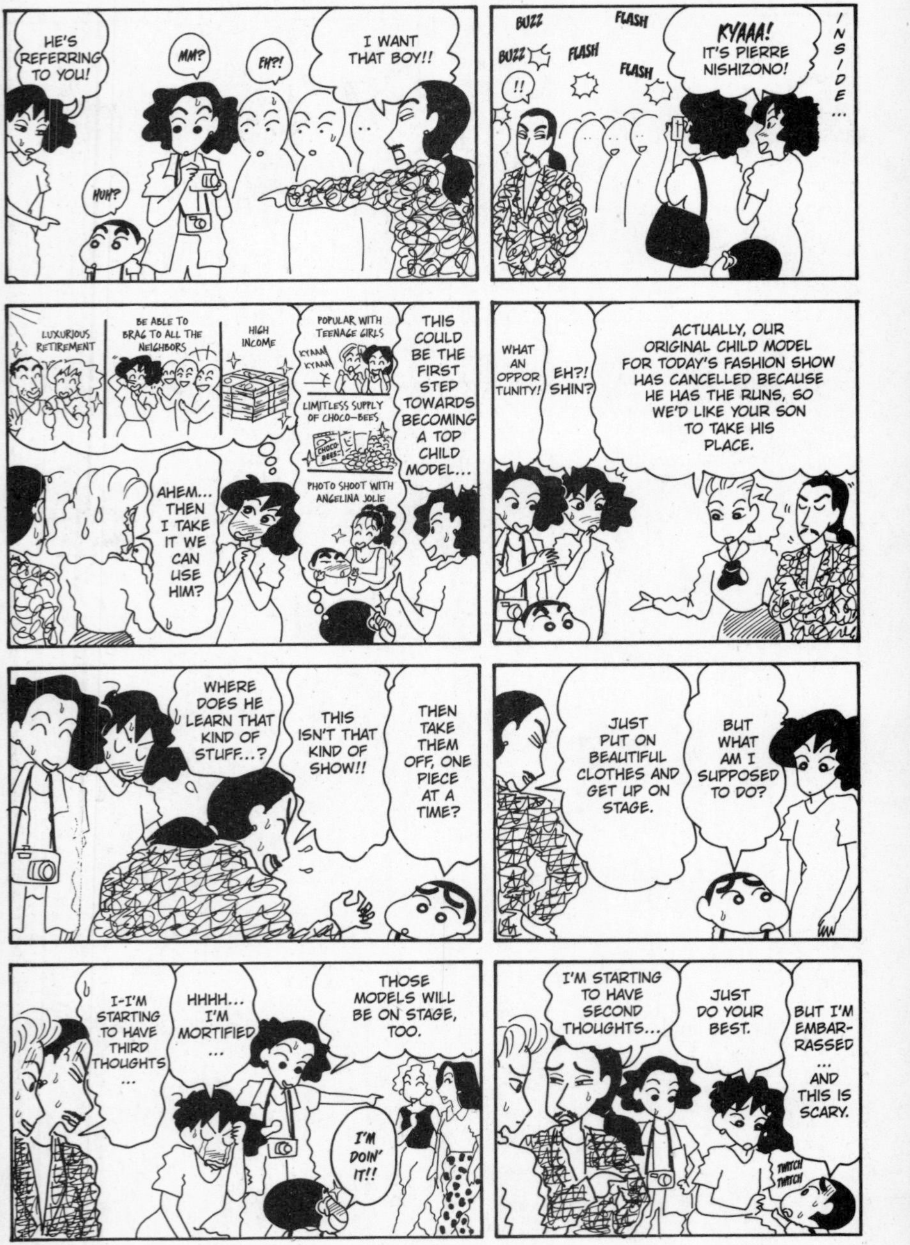
INSIDE...
KYAAA! IT'S PIERRE NISHIZONO!
FLASH
FLASH
FLASH
BUZZ
BUZZ
!!
I WANT THAT BOY!!
EH?!
MM?
HE'S REFERRING TO YOU!
HUH?
ACTUALLY, OUR ORIGINAL CHILD MODEL FOR TODAY'S FASHION SHOW HAS CANCELLED BECAUSE HE HAS THE RUNS, SO WE'D LIKE YOUR SON TO TAKE HIS PLACE.
EH?! SHIN?
WHAT AN OPPOR TUNITY!
THIS COULD BE THE FIRST STEP TOWARDS BECOMING A TOP CHILD MODEL...
POPULAR WITH TEENAGE GIRLS
KYAAA KYAAA
LIMITLESS SUPPLY OF CHOCO-BEES
CHOCO-BEES
PHOTO SHOOT WITH ANGELINA JOLIE
HIGH INCOME
BE ABLE TO BRAG TO ALL THE NEIGHBORS
LUXURIOUS RETIREMENT
AHEM... THEN I TAKE IT WE CAN USE HIM?
BUT WHAT AM I SUPPOSED TO DO?
JUST PUT ON BEAUTIFUL CLOTHES AND GET UP ON STAGE.
THEN TAKE THEM OFF, ONE PIECE AT A TIME?
THIS ISN'T THAT KIND OF SHOW!!
WHERE DOES HE LEARN THAT KIND OF STUFF...?
BUT I'M EMBAR-RASSED ... AND THIS IS SCARY.
JUST DO YOUR BEST.
I'M STARTING TO HAVE SECOND THOUGHTS...
TWITCH TWITCH
THOSE MODELS WILL BE ON STAGE, TOO.
I'M DOIN' IT!!
HHHH... I'M MORTIFIED ...
I-I'M STARTING TO HAVE THIRD THOUGHTS ...

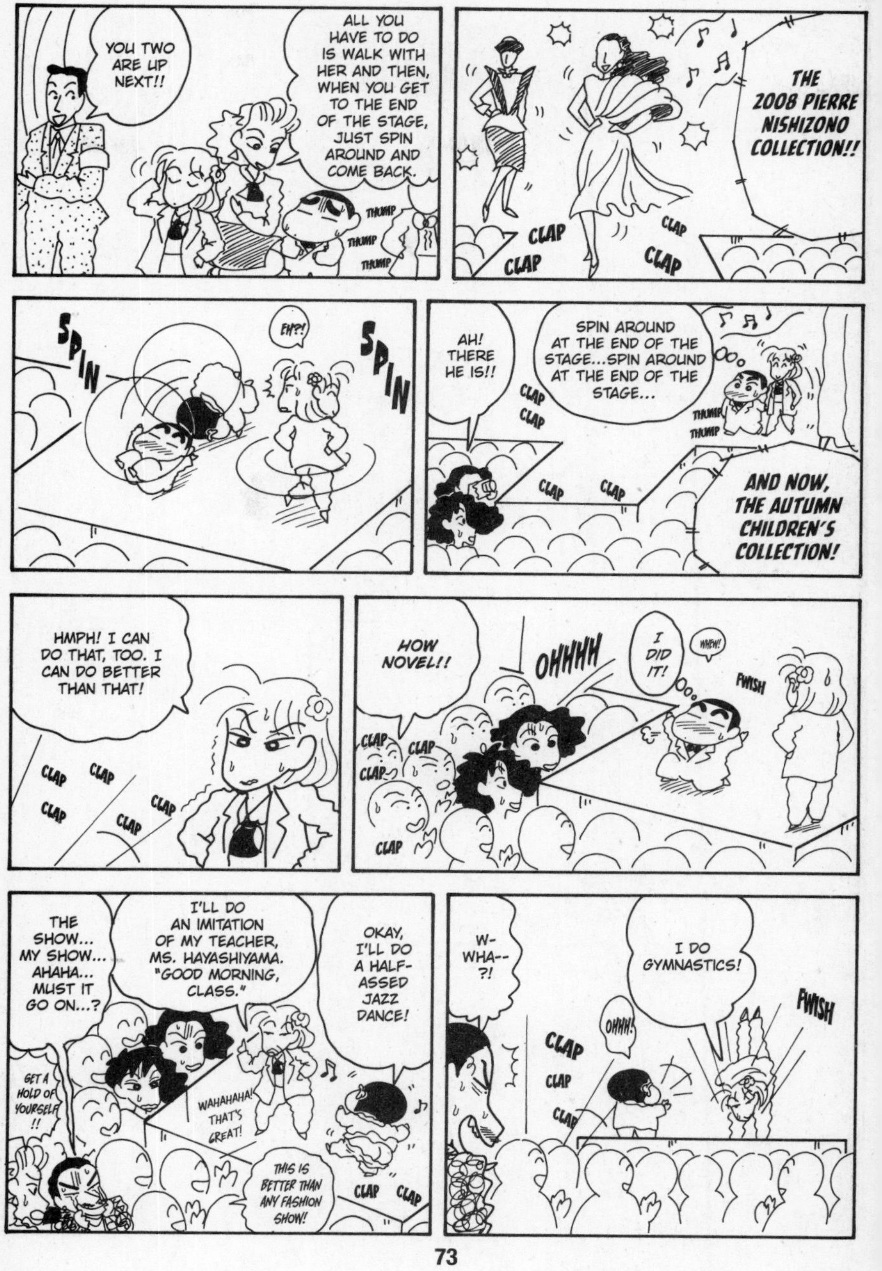
THE 2008 PIERRE NISHIZONO COLLECTION!!
CLAP
CLAP
CLAP
CLAP
YOU TWO ARE UP NEXT!!
ALL YOU HAVE TO DO IS WALK WITH HER AND THEN, WHEN YOU GET TO THE END OF THE STAGE, JUST SPIN AROUND AND COME BACK.
THUMP
THUMP
THUMP
AND NOW, THE AUTUMN CHILDREN'S COLLECTION!
SPIN AROUND AT THE END OF THE STAGE...SPIN AROUND AT THE END OF THE STAGE...
THUMP
THUMP
CLAP
CLAP
AH! THERE HE IS!!
CLAP
CLAP
SPIN
EH?!
SPIN
I DID IT!
WHEW!
FWISH
OHHHH
HOW NOVEL!!
CLAP
CLAP
CLAP
CLAP
HMPH! I CAN DO THAT, TOO. I CAN DO BETTER THAN THAT!
CLAP
CLAP
CLAP
CLAP
CLAP
I DO GYMNASTICS!
FWISH
OHHH!
CLAP
CLAP
CLAP
W-WHA--?!
OKAY, I'LL DO A HALF-ASSED JAZZ DANCE!
I'LL DO AN IMITATION OF MY TEACHER, MS. HAYASHIYAMA. "GOOD MORNING, CLASS."
THE SHOW... MY SHOW... AHAHA... MUST IT GO ON...?
GET A HOLD OF YOURSELF!!
WAHAHAHA! THAT'S GREAT!
THIS IS BETTER THAN ANY FASHION SHOW!
CLAP
CLAP

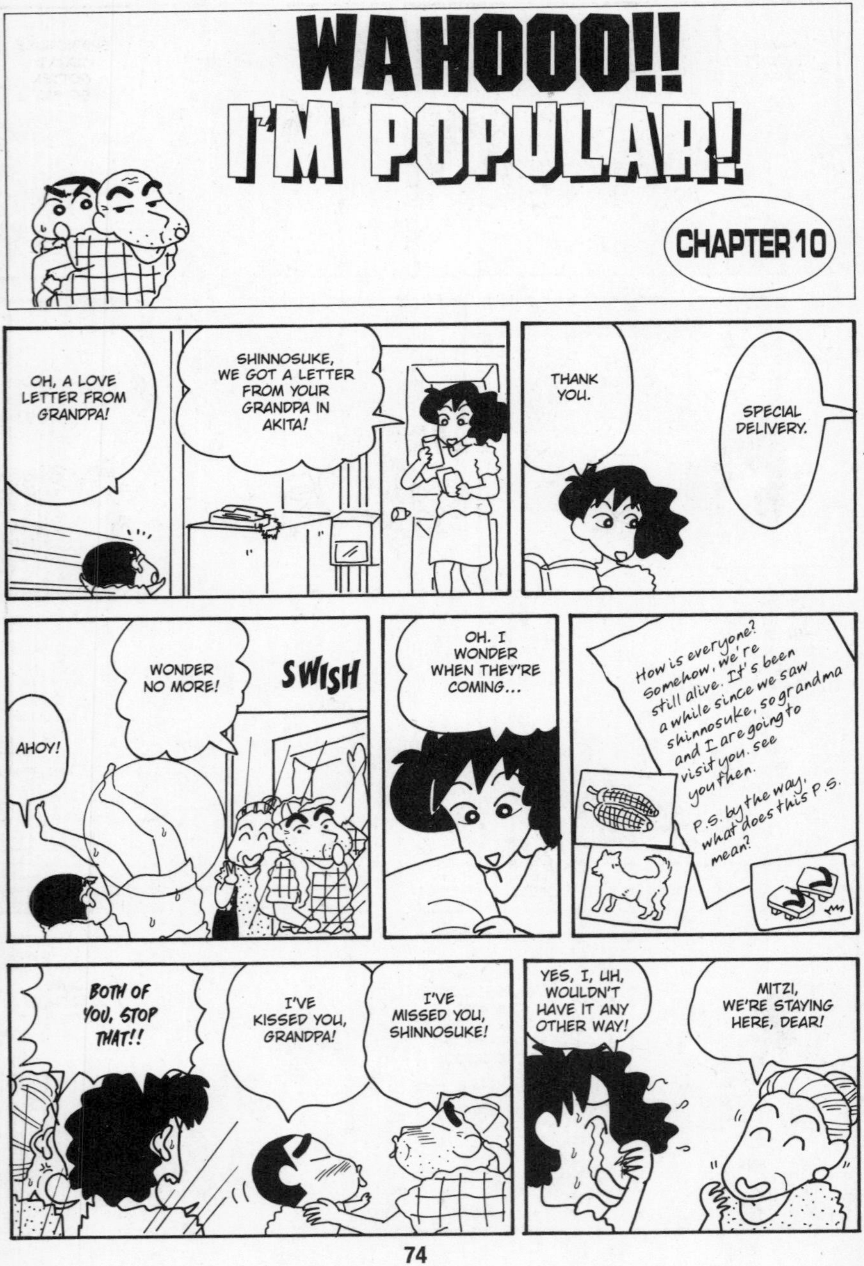
WAHOOO!! I'M POPULAR!
CHAPTER 10
SPECIAL DELIVERY.
THANK YOU.
SHINNOSUKE, WE GOT A LETTER FROM YOUR GRANDPA IN AKITA!
OH, A LOVE LETTER FROM GRANDPA!
How is everyone? Somehow, we're still alive. It's been a while since we saw shinnosuke, so grandma and I are going to visit you. see you then.
P.S. by the way, what does this P.S. mean?
OH. I WONDER WHEN THEY'RE COMING...
WONDER NO MORE!
SWISH
AHOY!
MITZI, WE'RE STAYING HERE, DEAR!
YES, I, UH, WOULDN'T HAVE IT ANY OTHER WAY!
I'VE MISSED YOU, SHINNOSUKE!
I'VE KISSED YOU, GRANDPA!
BOTH OF YOU, STOP THAT!!

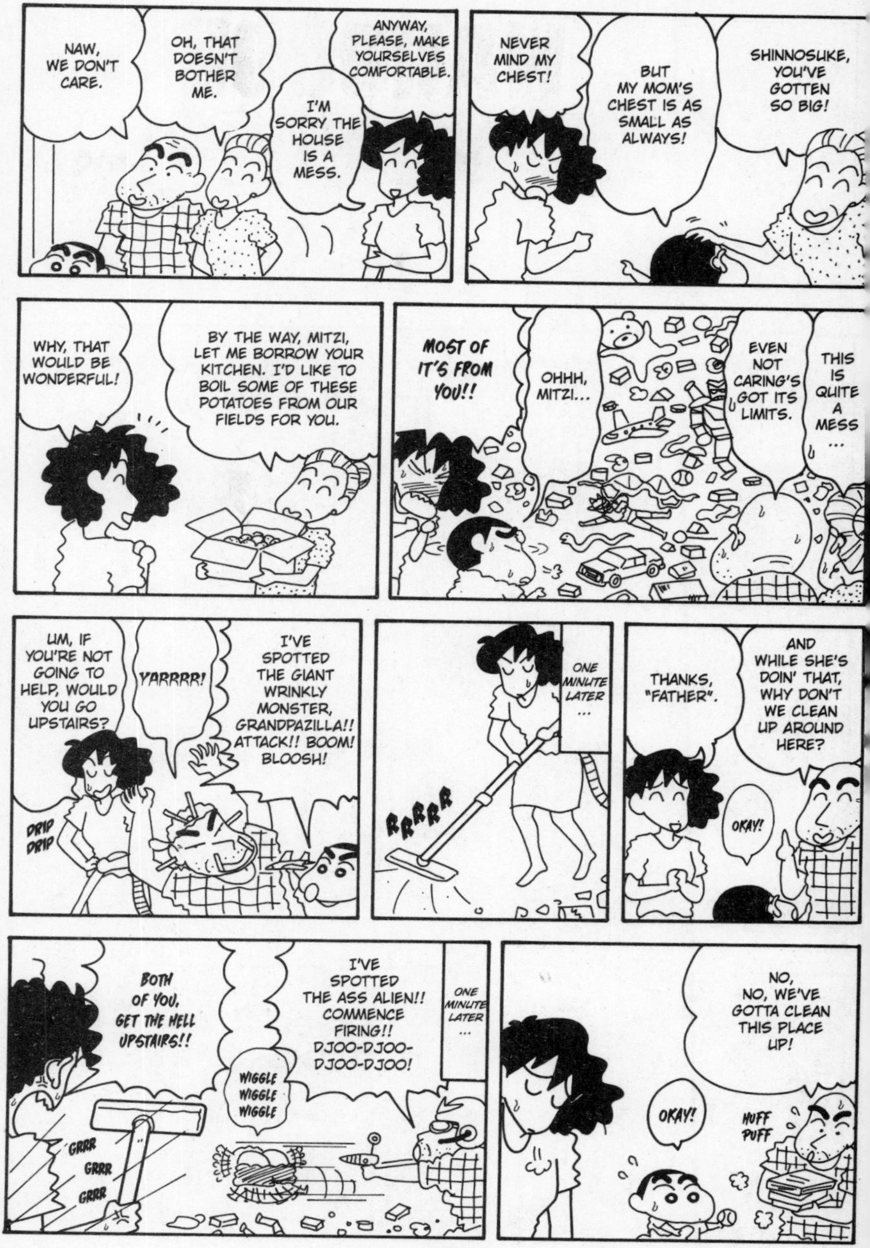
SHINNOSUKE, YOU'VE GOTTEN SO BIG!
BUT MY MOM'S CHEST IS AS SMALL AS ALWAYS!
NEVER MIND MY CHEST!
ANYWAY, PLEASE, MAKE YOURSELVES COMFORTABLE.
I'M SORRY THE HOUSE IS A MESS.
OH, THAT DOESN'T BOTHER ME.
NAW, WE DON'T CARE.
THIS IS QUITE A MESS ...
EVEN NOT CARING'S GOT ITS LIMITS.
OHHH, MITZI...
MOST OF IT'S FROM YOU!!
BY THE WAY, MITZI, LET ME BORROW YOUR KITCHEN. I'D LIKE TO BOIL SOME OF THESE POTATOES FROM OUR FIELDS FOR YOU.
WHY, THAT WOULD BE WONDERFUL!
AND WHILE SHE'S DOIN' THAT, WHY DON'T WE CLEAN UP AROUND HERE?
THANKS, "FATHER".
OKAY!
ONE MINUTE LATER ...
RRRRR
I'VE SPOTTED THE GIANT WRINKLY MONSTER, GRANDPAZILLA!! ATTACK!! BOOM! BLOOSH!
YARRRR!
UM, IF YOU'RE NOT GOING TO HELP, WOULD YOU GO UPSTAIRS?
DRIP DRIP
NO, NO, WE'VE GOTTA CLEAN THIS PLACE UP!
OKAY!
HUFF PUFF
ONE MINUTE LATER ...
I'VE SPOTTED THE ASS ALIEN!! COMMENCE FIRING!! DJOO-DJOO-DJOO-DJOO!
WIGGLE WIGGLE WIGGLE
BOTH OF YOU, GET THE HELL UPSTAIRS!!
GRRR GRRR GRRR

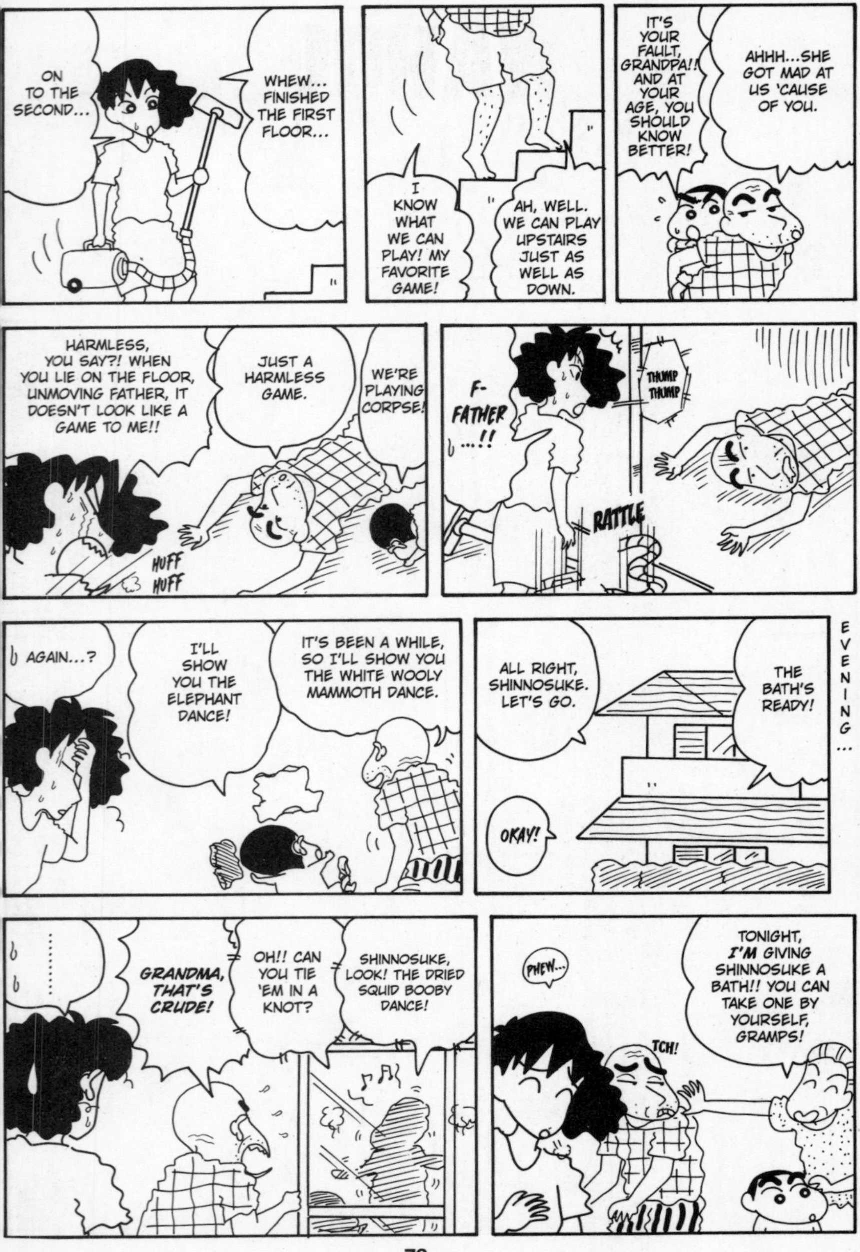
AHHH...SHE GOT MAD AT US 'CAUSE OF YOU.
IT'S YOUR FAULT, GRANDPA!! AND AT YOUR AGE, YOU SHOULD KNOW BETTER!
AH, WELL. WE CAN PLAY UPSTAIRS JUST AS WELL AS DOWN.
I KNOW WHAT WE CAN PLAY! MY FAVORITE GAME!
WHEW... FINISHED THE FIRST FLOOR...
ON TO THE SECOND...
THUMP THUMP
F-FATHER ...!!
RATTLE
WE'RE PLAYING CORPSE!
JUST A HARMLESS GAME.
HARMLESS, YOU SAY?! WHEN YOU LIE ON THE FLOOR, UNMOVING FATHER, IT DOESN'T LOOK LIKE A GAME TO ME!!
HUFF HUFF
EVENING...
THE BATH'S READY!
ALL RIGHT, SHINNOSUKE. LET'S GO.
OKAY!
IT'S BEEN A WHILE, SO I'LL SHOW YOU THE WHITE WOOLY MAMMOTH DANCE.
I'LL SHOW YOU THE ELEPHANT DANCE!
AGAIN...?
TONIGHT, I'M GIVING SHINNOSUKE A BATH!! YOU CAN TAKE ONE BY YOURSELF, GRAMPS!
TCH!
PHEW...
SHINNOSUKE, LOOK! THE DRIED SQUID BOOBY DANCE!
OH!! CAN YOU TIE 'EM IN A KNOT?
GRANDMA, THAT'S CRUDE!
......

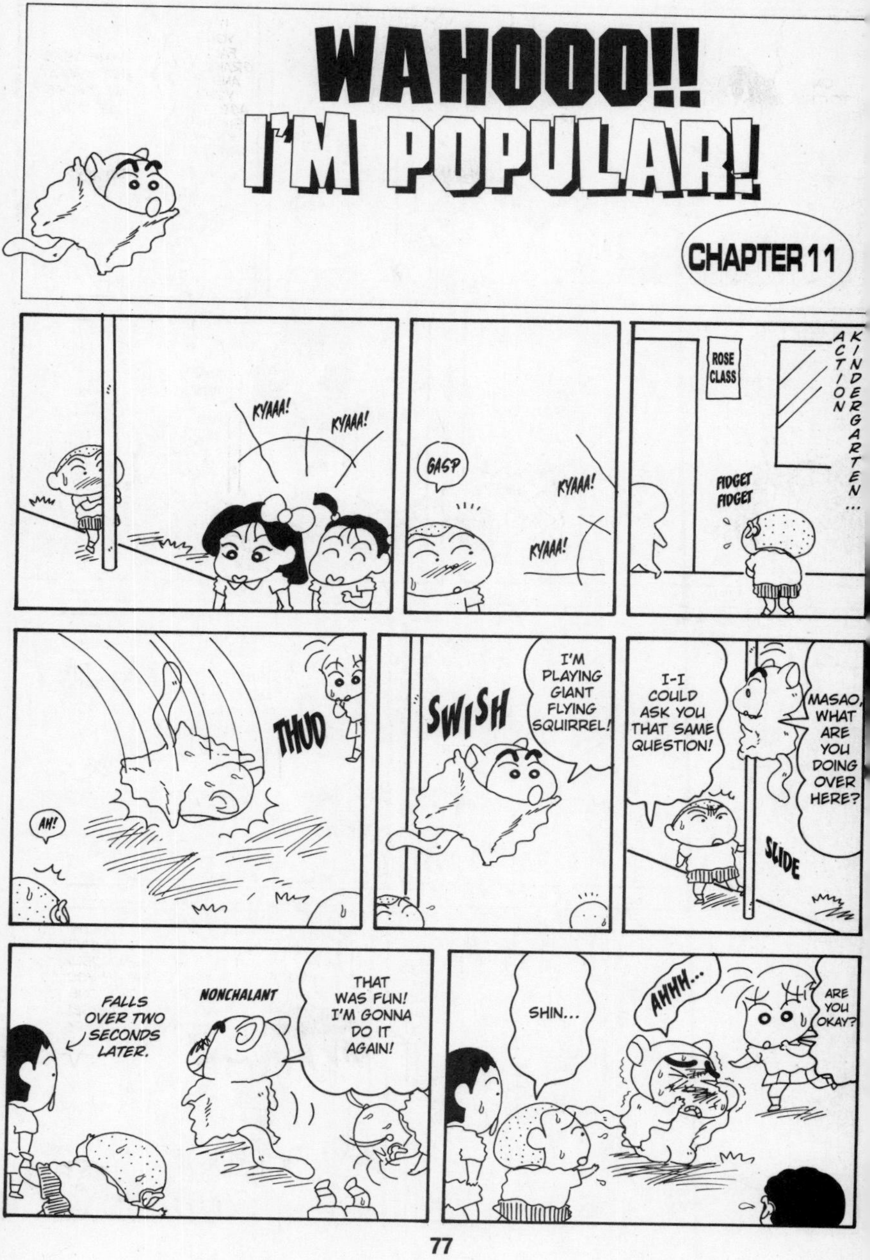
WAHOOO!! I'M POPULAR!
CHAPTER 11
ACTION KINDERGARTEN...
ROSE CLASS
FIDGET FIDGET
GASP
KYAAA!
KYAAA!
KYAAA!
KYAAA!
MASAO, WHAT ARE YOU DOING OVER HERE?
I-I COULD ASK YOU THAT SAME QUESTION!
SLIDE
I'M PLAYING GIANT FLYING SQUIRREL!
SWISH
THUD
AH!
ARE YOU OKAY?
AHHH...
SHIN...
THAT WAS FUN! I'M GONNA DO IT AGAIN!
NONCHALANT
FALLS OVER TWO SECONDS LATER.

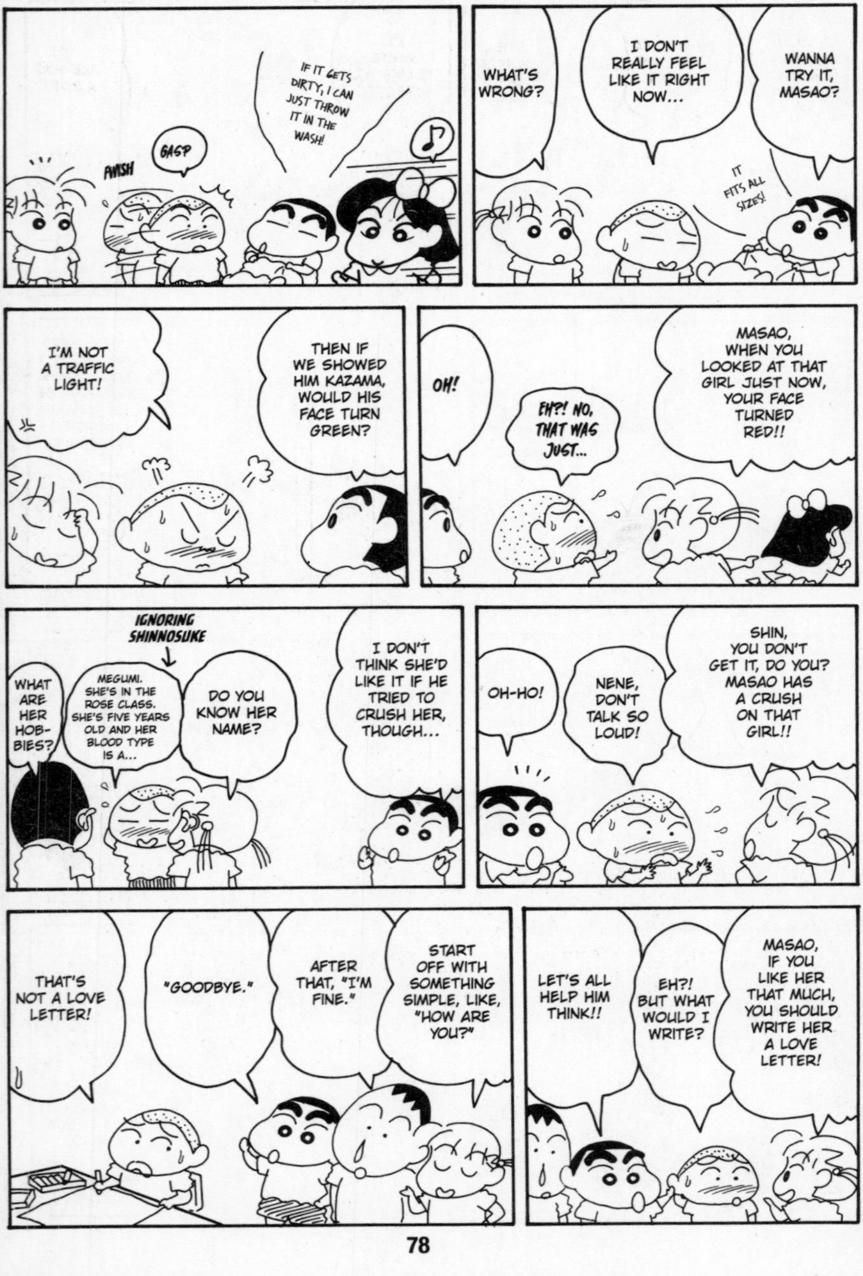
WANNA TRY IT, MASAO?
IT FITS ALL SIZES!
I DON'T REALLY FEEL LIKE IT RIGHT NOW…
WHAT'S WRONG?
IF IT GETS DIRTY, I CAN JUST THROW IT IN THE WASH!
GASP
FWISH
MASAO, WHEN YOU LOOKED AT THAT GIRL JUST NOW, YOUR FACE TURNED RED!!
EH?! NO, THAT WAS JUST…
OH!
THEN IF WE SHOWED HIM KAZAMA, WOULD HIS FACE TURN GREEN?
I'M NOT A TRAFFIC LIGHT!
SHIN, YOU DON'T GET IT, DO YOU? MASAO HAS A CRUSH ON THAT GIRL!!
NENE, DON'T TALK SO LOUD!
OH-HO!
I DON'T THINK SHE'D LIKE IT IF HE TRIED TO CRUSH HER, THOUGH…
DO YOU KNOW HER NAME?
IGNORING SHINNOSUKE
MEGUMI. SHE'S IN THE ROSE CLASS. SHE'S FIVE YEARS OLD AND HER BLOOD TYPE IS A…
WHAT ARE HER HOB-BIES?
MASAO, IF YOU LIKE HER THAT MUCH, YOU SHOULD WRITE HER A LOVE LETTER!
EH?! BUT WHAT WOULD I WRITE?
LET'S ALL HELP HIM THINK!!
START OFF WITH SOMETHING SIMPLE, LIKE, "HOW ARE YOU?"
AFTER THAT, "I'M FINE."
"GOODBYE."
THAT'S NOT A LOVE LETTER!

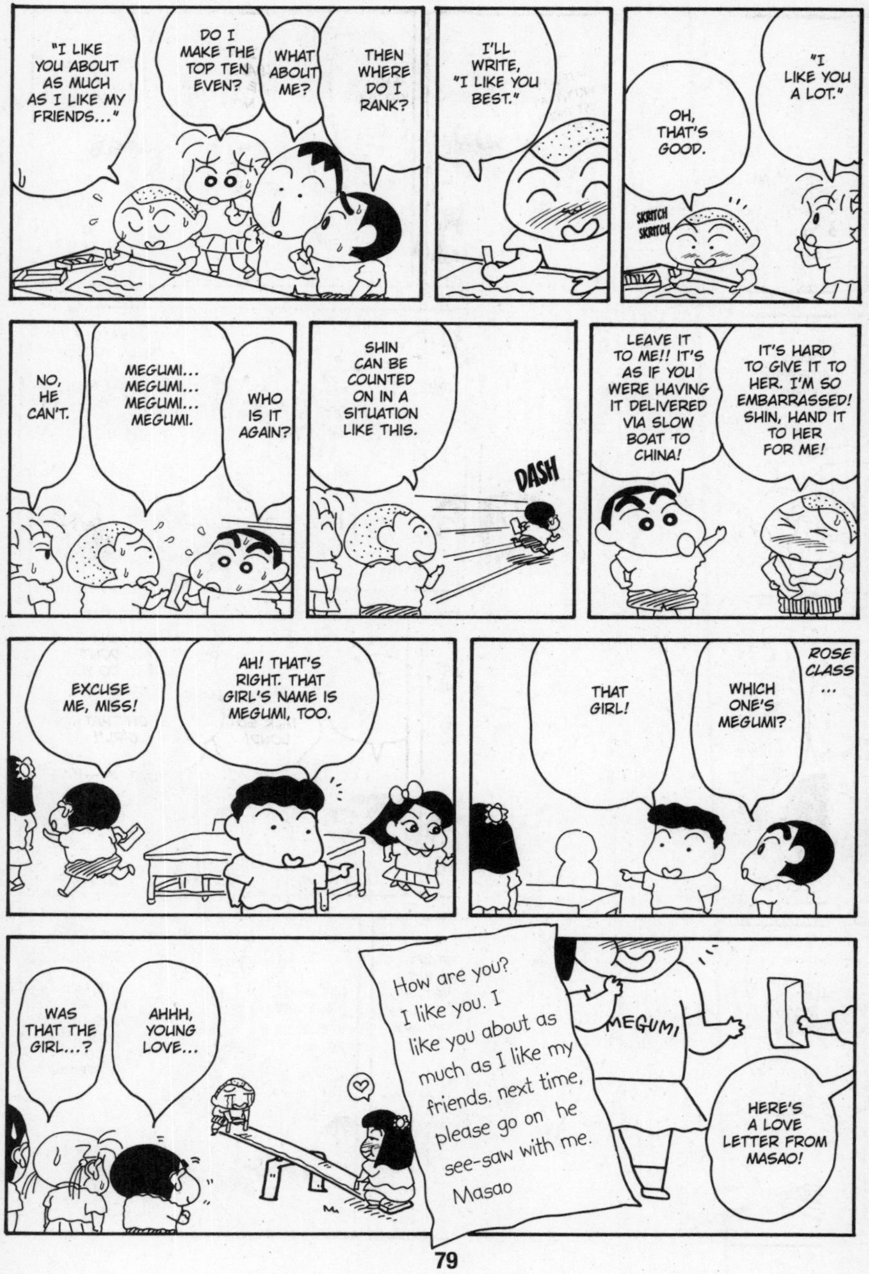
"I LIKE YOU A LOT."
OH, THAT'S GOOD.
SKRITCH SKRITCH
I'LL WRITE, "I LIKE YOU BEST."
THEN WHERE DO I RANK?
WHAT ABOUT ME?
DO I MAKE THE TOP TEN EVEN?
"I LIKE YOU ABOUT AS MUCH AS I LIKE MY FRIENDS..."
IT'S HARD TO GIVE IT TO HER. I'M SO EMBARRASSED! SHIN, HAND IT TO HER FOR ME!
LEAVE IT TO ME!! IT'S AS IF YOU WERE HAVING IT DELIVERED VIA SLOW BOAT TO CHINA!
SHIN CAN BE COUNTED ON IN A SITUATION LIKE THIS.
DASH
WHO IS IT AGAIN?
MEGUMI... MEGUMI... MEGUMI... MEGUMI.
NO, HE CAN'T.
ROSE CLASS ...
WHICH ONE'S MEGUMI?
THAT GIRL!
AH! THAT'S RIGHT. THAT GIRL'S NAME IS MEGUMI, TOO.
EXCUSE ME, MISS!
HERE'S A LOVE LETTER FROM MASAO!
MEGUMI
How are you? I like you. I like you about as much as I like my friends. next time, please go on he see-saw with me. Masao
AHHH, YOUNG LOVE...
WAS THAT THE GIRL...?

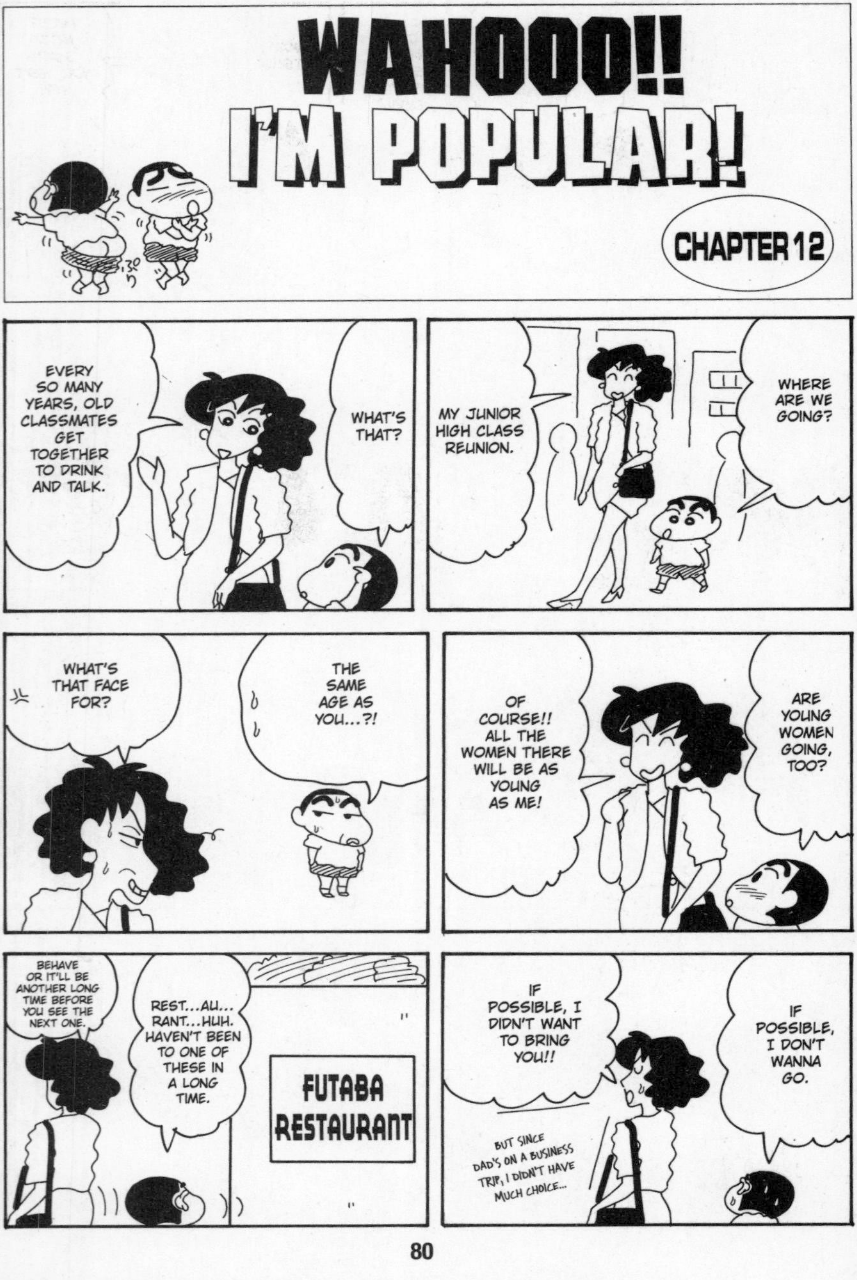
WAHOOO!! I'M POPULAR!
CHAPTER 12
WHERE ARE WE GOING?
MY JUNIOR HIGH CLASS REUNION.
WHAT'S THAT?
EVERY SO MANY YEARS, OLD CLASSMATES GET TOGETHER TO DRINK AND TALK.
ARE YOUNG WOMEN GOING, TOO?
OF COURSE!! ALL THE WOMEN THERE WILL BE AS YOUNG AS ME!
THE SAME AGE AS YOU...?!
WHAT'S THAT FACE FOR?
IF POSSIBLE, I DON'T WANNA GO.
IF POSSIBLE, I DIDN'T WANT TO BRING YOU!!
BUT SINCE DAD'S ON A BUSINESS TRIP, I DIDN'T HAVE MUCH CHOICE...
FUTABA RESTAURANT
REST...AU...RANT...HUH. HAVEN'T BEEN TO ONE OF THESE IN A LONG TIME.
BEHAVE OR IT'LL BE ANOTHER LONG TIME BEFORE YOU SEE THE NEXT ONE.

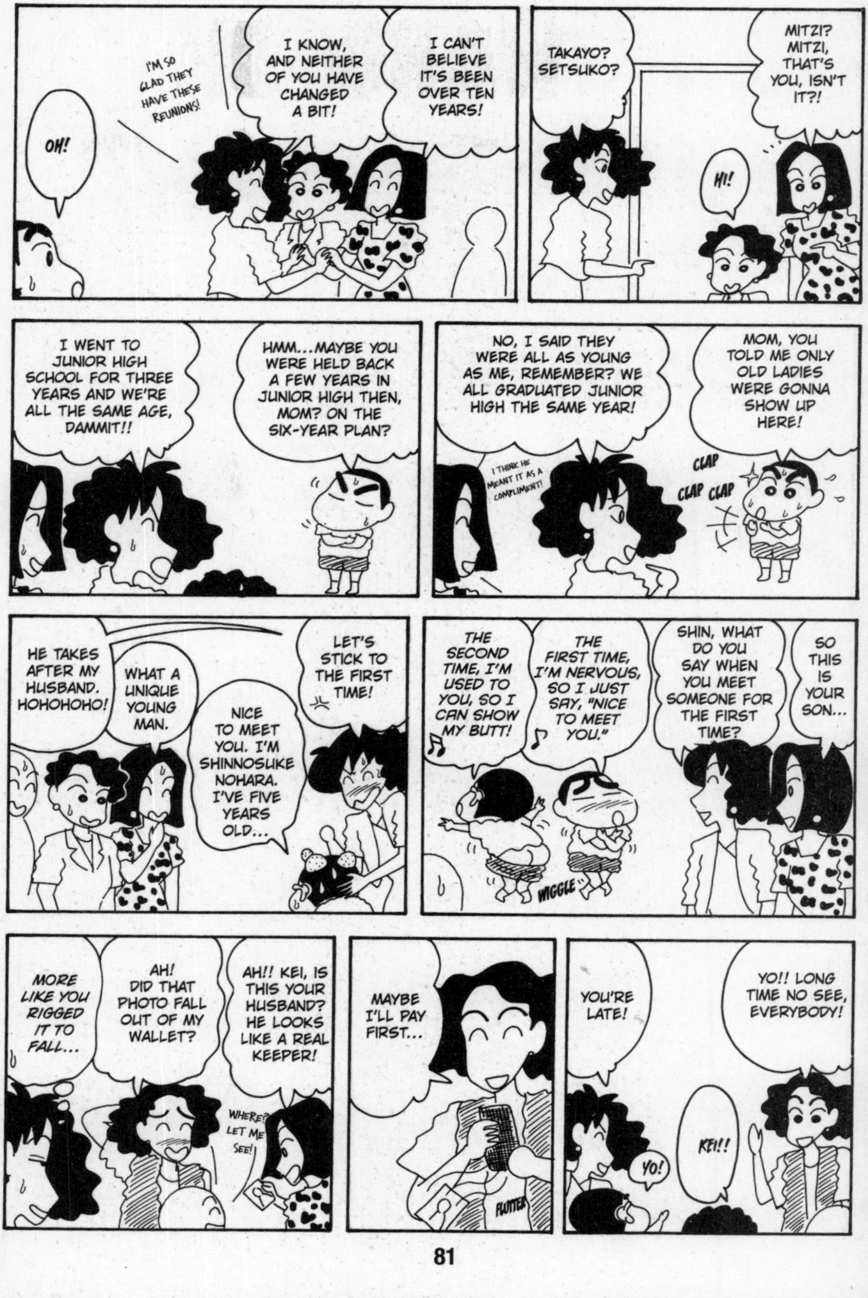
MITZI? MITZI, THAT'S YOU, ISN'T IT?!
TAKAYO? SETSUKO?
HI!
I CAN'T BELIEVE IT'S BEEN OVER TEN YEARS!
I KNOW, AND NEITHER OF YOU HAVE CHANGED A BIT!
I'M SO GLAD THEY HAVE THESE REUNIONS!
OH!
MOM, YOU TOLD ME ONLY OLD LADIES WERE GONNA SHOW UP HERE!
NO, I SAID THEY WERE ALL AS YOUNG AS ME, REMEMBER? WE ALL GRADUATED JUNIOR HIGH THE SAME YEAR!
CLAP CLAP CLAP
I THINK HE MEANT IT AS A COMPLIMENT!
HMM...MAYBE YOU WERE HELD BACK A FEW YEARS IN JUNIOR HIGH THEN, MOM? ON THE SIX-YEAR PLAN?
I WENT TO JUNIOR HIGH SCHOOL FOR THREE YEARS AND WE'RE ALL THE SAME AGE, DAMMIT!!
SO THIS IS YOUR SON...
SHIN, WHAT DO YOU SAY WHEN YOU MEET SOMEONE FOR THE FIRST TIME?
THE FIRST TIME, I'M NERVOUS, SO I JUST SAY, "NICE TO MEET YOU."
THE SECOND TIME, I'M USED TO YOU, SO I CAN SHOW MY BUTT!
WIGGLE
LET'S STICK TO THE FIRST TIME!
NICE TO MEET YOU. I'M SHINNOSUKE NOHARA. I'VE FIVE YEARS OLD...
WHAT A UNIQUE YOUNG MAN.
HE TAKES AFTER MY HUSBAND. HOHOHOHO!
YO!! LONG TIME NO SEE, EVERYBODY!
YOU'RE LATE!
KEI!!
YO!
MAYBE I'LL PAY FIRST...
FLUTTER
AH!! KEI, IS THIS YOUR HUSBAND? HE LOOKS LIKE A REAL KEEPER!
WHERE? LET ME SEE!
AH! DID THAT PHOTO FALL OUT OF MY WALLET?
MORE LIKE YOU RIGGED IT TO FALL...

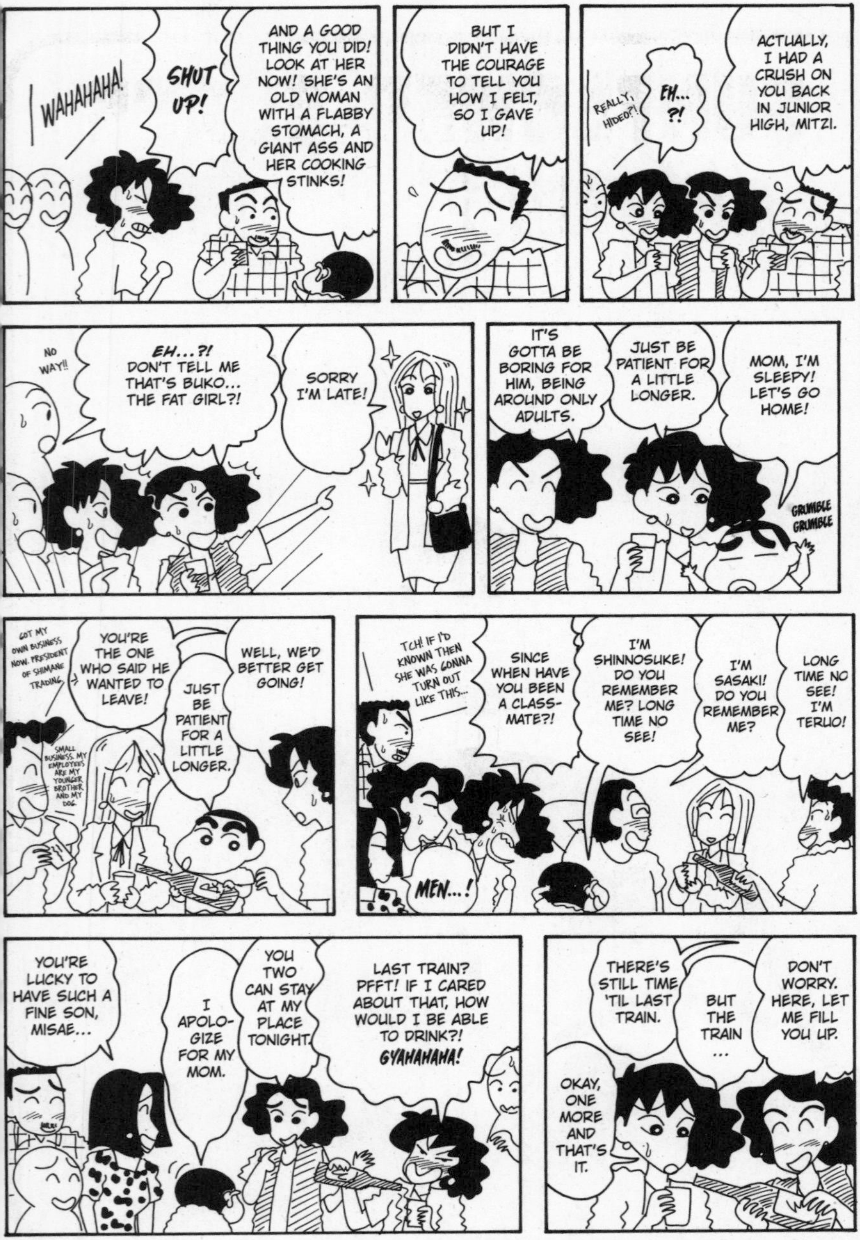
ACTUALLY, I HAD A CRUSH ON YOU BACK IN JUNIOR HIGH, MITZI.
EH...?!
REALLY, HIDEO?!
BUT I DIDN'T HAVE THE COURAGE TO TELL YOU HOW I FELT, SO I GAVE UP!
AND A GOOD THING YOU DID! LOOK AT HER NOW! SHE'S AN OLD WOMAN WITH A FLABBY STOMACH, A GIANT ASS AND HER COOKING STINKS!
SHUT UP!
WAHAHAHA!
MOM, I'M SLEEPY! LET'S GO HOME!
JUST BE PATIENT FOR A LITTLE LONGER.
IT'S GOTTA BE BORING FOR HIM, BEING AROUND ONLY ADULTS.
GRUMBLE GRUMBLE
SORRY I'M LATE!
EH...?! DON'T TELL ME THAT'S BUKO... THE FAT GIRL?!
NO WAY!!
LONG TIME NO SEE! I'M TERUO!
I'M SASAKI! DO YOU REMEMBER ME?
I'M SHINNOSUKE! DO YOU REMEMBER ME? LONG TIME NO SEE!
SINCE WHEN HAVE YOU BEEN A CLASS-MATE?!
TCH! IF I'D KNOWN THEN SHE WAS GONNA TURN OUT LIKE THIS...
MEN...!
WELL, WE'D BETTER GET GOING!
JUST BE PATIENT FOR A LITTLE LONGER.
YOU'RE THE ONE WHO SAID HE WANTED TO LEAVE!
GOT MY OWN BUSINESS NOW. PRESIDENT OF SHIMANE TRADING.
SMALL BUSINESS. MY EMPLOYEES ARE MY YOUNGER BROTHER AND MY DOG.
DON'T WORRY. HERE, LET ME FILL YOU UP.
BUT THE TRAIN ...
THERE'S STILL TIME 'TIL LAST TRAIN.
OKAY, ONE MORE AND THAT'S IT.
LAST TRAIN? PFFT! IF I CARED ABOUT THAT, HOW WOULD I BE ABLE TO DRINK?! GYAHAHAHA!
YOU TWO CAN STAY AT MY PLACE TONIGHT.
I APOLO-GIZE FOR MY MOM.
YOU'RE LUCKY TO HAVE SUCH A FINE SON, MISAE...

SUNFLOWER CLASS VS. ROSE CLASS

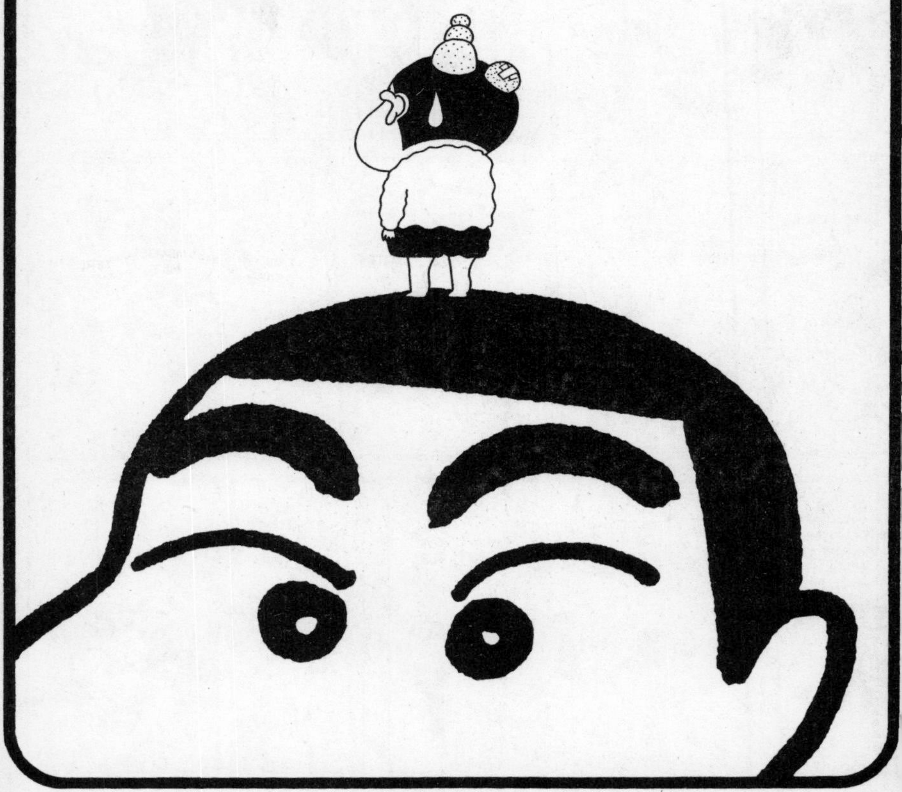

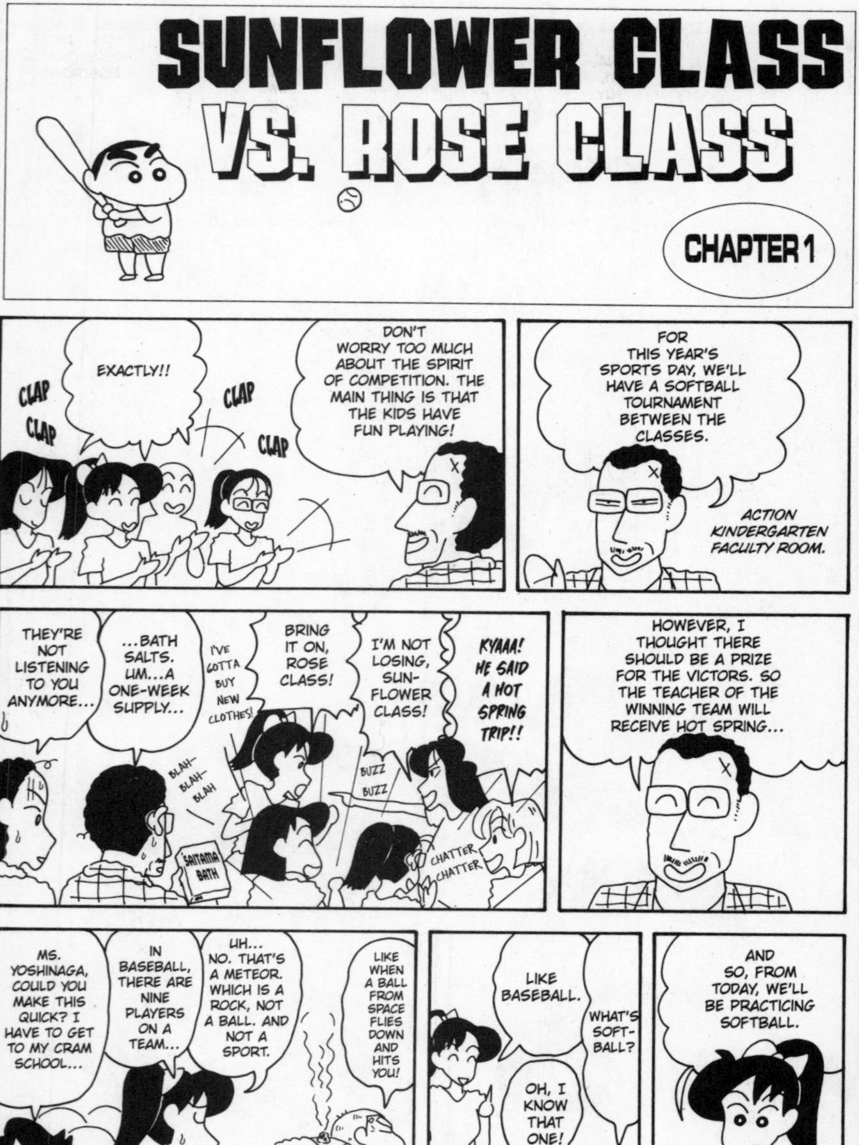
SUNFLOWER CLASS
VS. ROSE CLASS
CHAPTER 1
FOR THIS YEAR'S SPORTS DAY, WE'LL HAVE A SOFTBALL TOURNAMENT BETWEEN THE CLASSES.
ACTION KINDERGARTEN FACULTY ROOM.
DON'T WORRY TOO MUCH ABOUT THE SPIRIT OF COMPETITION. THE MAIN THING IS THAT THE KIDS HAVE FUN PLAYING!
CLAP
CLAP
EXACTLY!!
CLAP
CLAP
HOWEVER, I THOUGHT THERE SHOULD BE A PRIZE FOR THE VICTORS. SO THE TEACHER OF THE WINNING TEAM WILL RECEIVE HOT SPRING...
KYAAA! HE SAID A HOT SPRING TRIP!!
I'M NOT LOSING, SUN-FLOWER CLASS!
BRING IT ON, ROSE CLASS!
I'VE GOTTA BUY NEW CLOTHES!
...BATH SALTS. UM...A ONE-WEEK SUPPLY...
THEY'RE NOT LISTENING TO YOU ANYMORE...
CHATTER CHATTER
BUZZ BUZZ
BLAH-BLAH-BLAH
SAITAMA BATH
AND SO, FROM TODAY, WE'LL BE PRACTICING SOFTBALL.
WHAT'S SOFT-BALL?
OH, I KNOW THAT ONE!
LIKE BASEBALL.
LIKE WHEN A BALL FROM SPACE FLIES DOWN AND HITS YOU!
UH... NO. THAT'S A METEOR. WHICH IS A ROCK, NOT A BALL. AND NOT A SPORT.
IN BASEBALL, THERE ARE NINE PLAYERS ON A TEAM...
MS. YOSHINAGA, COULD YOU MAKE THIS QUICK? I HAVE TO GET TO MY CRAM SCHOOL...

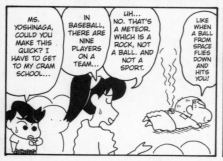

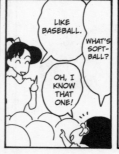

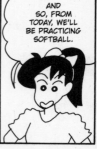

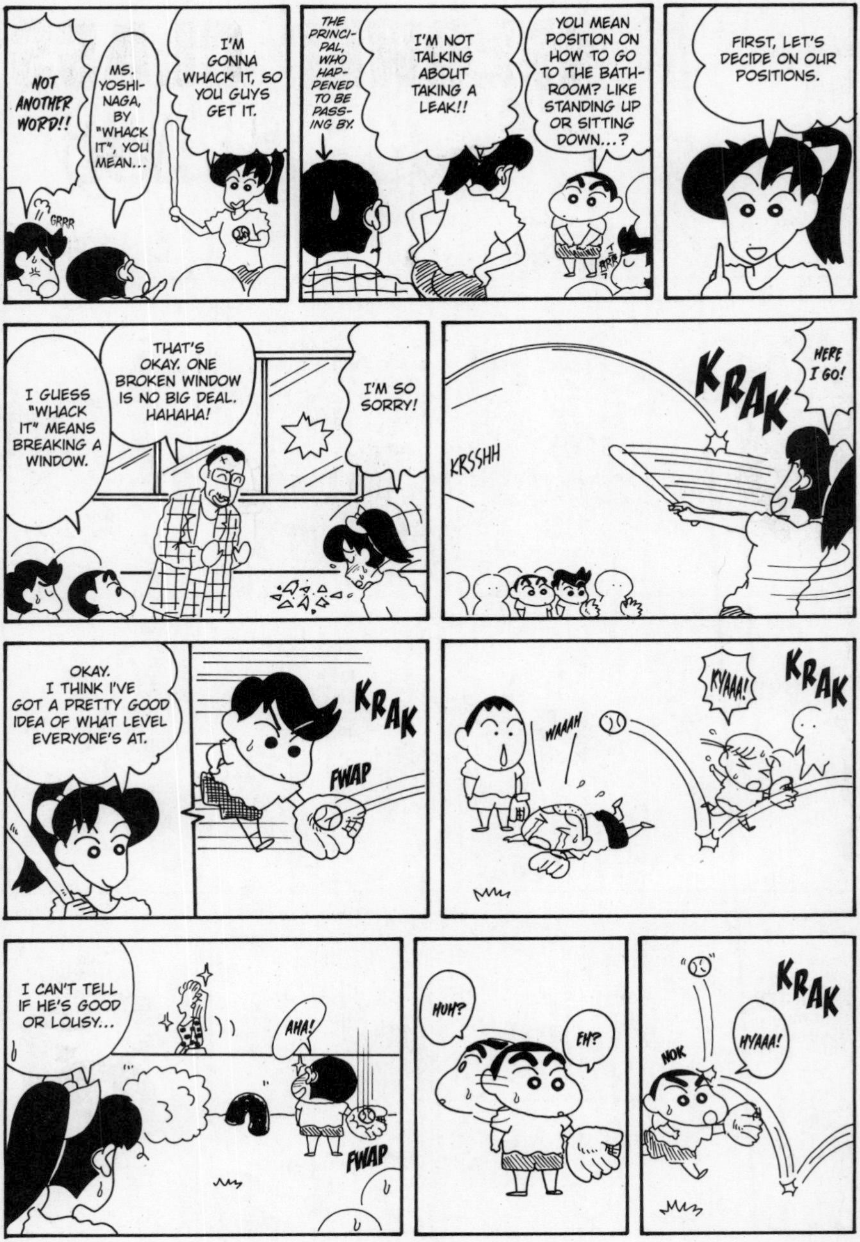
FIRST, LET'S DECIDE ON OUR POSITIONS.
YOU MEAN POSITION ON HOW TO GO TO THE BATH-ROOM? LIKE STANDING UP OR SITTING DOWN...?
I'M NOT TALKING ABOUT TAKING A LEAK!!
THE PRINCIPAL, WHO HAPPENED TO BE PASSING BY.
I'M GONNA WHACK IT, SO YOU GUYS GET IT.
MS. YOSHINAGA, BY "WHACK IT", YOU MEAN...
NOT ANOTHER WORD!!
GRRR
HERE I GO!
KRAK
KRSSHH
I'M SO SORRY!
THAT'S OKAY. ONE BROKEN WINDOW IS NO BIG DEAL. HAHAHA!
I GUESS "WHACK IT" MEANS BREAKING A WINDOW.
KRAK
KYAAA!
WAAAH
KRAK
FWAP
OKAY. I THINK I'VE GOT A PRETTY GOOD IDEA OF WHAT LEVEL EVERYONE'S AT.
KRAK
HYAAA!
NOK
EH?
HUH?
AHA!
FWAP
I CAN'T TELL IF HE'S GOOD OR LOUSY...

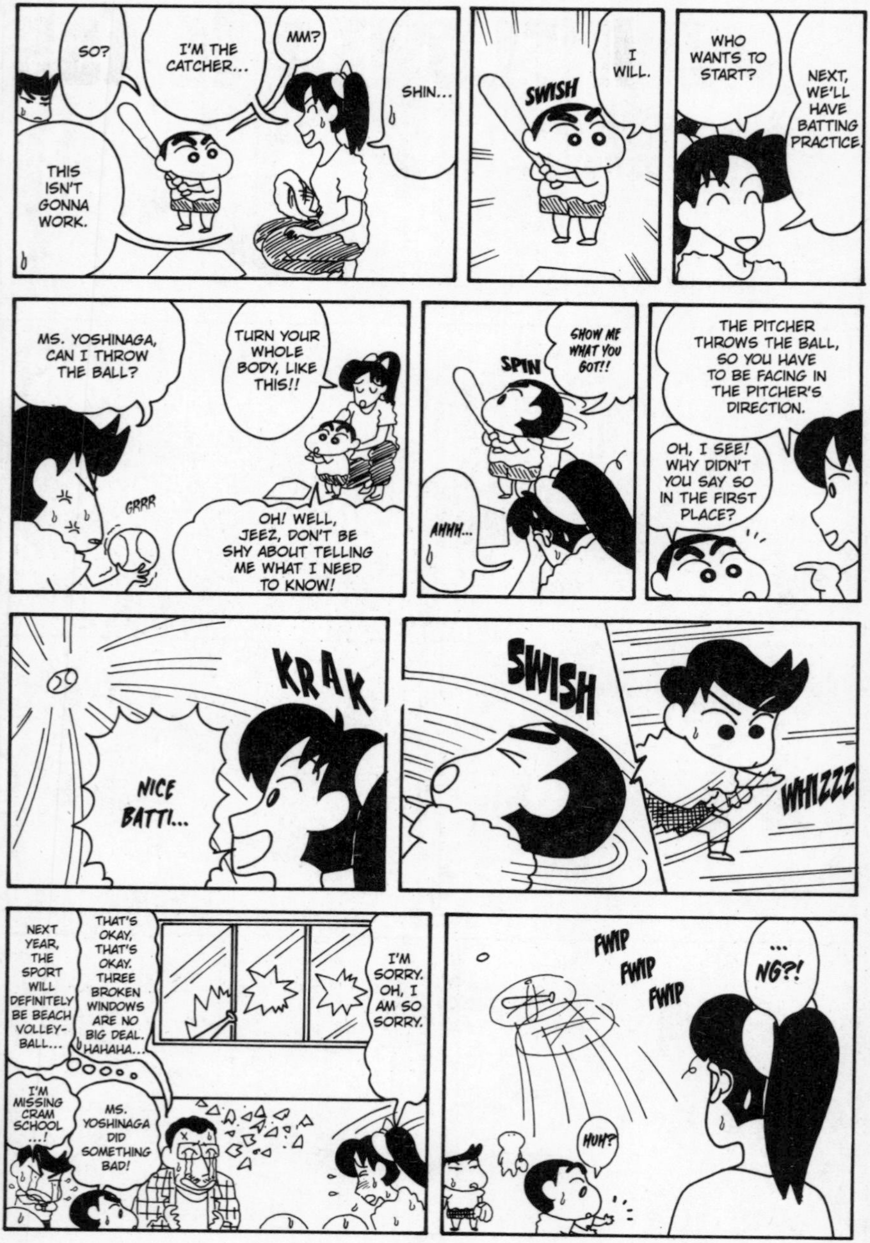
NEXT, WE'LL HAVE BATTING PRACTICE.
WHO WANTS TO START?
I WILL.
SWISH
SHIN...
MM?
I'M THE CATCHER...
SO?
THIS ISN'T GONNA WORK.
THE PITCHER THROWS THE BALL, SO YOU HAVE TO BE FACING IN THE PITCHER'S DIRECTION.
OH, I SEE! WHY DIDN'T YOU SAY SO IN THE FIRST PLACE?
SHOW ME WHAT YOU GOT!!
SPIN
AHHH...
TURN YOUR WHOLE BODY, LIKE THIS!!
MS. YOSHINAGA, CAN I THROW THE BALL?
GRRR
OH! WELL, JEEZ, DON'T BE SHY ABOUT TELLING ME WHAT I NEED TO KNOW!
SWISH
WHIZZZ
KRAK
NICE BATTI...
...NG?!
FWIP
FWIP
FWIP
HUH?
I'M SORRY. OH, I AM SO SORRY.
THAT'S OKAY, THAT'S OKAY. THREE BROKEN WINDOWS ARE NO BIG DEAL. HAHAHA...
NEXT YEAR, THE SPORT WILL DEFINITELY BE BEACH VOLLEY-BALL...
MS. YOSHINAGA DID SOMETHING BAD!
I'M MISSING CRAM SCHOOL...!

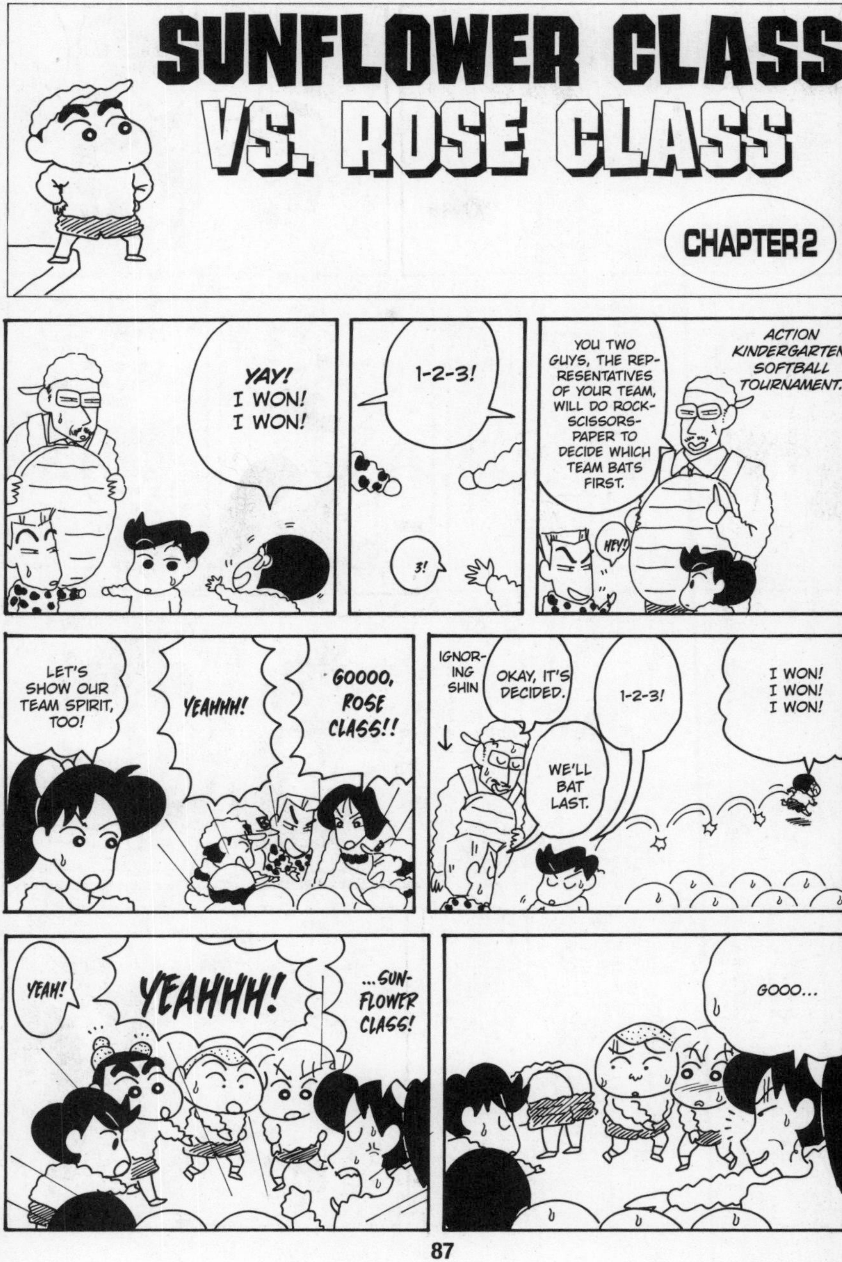
SUNFLOWER CLASS VS. ROSE CLASS
CHAPTER 2
ACTION KINDERGARTEN, SOFTBALL TOURNAMENT.
YOU TWO GUYS, THE REPRESENTATIVES OF YOUR TEAM, WILL DO ROCK-SCISSORS-PAPER TO DECIDE WHICH TEAM BATS FIRST.
HEY!
1-2-3!
3!
YAY! I WON! I WON!
I WON! I WON! I WON!
1-2-3!
OKAY, IT'S DECIDED.
IGNORING SHIN
WE'LL BAT LAST.
GOOOO, ROSE CLASS!!
YEAHHH!
LET'S SHOW OUR TEAM SPIRIT, TOO!
GOOO...
...SUNFLOWER CLASS!
YEAHHH!
YEAH!

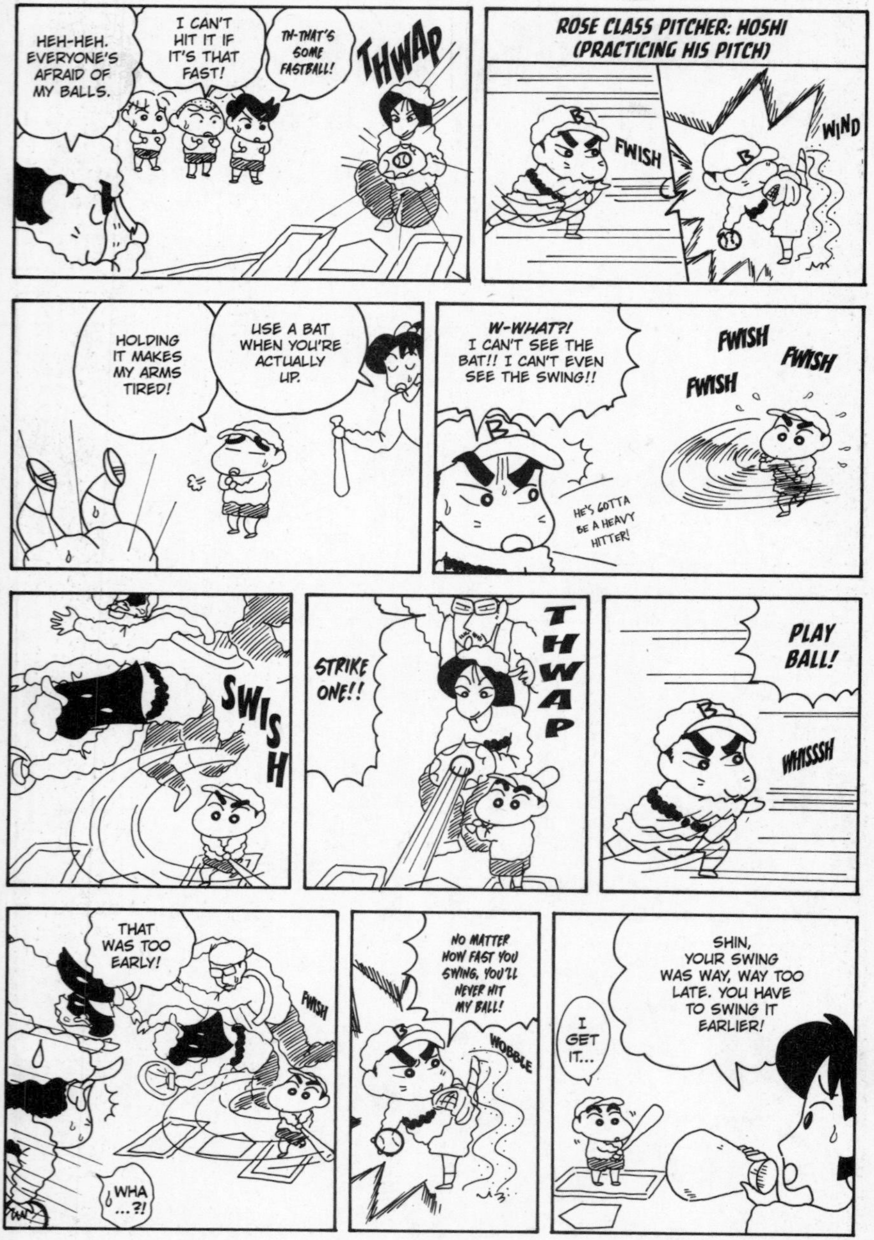
ROSE CLASS PITCHER: HOSHI (PRACTICING HIS PITCH)
WIND
FWISH
THWAP
TH-THAT'S SOME FASTBALL!
I CAN'T HIT IT IF IT'S THAT FAST!
HEH-HEH. EVERYONE'S AFRAID OF MY BALLS.
W-WHAT?! I CAN'T SEE THE BAT!! I CAN'T EVEN SEE THE SWING!!
FWISH
FWISH
FWISH
HE'S GOTTA BE A HEAVY HITTER!
USE A BAT WHEN YOU'RE ACTUALLY UP.
HOLDING IT MAKES MY ARMS TIRED!
PLAY BALL!
WHISSSH
THWAP
STRIKE ONE!!
SWISH
SHIN, YOUR SWING WAS WAY, WAY TOO LATE. YOU HAVE TO SWING IT EARLIER!
I GET IT...
NO MATTER HOW FAST YOU SWING, YOU'LL NEVER HIT MY BALL!
WOBBLE
FWISH
THAT WAS TOO EARLY!
WHA ...?!

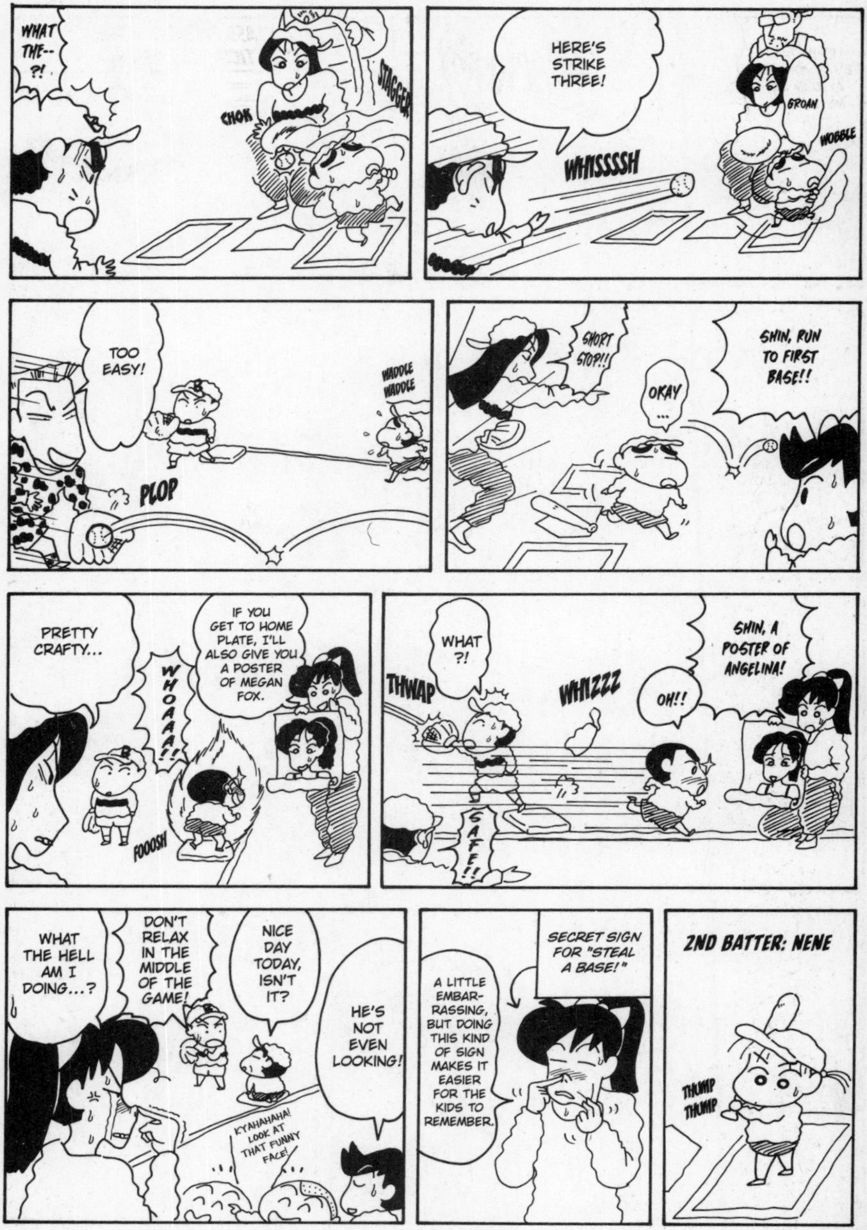
HERE'S STRIKE THREE!
WHISSSSH
GROAN
WOBBLE
WHAT THE-- ?!
CHOK
STAGGER
SHIN, RUN TO FIRST BASE!!
SHORT STOP!!
OKAY ...
TOO EASY!
WADDLE WADDLE
PLOP
SHIN, A POSTER OF ANGELINA!
WHAT ?!
OH!!
THWAP
WHIZZZ
SAFE!!
IF YOU GET TO HOME PLATE, I'LL ALSO GIVE YOU A POSTER OF MEGAN FOX.
PRETTY CRAFTY...
WHOAAAA!!
FOOOSH
2ND BATTER: NENE
THUMP THUMP
SECRET SIGN FOR "STEAL A BASE!"
A LITTLE EMBAR-RASSING, BUT DOING THIS KIND OF SIGN MAKES IT EASIER FOR THE KIDS TO REMEMBER.
HE'S NOT EVEN LOOKING!
NICE DAY TODAY, ISN'T IT?
DON'T RELAX IN THE MIDDLE OF THE GAME!
WHAT THE HELL AM I DOING...?
KYAHAHAHA! LOOK AT THAT FUNNY FACE!

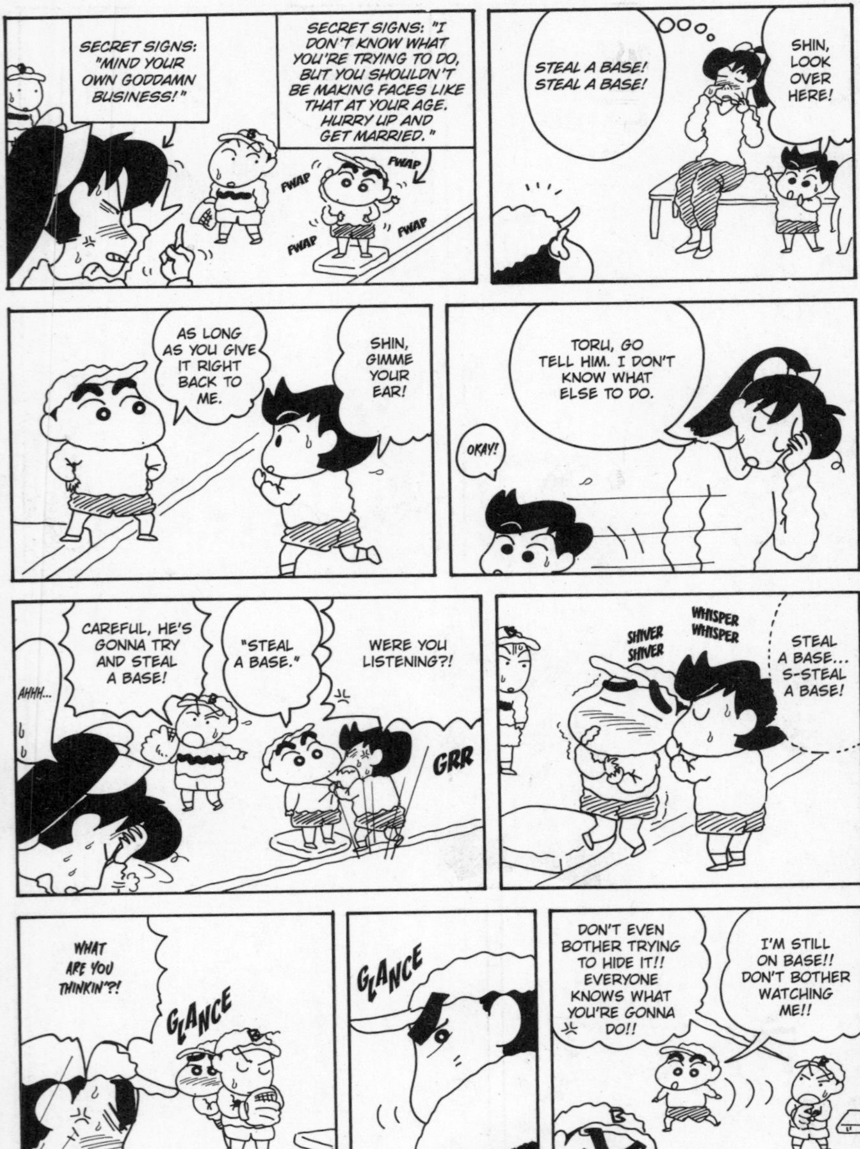
SHIN, LOOK OVER HERE!
STEAL A BASE! STEAL A BASE!
SECRET SIGNS: "I DON'T KNOW WHAT YOU'RE TRYING TO DO, BUT YOU SHOULDN'T BE MAKING FACES LIKE THAT AT YOUR AGE. HURRY UP AND GET MARRIED."
FWAP
FWAP
FWAP
FWAP
SECRET SIGNS: "MIND YOUR OWN GODDAMN BUSINESS!"
TORU, GO TELL HIM. I DON'T KNOW WHAT ELSE TO DO.
OKAY!
SHIN, GIMME YOUR EAR!
AS LONG AS YOU GIVE IT RIGHT BACK TO ME.
STEAL A BASE... S-STEAL A BASE!
WHISPER WHISPER
SHIVER SHIVER
WERE YOU LISTENING?!
"STEAL A BASE."
CAREFUL, HE'S GONNA TRY AND STEAL A BASE!
GRR
AHHH...
I'M STILL ON BASE!! DON'T BOTHER WATCHING ME!!
DON'T EVEN BOTHER TRYING TO HIDE IT!! EVERYONE KNOWS WHAT YOU'RE GONNA DO!!
GLANCE
GLANCE
WHAT ARE YOU THINKIN'?!

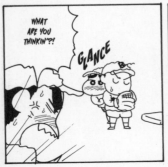

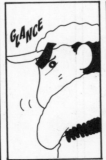

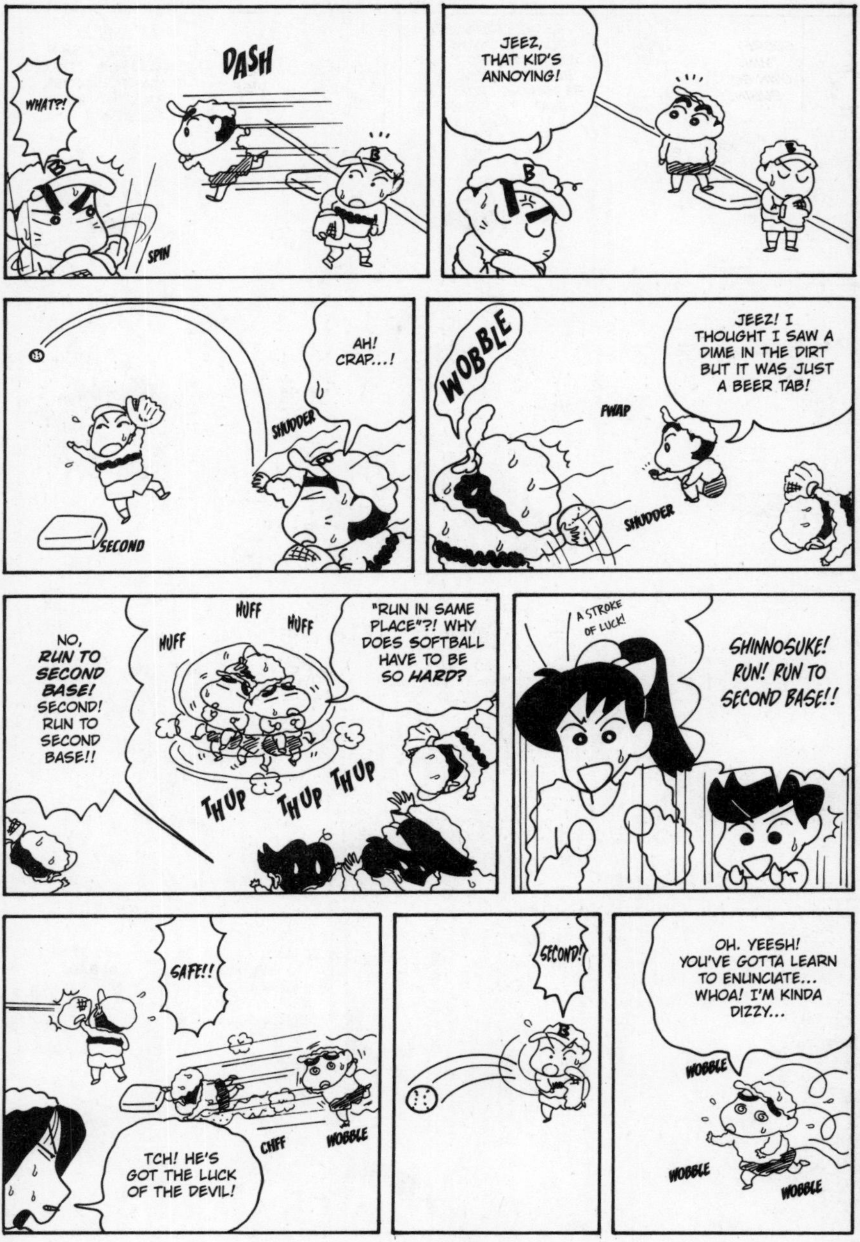
JEEZ, THAT KID'S ANNOYING!
DASH
WHAT?!
SPIN
JEEZ! I THOUGHT I SAW A DIME IN THE DIRT BUT IT WAS JUST A BEER TAB!
WOBBLE
FWAP
SHUDDER
AH! CRAP...!
SHUDDER
SECOND
SHINNOSUKE! RUN! RUN TO SECOND BASE!!
A STROKE OF LUCK!
"RUN IN SAME PLACE"?! WHY DOES SOFTBALL HAVE TO BE SO *HARD?*
HUFF
HUFF
HUFF
NO, ***RUN TO SECOND BASE!*** SECOND! RUN TO SECOND BASE!!
THUP
THUP
THUP
OH. YEESH! YOU'VE GOTTA LEARN TO ENUNCIATE... WHOA! I'M KINDA DIZZY...
WOBBLE
WOBBLE
WOBBLE
SECOND!
SAFE!!
WOBBLE
CHFF
TCH! HE'S GOT THE LUCK OF THE DEVIL!

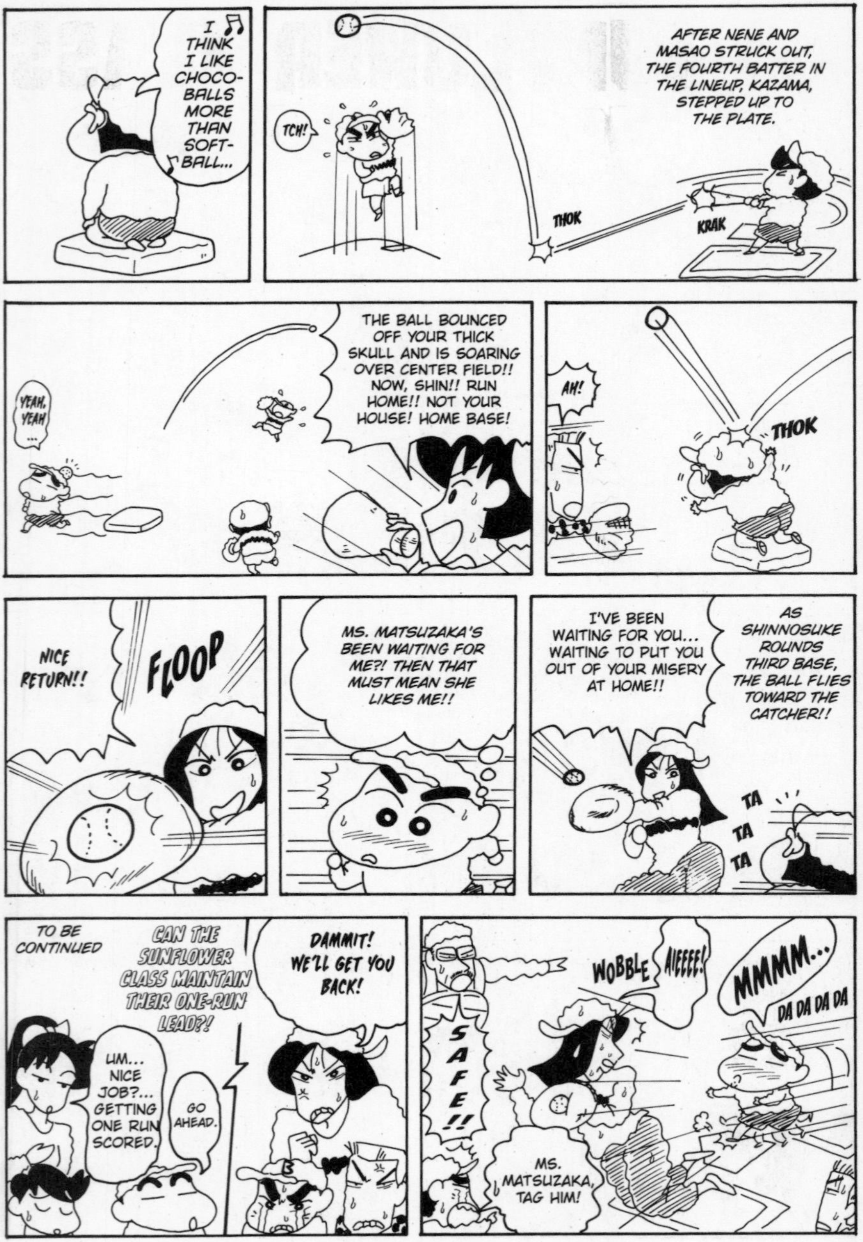
AFTER NENE AND MASAO STRUCK OUT, THE FOURTH BATTER IN THE LINEUP, KAZAMA, STEPPED UP TO THE PLATE.
KRAK
THOK
TCH!
I THINK I LIKE CHOCO-BALLS MORE THAN SOFT-BALL...
THOK
AH!
THE BALL BOUNCED OFF YOUR THICK SKULL AND IS SOARING OVER CENTER FIELD!! NOW, SHIN!! RUN HOME!! NOT YOUR HOUSE! HOME BASE!
YEAH, YEAH ...
AS SHINNOSUKE ROUNDS THIRD BASE, THE BALL FLIES TOWARD THE CATCHER!!
I'VE BEEN WAITING FOR YOU... WAITING TO PUT YOU OUT OF YOUR MISERY AT HOME!!
TA TA TA
MS. MATSUZAKA'S BEEN WAITING FOR ME?! THEN THAT MUST MEAN SHE LIKES ME!!
FLOOP
NICE RETURN!!
MMMM...
DA DA DA DA
AIEEEE!
WOBBLE
SAFE!!
MS. MATSUZAKA, TAG HIM!
DAMMIT! WE'LL GET YOU BACK!
CAN THE SUNFLOWER CLASS MAINTAIN THEIR ONE-RUN LEAD?!
TO BE CONTINUED
UM... NICE JOB?... GETTING ONE RUN SCORED.
GO AHEAD.

SUNFLOWER CLASS VS. ROSE CLASS

CHAPTER 3

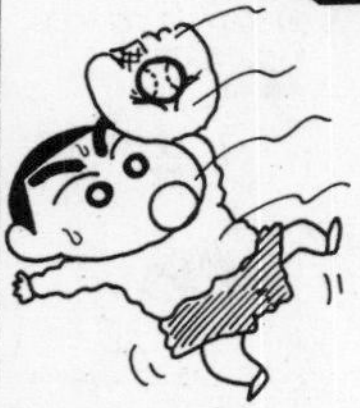

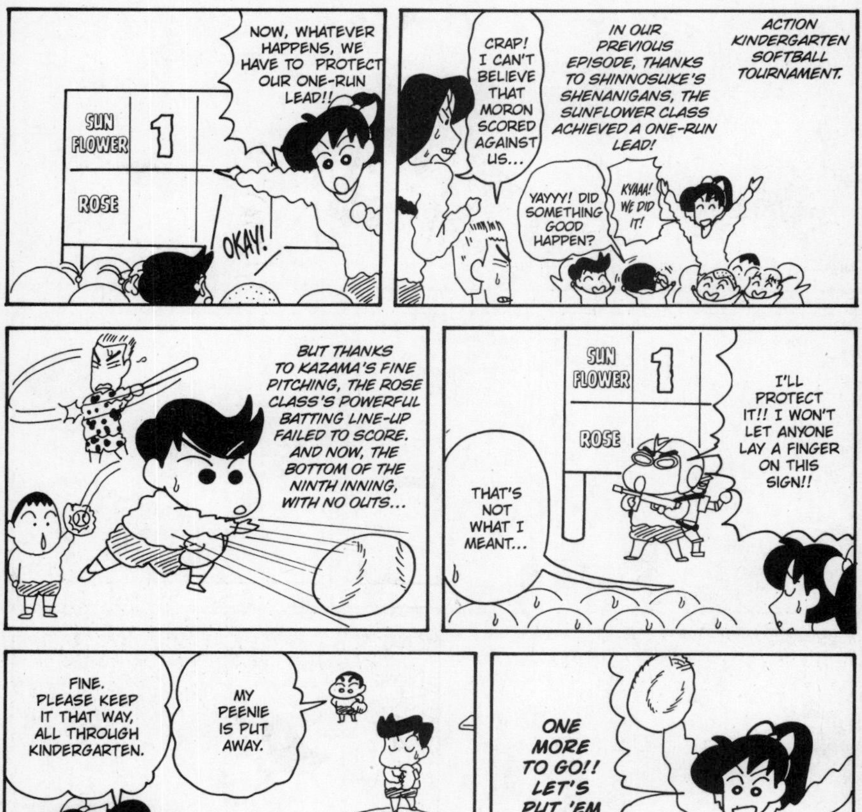
ACTION KINDERGARTEN SOFTBALL TOURNAMENT.
IN OUR PREVIOUS EPISODE, THANKS TO SHINNOSUKE'S SHENANIGANS, THE SUNFLOWER CLASS ACHIEVED A ONE-RUN LEAD!
CRAP! I CAN'T BELIEVE THAT MORON SCORED AGAINST US...
KYAAA! WE DID IT!
YAYYY! DID SOMETHING GOOD HAPPEN?
NOW, WHATEVER HAPPENS, WE HAVE TO PROTECT OUR ONE-RUN LEAD!!
SUN FLOWER
1
ROSE
OKAY!
SUN FLOWER
1
ROSE
I'LL PROTECT IT!! I WON'T LET ANYONE LAY A FINGER ON THIS SIGN!!
THAT'S NOT WHAT I MEANT...
BUT THANKS TO KAZAMA'S FINE PITCHING, THE ROSE CLASS'S POWERFUL BATTING LINE-UP FAILED TO SCORE. AND NOW, THE BOTTOM OF THE NINTH INNING, WITH NO OUTS...
ONE MORE TO GO!! LET'S PUT 'EM AWAY!!
MY PEENIE IS PUT AWAY.
FINE. PLEASE KEEP IT THAT WAY, ALL THROUGH KINDERGARTEN.

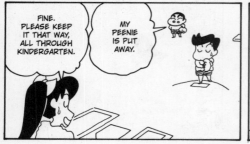

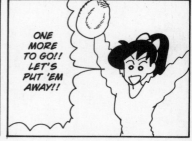

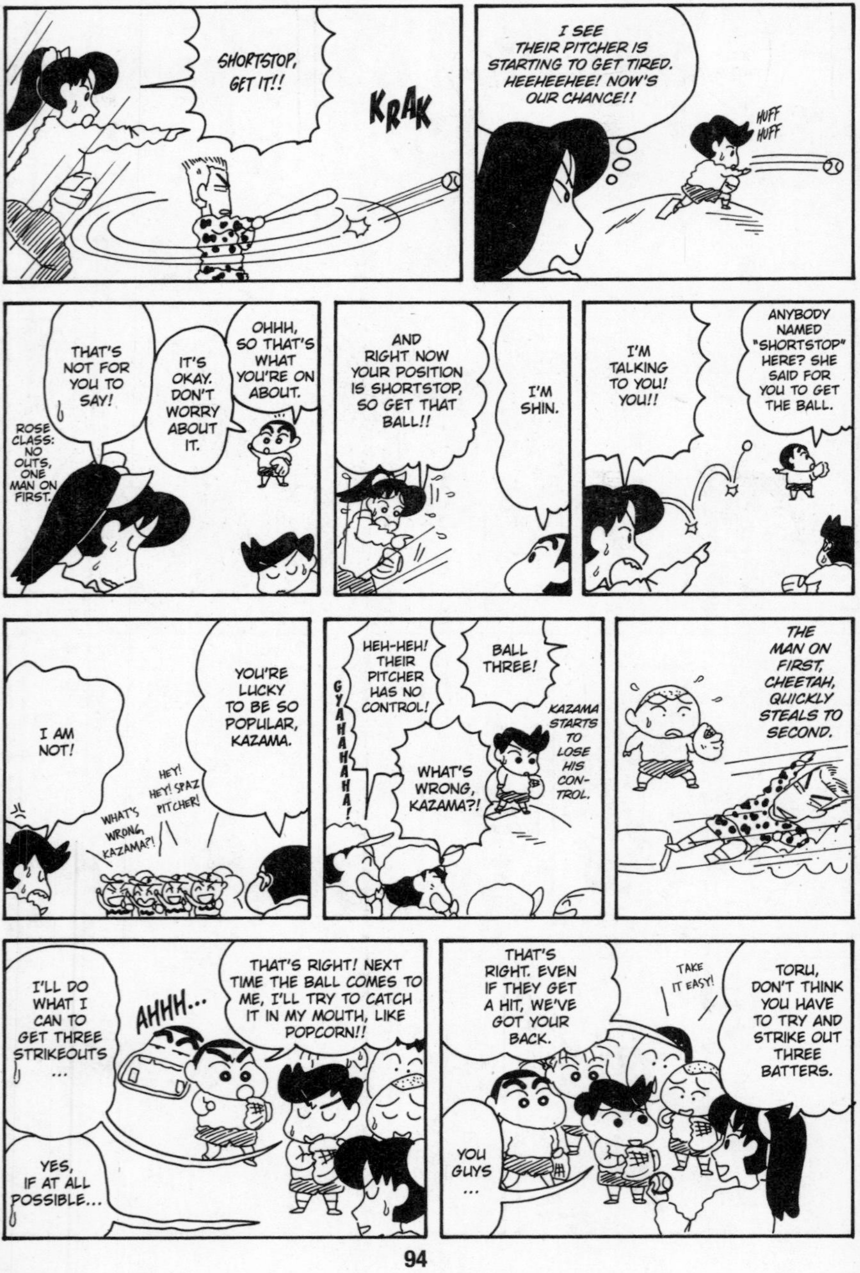
I SEE THEIR PITCHER IS STARTING TO GET TIRED. HEEHEEHEE! NOW'S OUR CHANCE!!
HUFF HUFF
KRAK
SHORTSTOP, GET IT!!
ANYBODY NAMED "SHORTSTOP" HERE? SHE SAID FOR YOU TO GET THE BALL.
I'M TALKING TO YOU! YOU!!
I'M SHIN.
AND RIGHT NOW YOUR POSITION IS SHORTSTOP, SO GET THAT BALL!!
OHHH, SO THAT'S WHAT YOU'RE ON ABOUT.
IT'S OKAY. DON'T WORRY ABOUT IT.
THAT'S NOT FOR YOU TO SAY!
ROSE CLASS: NO OUTS, ONE MAN ON FIRST.
THE MAN ON FIRST, CHEETAH, QUICKLY STEALS TO SECOND.
BALL THREE!
HEH-HEH! THEIR PITCHER HAS NO CONTROL!
KAZAMA STARTS TO LOSE HIS CON-TROL.
GYAHAHAHAHA!
WHAT'S WRONG, KAZAMA?!
YOU'RE LUCKY TO BE SO POPULAR, KAZAMA.
I AM NOT!
HEY! HEY! SPAZ PITCHER!
WHAT'S WRONG KAZAMA?!
TORU, DON'T THINK YOU HAVE TO TRY AND STRIKE OUT THREE BATTERS.
TAKE IT EASY!
THAT'S RIGHT. EVEN IF THEY GET A HIT, WE'VE GOT YOUR BACK.
YOU GUYS ...
THAT'S RIGHT! NEXT TIME THE BALL COMES TO ME, I'LL TRY TO CATCH IT IN MY MOUTH, LIKE POPCORN!!
AHHH...
I'LL DO WHAT I CAN TO GET THREE STRIKEOUTS ...
YES, IF AT ALL POSSIBLE...

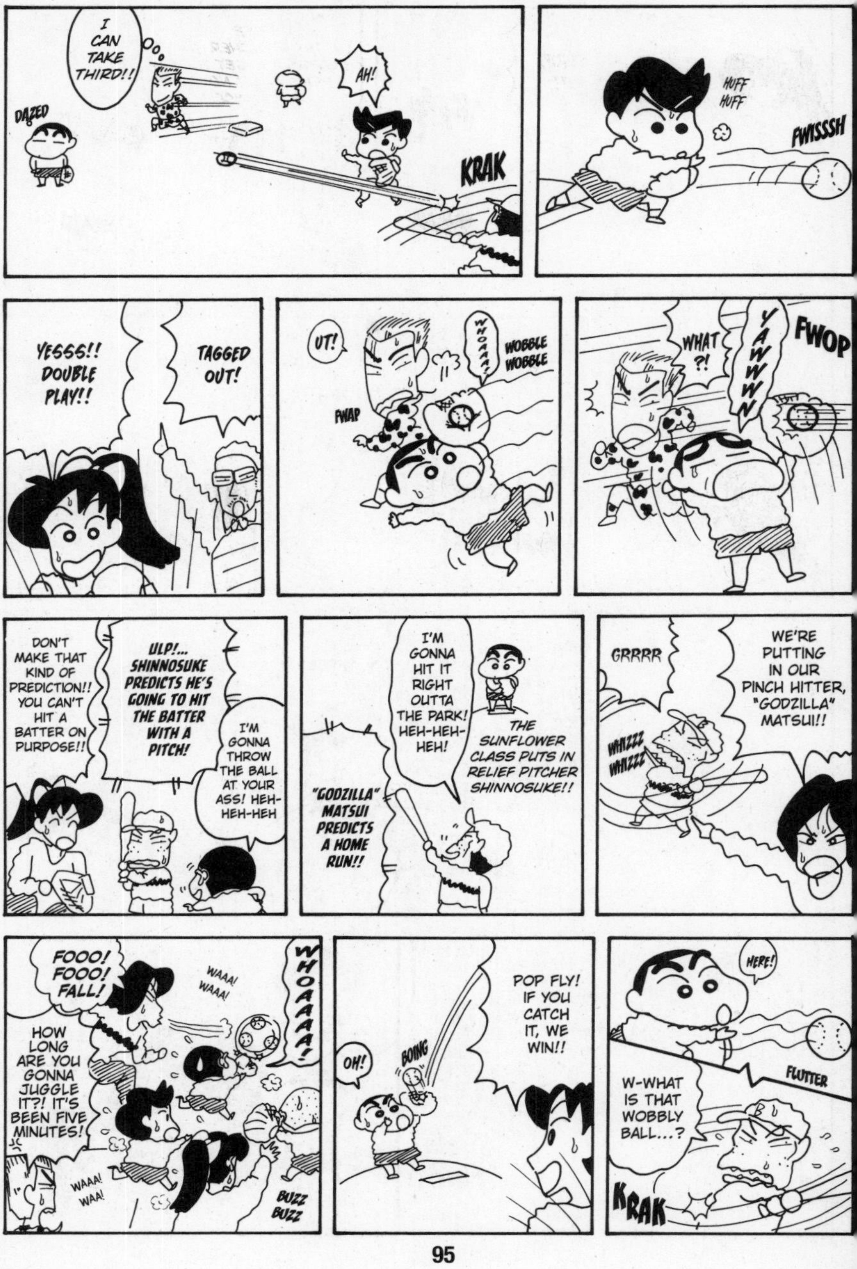
HUFF HUFF
FWISSSH
AH!
I CAN TAKE THIRD!!
DAZED
KRAK
FWOP
YAWWWN
WHAT ?!
WHOAAAA?
WOBBLE WOBBLE
UT!
FWAP
TAGGED OUT!
YESSS!! DOUBLE PLAY!!
WE'RE PUTTING IN OUR PINCH HITTER, "GODZILLA" MATSUI!!
GRRRR
WHIZZZ WHIZZZ
I'M GONNA HIT IT RIGHT OUTTA THE PARK! HEH-HEH-HEH!
THE SUNFLOWER CLASS PUTS IN RELIEF PITCHER SHINNOSUKE!!
"GODZILLA" MATSUI PREDICTS A HOME RUN!!
ULP!... SHINNOSUKE PREDICTS HE'S GOING TO HIT THE BATTER WITH A PITCH!
DON'T MAKE THAT KIND OF PREDICTION!! YOU CAN'T HIT A BATTER ON PURPOSE!!
I'M GONNA THROW THE BALL AT YOUR ASS! HEH-HEH-HEH
HERE!
FLUTTER
W-WHAT IS THAT WOBBLY BALL...?
KRAK
POP FLY! IF YOU CATCH IT, WE WIN!!
BOING
OH!
WHOAAAAA!
WAAA! WAAA!
FOOO! FOOO! FALL!
HOW LONG ARE YOU GONNA JUGGLE IT?! IT'S BEEN FIVE MINUTES!
WAAA! WAA!
BUZZ BUZZ

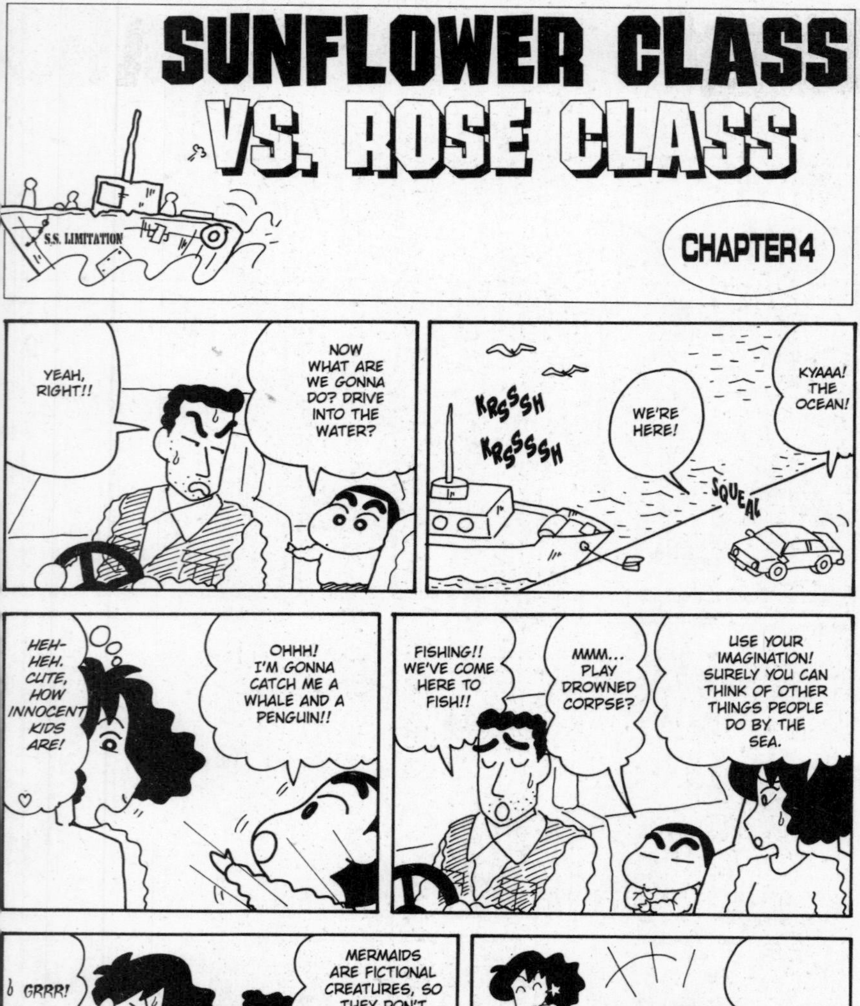
SUNFLOWER CLASS VS. ROSE CLASS
S.S. LIMITATION
CHAPTER 4
KYAAA! THE OCEAN!
WE'RE HERE!
KRSSSH
KRSSSSH
SQUEAL
NOW WHAT ARE WE GONNA DO? DRIVE INTO THE WATER?
YEAH, RIGHT!!
USE YOUR IMAGINATION! SURELY YOU CAN THINK OF OTHER THINGS PEOPLE DO BY THE SEA.
MMM... PLAY DROWNED CORPSE?
FISHING!! WE'VE COME HERE TO FISH!!
OHHH! I'M GONNA CATCH ME A WHALE AND A PENGUIN!!
HEH-HEH. CUTE, HOW INNOCENT KIDS ARE!
THEN MAYBE I'LL CATCH A MERMAID!!
MERMAIDS ARE FICTIONAL CREATURES, SO THEY DON'T ACTUALLY EXIST!! YOU SHOULDN'T TALK LIKE A CHILD AT YOUR AGE, MITZI.
GRRR!
OKAY, OKAY. LET'S CALM DOWN.

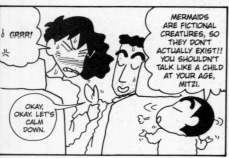

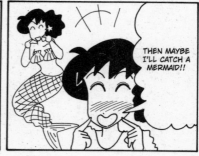

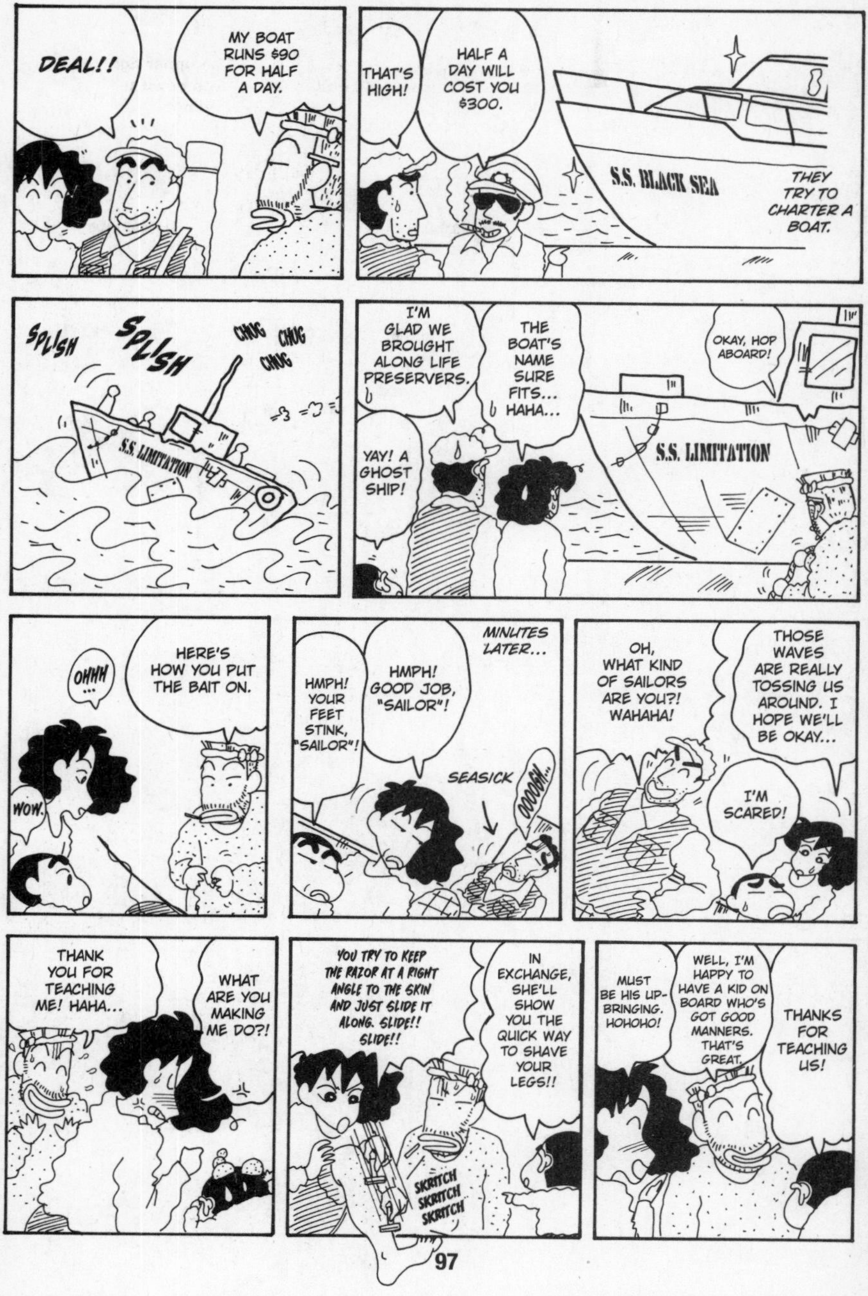
THEY TRY TO CHARTER A BOAT.
S.S. BLACK SEA
HALF A DAY WILL COST YOU $300.
THAT'S HIGH!
MY BOAT RUNS $90 FOR HALF A DAY.
DEAL!!
OKAY, HOP ABOARD!
S.S. LIMITATION
THE BOAT'S NAME SURE FITS... HAHA...
I'M GLAD WE BROUGHT ALONG LIFE PRESERVERS.
YAY! A GHOST SHIP!
CHUG CHUG CHUG
SPLISH
SPLISH
S.S. LIMITATION
THOSE WAVES ARE REALLY TOSSING US AROUND. I HOPE WE'LL BE OKAY...
OH, WHAT KIND OF SAILORS ARE YOU?! WAHAHA!
I'M SCARED!
MINUTES LATER...
HMPH! GOOD JOB, "SAILOR"!
HMPH! YOUR FEET STINK, "SAILOR"!
OOOOGH...
SEASICK
HERE'S HOW YOU PUT THE BAIT ON.
OHHH ...
WOW.
THANKS FOR TEACHING US!
WELL, I'M HAPPY TO HAVE A KID ON BOARD WHO'S GOT GOOD MANNERS. THAT'S GREAT.
MUST BE HIS UP-BRINGING. HOHOHO!
IN EXCHANGE, SHE'LL SHOW YOU THE QUICK WAY TO SHAVE YOUR LEGS!!
YOU TRY TO KEEP THE RAZOR AT A RIGHT ANGLE TO THE SKIN AND JUST SLIDE IT ALONG. SLIDE!! SLIDE!!
SKRITCH SKRITCH SKRITCH
WHAT ARE YOU MAKING ME DO?!
THANK YOU FOR TEACHING ME! HAHA...

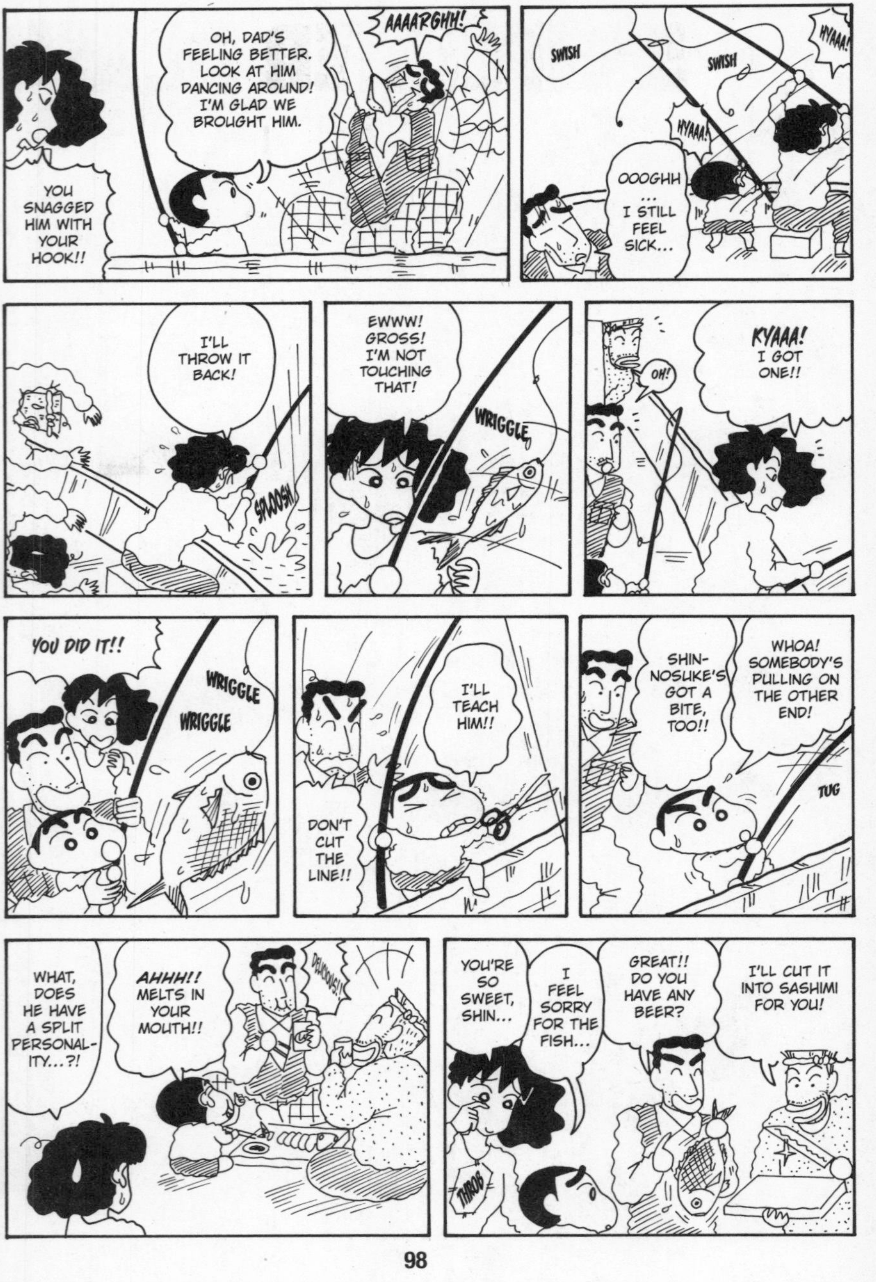
HYAAA!
SWISH
SWISH
HYAAA!
OOOGHH ... I STILL FEEL SICK...
AAAARGHH!
OH, DAD'S FEELING BETTER. LOOK AT HIM DANCING AROUND! I'M GLAD WE BROUGHT HIM.
YOU SNAGGED HIM WITH YOUR HOOK!!
KYAAA! I GOT ONE!!
OH!
EWWW! GROSS! I'M NOT TOUCHING THAT!
WRIGGLE
I'LL THROW IT BACK!
SPLOOSH
WHOA! SOMEBODY'S PULLING ON THE OTHER END!
SHIN-NOSUKE'S GOT A BITE, TOO!!
TUG
I'LL TEACH HIM!!
DON'T CUT THE LINE!!
WRIGGLE
WRIGGLE
YOU DID IT!!
I'LL CUT IT INTO SASHIMI FOR YOU!
GREAT!! DO YOU HAVE ANY BEER?
I FEEL SORRY FOR THE FISH...
YOU'RE SO SWEET, SHIN...
THROB
DELICIOUS!!
AHHH!! MELTS IN YOUR MOUTH!!
WHAT, DOES HE HAVE A SPLIT PERSONAL-ITY...?!

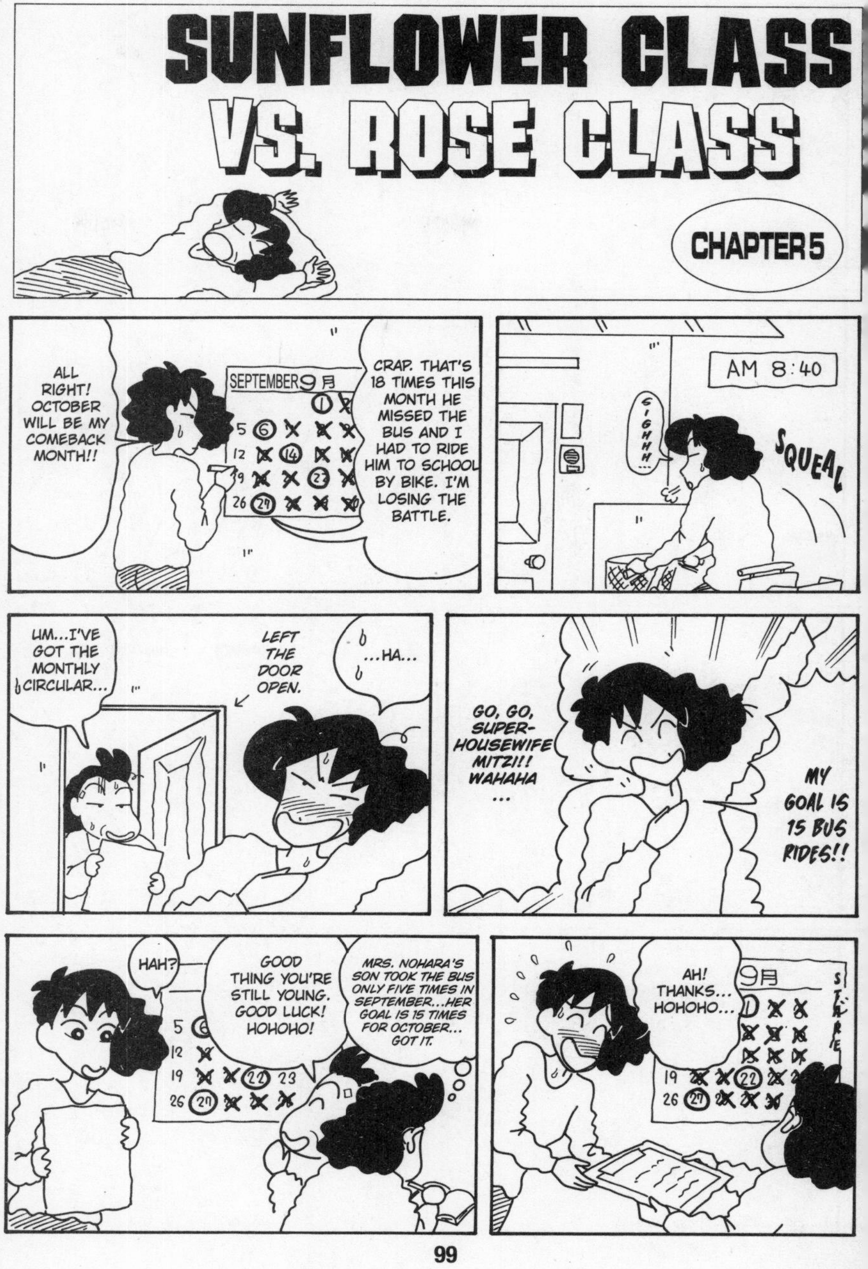
SUNFLOWER CLASS VS. ROSE CLASS
CHAPTER 5
AM 8:40
SIGHHH...
SQUEAL
CRAP. THAT'S 18 TIMES THIS MONTH HE MISSED THE BUS AND I HAD TO RIDE HIM TO SCHOOL BY BIKE. I'M LOSING THE BATTLE.
SEPTEMBER 9月
ALL RIGHT! OCTOBER WILL BE MY COMEBACK MONTH!!
MY GOAL IS 15 BUS RIDES!!
GO, GO, SUPER-HOUSEWIFE MITZI!! WAHAHA ...
...HA...
LEFT THE DOOR OPEN.
UM...I'VE GOT THE MONTHLY CIRCULAR...
STARE
AH! THANKS... HOHOHO...
MRS. NOHARA'S SON TOOK THE BUS ONLY FIVE TIMES IN SEPTEMBER...HER GOAL IS 15 TIMES FOR OCTOBER... GOT IT.
GOOD THING YOU'RE STILL YOUNG. GOOD LUCK! HOHOHO!
HAH?

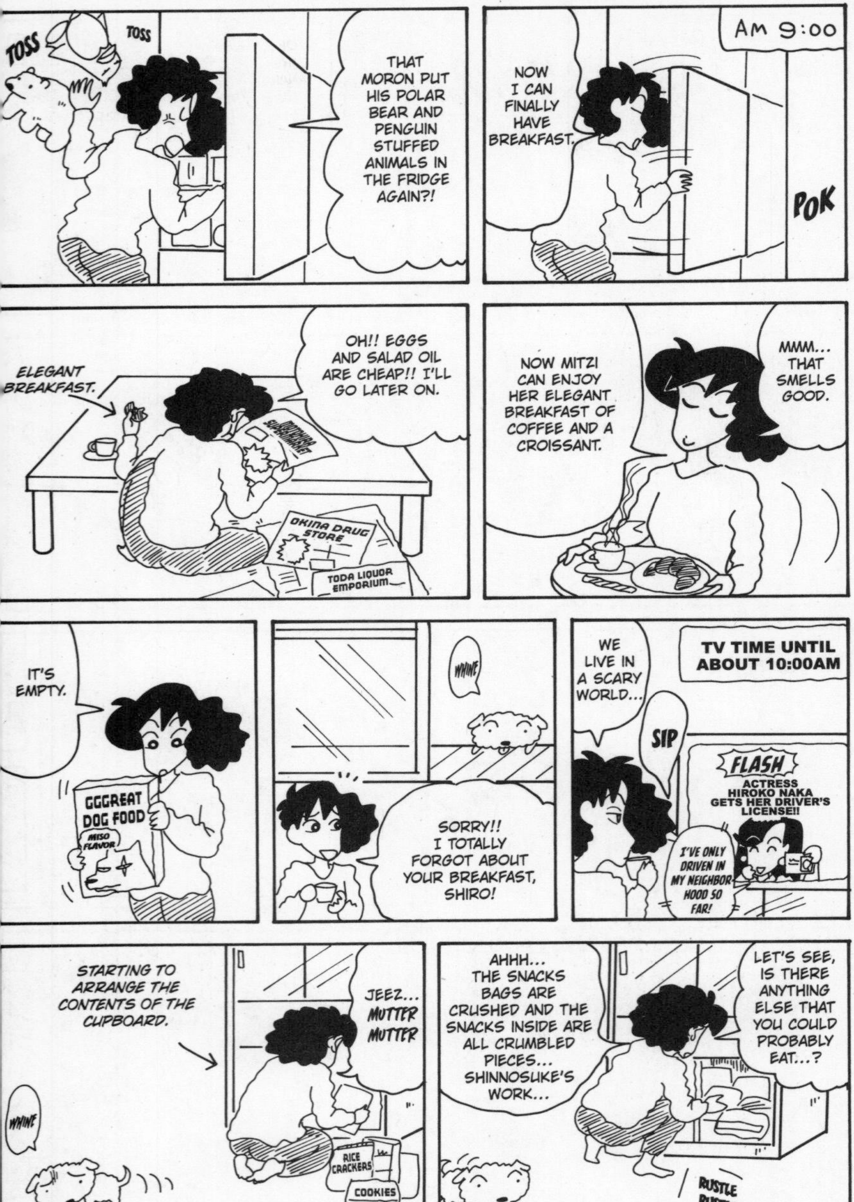
AM 9:00
NOW I CAN FINALLY HAVE BREAKFAST.
POK
THAT MORON PUT HIS POLAR BEAR AND PENGUIN STUFFED ANIMALS IN THE FRIDGE AGAIN?!
TOSS
TOSS
MMM... THAT SMELLS GOOD.
NOW MITZI CAN ENJOY HER ELEGANT BREAKFAST OF COFFEE AND A CROISSANT.
OH!! EGGS AND SALAD OIL ARE CHEAP!! I'LL GO LATER ON.
ELEGANT BREAKFAST.
OKINA DRUG STORE
TODA LIQUOR EMPORIUM
TV TIME UNTIL ABOUT 10:00AM
WE LIVE IN A SCARY WORLD...
SIP
FLASH
ACTRESS HIROKO NAKA GETS HER DRIVER'S LICENSE!!
I'VE ONLY DRIVEN IN MY NEIGHBORHOOD SO FAR!
WHINE
SORRY!! I TOTALLY FORGOT ABOUT YOUR BREAKFAST, SHIRO!
IT'S EMPTY.
GGGREAT DOG FOOD
MISO FLAVOR
LET'S SEE, IS THERE ANYTHING ELSE THAT YOU COULD PROBABLY EAT...?
AHHH... THE SNACKS BAGS ARE CRUSHED AND THE SNACKS INSIDE ARE ALL CRUMBLED PIECES... SHINNOSUKE'S WORK...
RUSTLE RUSTLE
STARTING TO ARRANGE THE CONTENTS OF THE CUPBOARD.
JEEZ... MUTTER MUTTER
WHINE
RICE CRACKERS
COOKIES

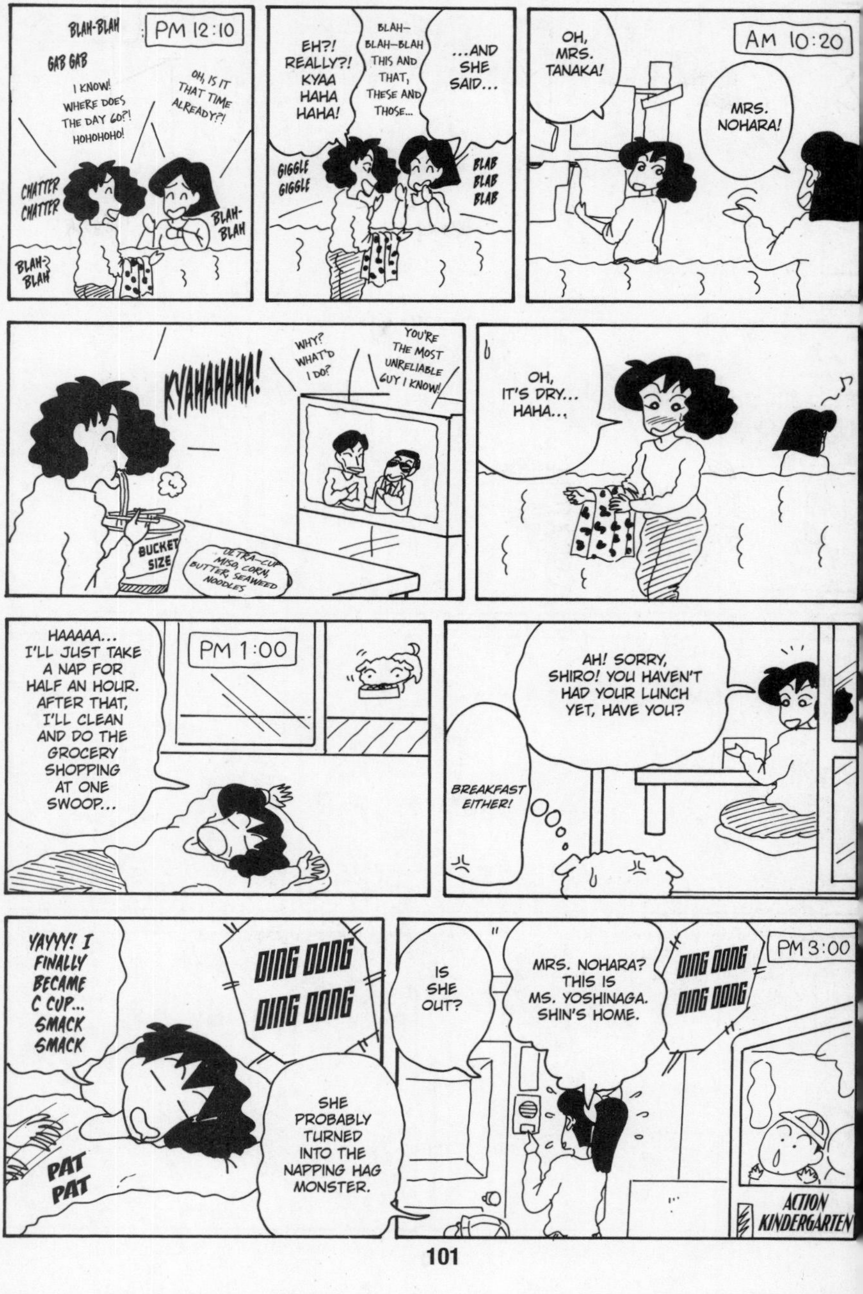
AM 10:20
MRS. NOHARA!
OH, MRS. TANAKA!
...AND SHE SAID...
BLAH-BLAH-BLAH THIS AND THAT, THESE AND THOSE...
EH?! REALLY?! KYAA HAHA HAHA!
BLAB BLAB BLAB
GIGGLE GIGGLE
PM 12:10
OH, IS IT THAT TIME ALREADY?!
BLAH-BLAH
GAB GAB
I KNOW! WHERE DOES THE DAY GO?! HOHOHOHO!
CHATTER CHATTER
BLAH-BLAH
BLAH-BLAH
OH, IT'S DRY... HAHA...
YOU'RE THE MOST UNRELIABLE GUY I KNOW!
WHY? WHAT'D I DO?
KYAHAHAHA!
BUCKET SIZE
ULTRA-CUP MISO, CORN, BUTTER, SEAWEED NOODLES
AH! SORRY, SHIRO! YOU HAVEN'T HAD YOUR LUNCH YET, HAVE YOU?
BREAKFAST EITHER!
PM 1:00
HAAAAA... I'LL JUST TAKE A NAP FOR HALF AN HOUR. AFTER THAT, I'LL CLEAN AND DO THE GROCERY SHOPPING AT ONE SWOOP...
PM 3:00
DING DONG DING DONG
MRS. NOHARA? THIS IS MS. YOSHINAGA. SHIN'S HOME.
IS SHE OUT?
ACTION KINDERGARTEN
DING DONG DING DONG
YAYYY! I FINALLY BECAME C CUP... SMACK SMACK
SHE PROBABLY TURNED INTO THE NAPPING HAG MONSTER.
PAT PAT

SUNFLOWER CLASS VS. ROSE CLASS

CHAPTER 6

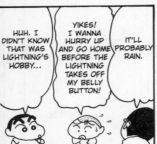

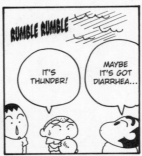

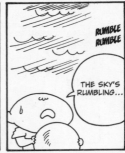

RUMBLE RUMBLE
THE SKY'S RUMBLING...
RUMBLE RUMBLE
MAYBE IT'S GOT DIARRHEA...
IT'S THUNDER!
IT'LL PROBABLY RAIN.
YIKES! I WANNA HURRY UP AND GO HOME BEFORE THE LIGHTNING TAKES OFF MY BELLY BUTTON!
HUH. I DIDN'T KNOW THAT WAS LIGHTNING'S HOBBY...
SEE YOU LATER!
BYE-BYE!
BYE!
FLASH
CRACKKKLE
TWITCH
OH...
CAN I HAVE A LITTLE TAPE?
UMBRELLAS FROM $10.
YEAH, SURE.
?
THANK YOU. I WON'T FORGET YOUR KINDNESS UNTIL I FORGET ABOUT IT.
BYE!

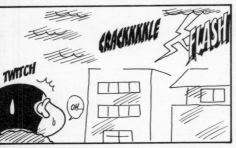

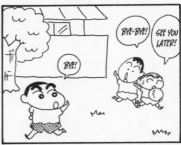

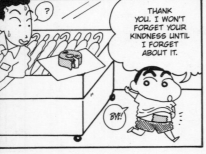

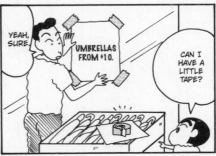

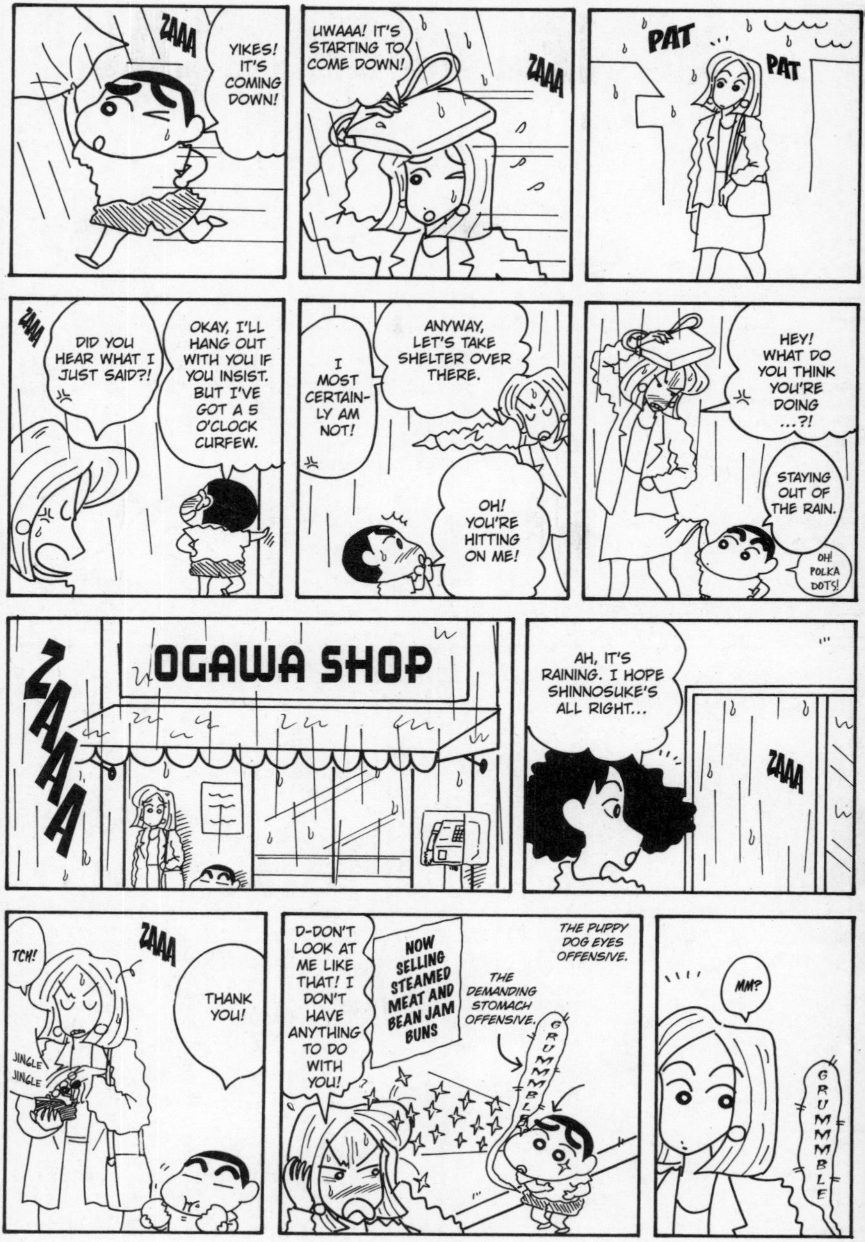
PAT
PAT
UWAAA! IT'S STARTING TO COME DOWN!
ZAAA
ZAAA
YIKES! IT'S COMING DOWN!
HEY! WHAT DO YOU THINK YOU'RE DOING ...?!
STAYING OUT OF THE RAIN.
OH! POLKA DOTS!
ANYWAY, LET'S TAKE SHELTER OVER THERE.
OH! YOU'RE HITTING ON ME!
I MOST CERTAIN-LY AM NOT!
ZAAA
OKAY, I'LL HANG OUT WITH YOU IF YOU INSIST. BUT I'VE GOT A 5 O'CLOCK CURFEW.
DID YOU HEAR WHAT I JUST SAID?!
AH, IT'S RAINING. I HOPE SHINNOSUKE'S ALL RIGHT...
ZAAA
OGAWA SHOP
ZAAAA
MM?
GRUMMBLE
THE PUPPY DOG EYES OFFENSIVE.
NOW SELLING STEAMED MEAT AND BEAN JAM BUNS
D-DON'T LOOK AT ME LIKE THAT! I DON'T HAVE ANYTHING TO DO WITH YOU!
THE DEMANDING STOMACH OFFENSIVE.
GRUMMBLE
ZAAA
THANK YOU!
TCH!
JINGLE JINGLE

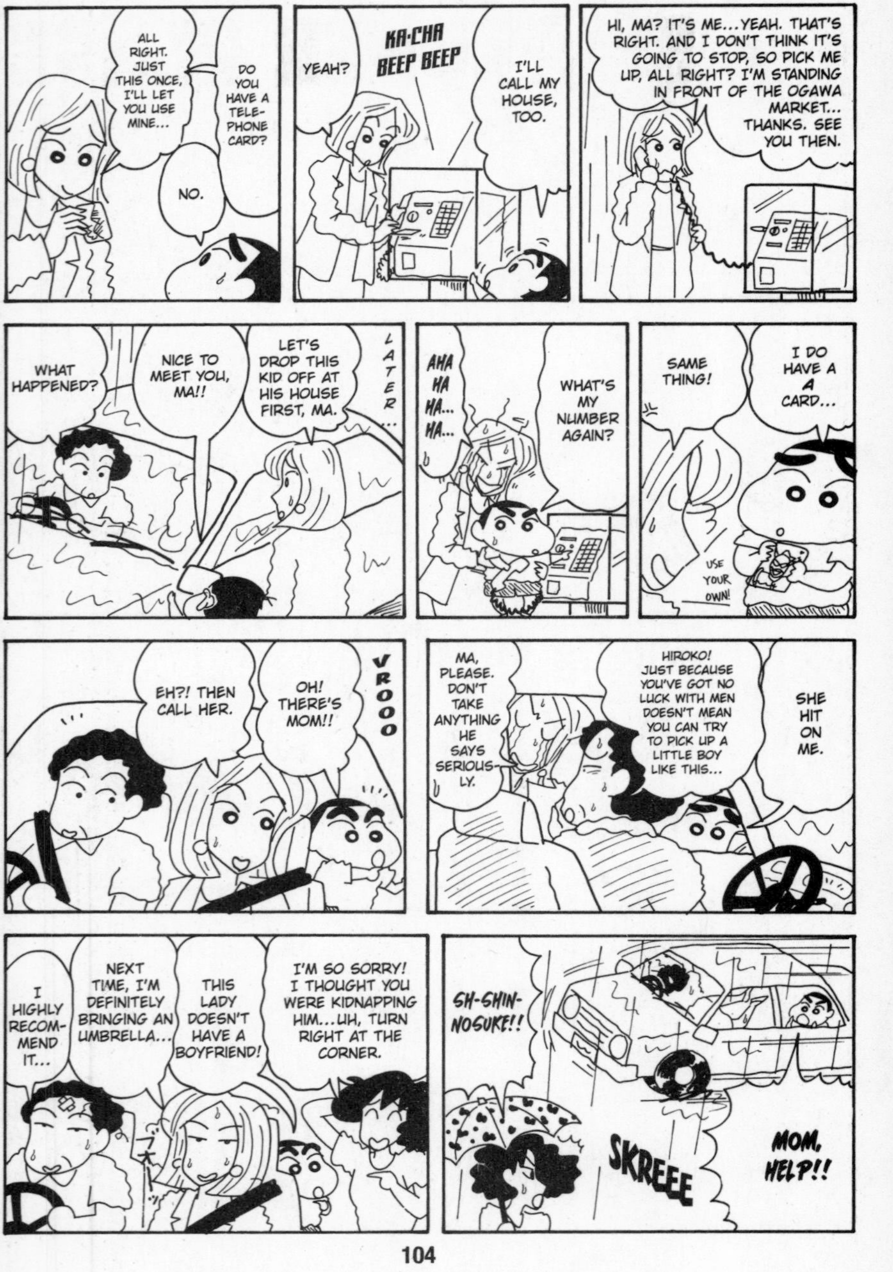
HI, MA? IT'S ME...YEAH. THAT'S RIGHT. AND I DON'T THINK IT'S GOING TO STOP, SO PICK ME UP, ALL RIGHT? I'M STANDING IN FRONT OF THE OGAWA MARKET... THANKS. SEE YOU THEN.
I'LL CALL MY HOUSE, TOO.
KA-CHA BEEP BEEP
YEAH?
DO YOU HAVE A TELE-PHONE CARD?
NO.
ALL RIGHT. JUST THIS ONCE, I'LL LET YOU USE MINE...
I DO HAVE A A CARD...
SAME THING!
USE YOUR OWN!
WHAT'S MY NUMBER AGAIN?
AHA HA HA... HA...
LATER...
LET'S DROP THIS KID OFF AT HIS HOUSE FIRST, MA.
NICE TO MEET YOU, MA!!
WHAT HAPPENED?
SHE HIT ON ME.
HIROKO! JUST BECAUSE YOU'VE GOT NO LUCK WITH MEN DOESN'T MEAN YOU CAN TRY TO PICK UP A LITTLE BOY LIKE THIS...
MA, PLEASE. DON'T TAKE ANYTHING HE SAYS SERIOUS-LY.
VROOO
OH! THERE'S MOM!!
EH?! THEN CALL HER.
SH-SHIN-NOSUKE!!
MOM, HELP?!!
SKREEE
I'M SO SORRY! I THOUGHT YOU WERE KIDNAPPING HIM...UH, TURN RIGHT AT THE CORNER.
THIS LADY DOESN'T HAVE A BOYFRIEND!
NEXT TIME, I'M DEFINITELY BRINGING AN UMBRELLA...
I HIGHLY RECOM-MEND IT...

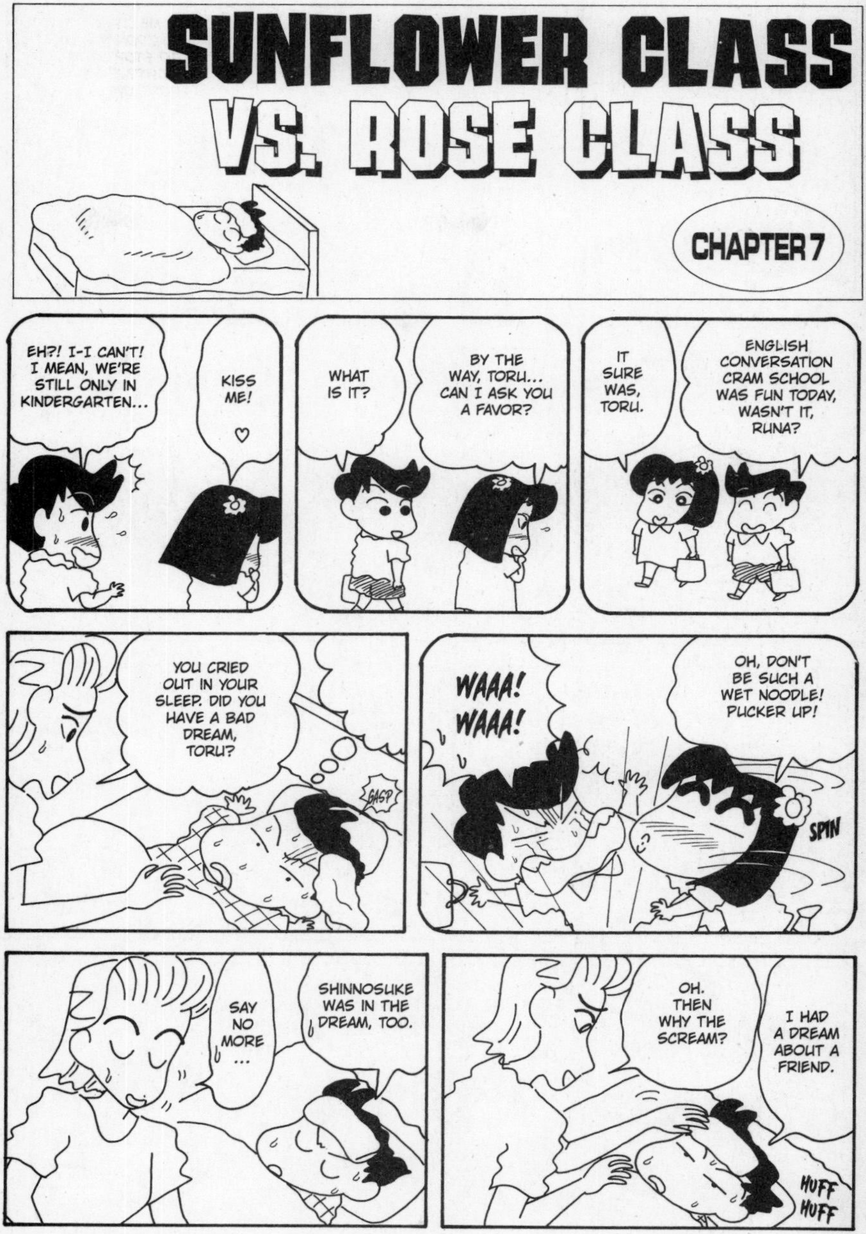
SUNFLOWER CLASS VS. ROSE CLASS
CHAPTER 7
ENGLISH CONVERSATION CRAM SCHOOL WAS FUN TODAY, WASN'T IT, RUNA?
IT SURE WAS, TORU.
BY THE WAY, TORU... CAN I ASK YOU A FAVOR?
WHAT IS IT?
KISS ME! ♡
EH?! I-I CAN'T! I MEAN, WE'RE STILL ONLY IN KINDERGARTEN...
OH, DON'T BE SUCH A WET NOODLE! PUCKER UP!
SPIN
WAAA! WAAA!
GASP
YOU CRIED OUT IN YOUR SLEEP. DID YOU HAVE A BAD DREAM, TORU?
I HAD A DREAM ABOUT A FRIEND.
OH. THEN WHY THE SCREAM?
HUFF HUFF
SHINNOSUKE WAS IN THE DREAM, TOO.
SAY NO MORE...

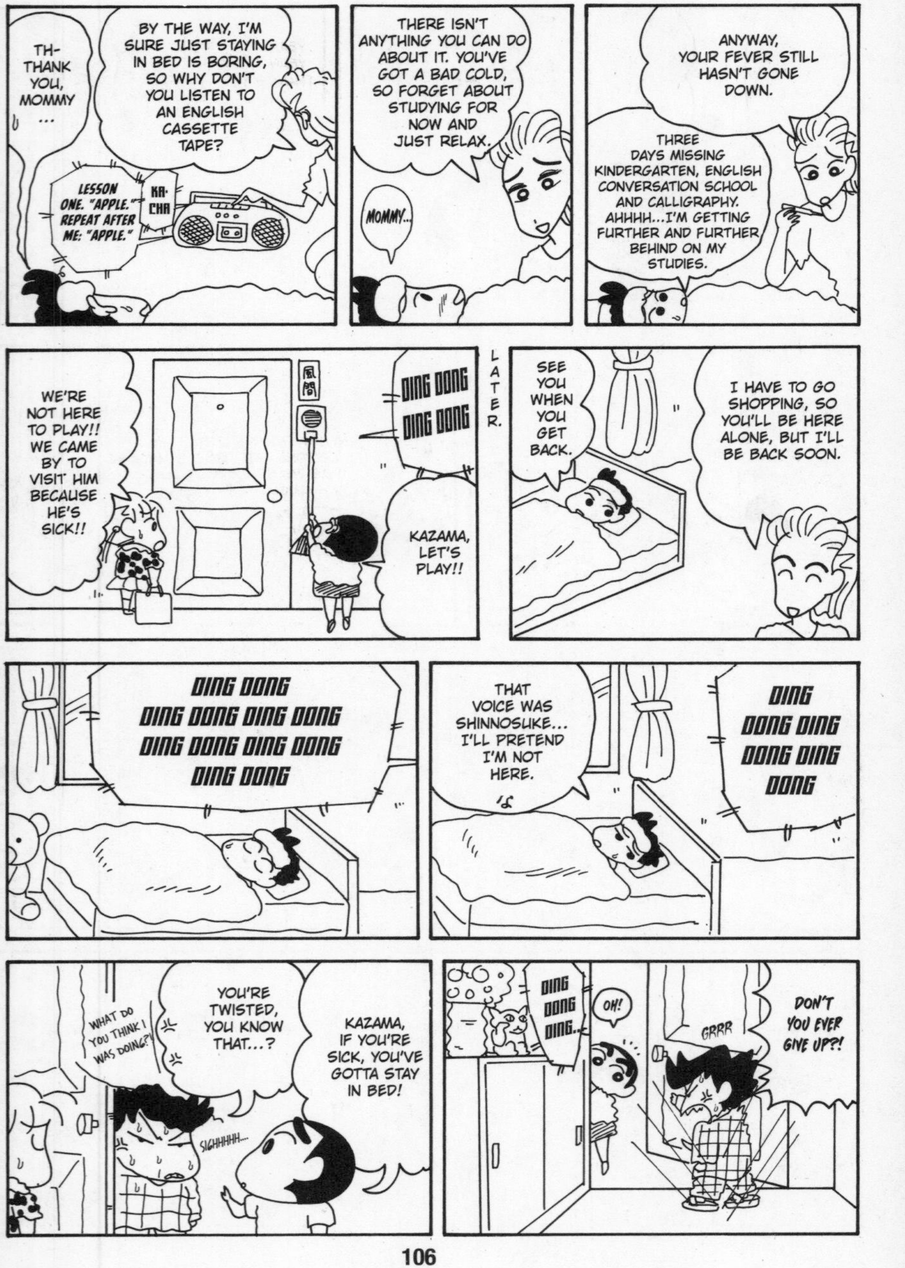
ANYWAY, YOUR FEVER STILL HASN'T GONE DOWN.
THREE DAYS MISSING KINDERGARTEN, ENGLISH CONVERSATION SCHOOL AND CALLIGRAPHY. AHHHH...I'M GETTING FURTHER AND FURTHER BEHIND ON MY STUDIES.
THERE ISN'T ANYTHING YOU CAN DO ABOUT IT. YOU'VE GOT A BAD COLD, SO FORGET ABOUT STUDYING FOR NOW AND JUST RELAX.
MOMMY...
BY THE WAY, I'M SURE JUST STAYING IN BED IS BORING, SO WHY DON'T YOU LISTEN TO AN ENGLISH CASSETTE TAPE?
TH- THANK YOU, MOMMY ...
KA-CHA
LESSON ONE. "APPLE." REPEAT AFTER ME: "APPLE."
I HAVE TO GO SHOPPING, SO YOU'LL BE HERE ALONE, BUT I'LL BE BACK SOON.
SEE YOU WHEN YOU GET BACK.
LATER.
DING DONG DING DONG
KAZAMA, LET'S PLAY!!
WE'RE NOT HERE TO PLAY!! WE CAME BY TO VISIT HIM BECAUSE HE'S SICK!!
DING DONG DING DONG DING DONG
THAT VOICE WAS SHINNOSUKE... I'LL PRETEND I'M NOT HERE.
DING DONG DING DONG DING DONG DING DONG DING DONG DING DONG
DON'T YOU EVER GIVE UP?!
GRRR
OH!
DING DONG DING...
KAZAMA, IF YOU'RE SICK, YOU'VE GOTTA STAY IN BED!
SIGHHHHH...
YOU'RE TWISTED, YOU KNOW THAT...?
WHAT DO YOU THINK I WAS DOING?!

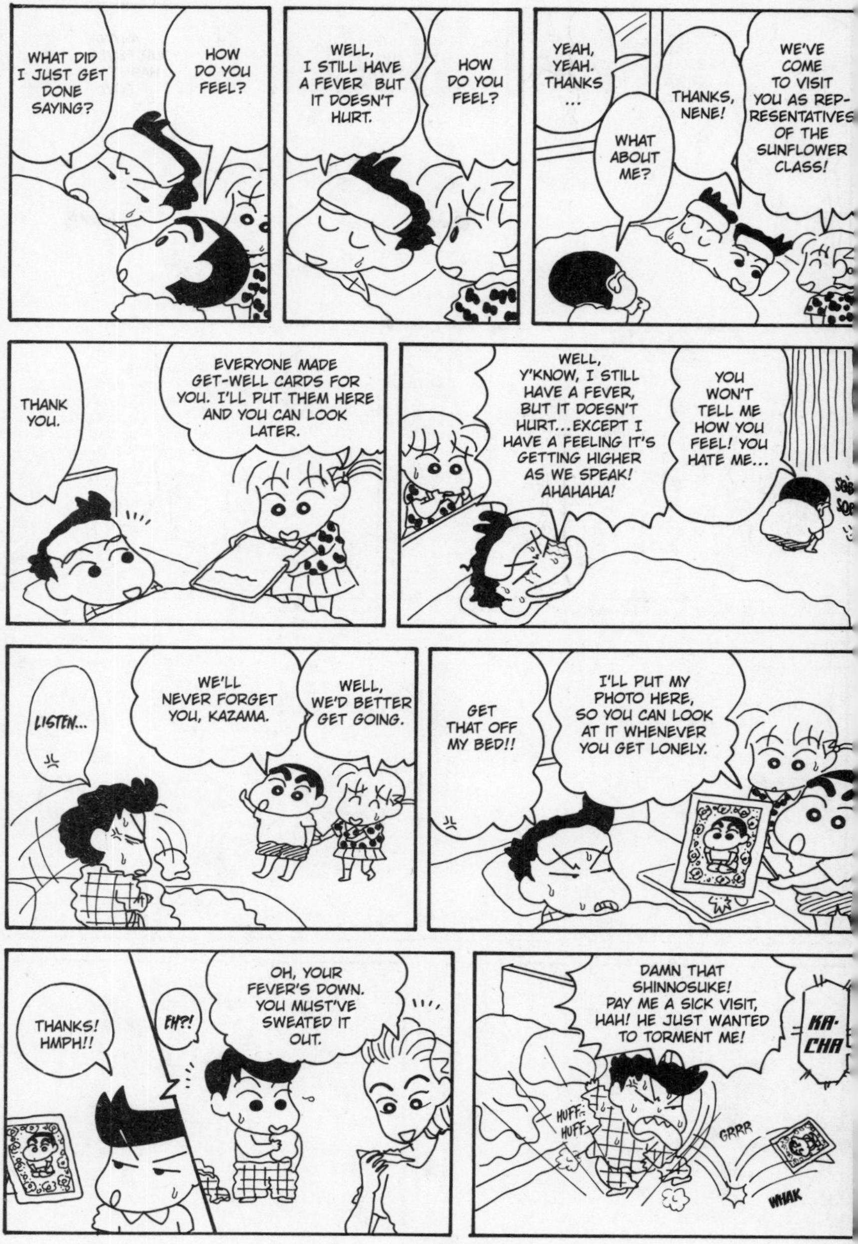
WE'VE COME TO VISIT YOU AS REPRESENTATIVES OF THE SUNFLOWER CLASS!
THANKS, NENE!
WHAT ABOUT ME?
YEAH, YEAH. THANKS ...
HOW DO YOU FEEL?
WELL, I STILL HAVE A FEVER BUT IT DOESN'T HURT.
HOW DO YOU FEEL?
WHAT DID I JUST GET DONE SAYING?
YOU WON'T TELL ME HOW YOU FEEL! YOU HATE ME...
WELL, Y'KNOW, I STILL HAVE A FEVER, BUT IT DOESN'T HURT...EXCEPT I HAVE A FEELING IT'S GETTING HIGHER AS WE SPEAK! AHAHAHA!
EVERYONE MADE GET-WELL CARDS FOR YOU. I'LL PUT THEM HERE AND YOU CAN LOOK LATER.
THANK YOU.
I'LL PUT MY PHOTO HERE, SO YOU CAN LOOK AT IT WHENEVER YOU GET LONELY.
GET THAT OFF MY BED!!
WELL, WE'D BETTER GET GOING.
WE'LL NEVER FORGET YOU, KAZAMA.
LISTEN...
KA-CHA
DAMN THAT SHINNOSUKE! PAY ME A SICK VISIT, HAH! HE JUST WANTED TO TORMENT ME!
HUFF HUFF
GRRR
WHAK
OH, YOUR FEVER'S DOWN. YOU MUST'VE SWEATED IT OUT.
EH?!
THANKS! HMPH!!

SUNFLOWER CLASS VS. ROSE CLASS

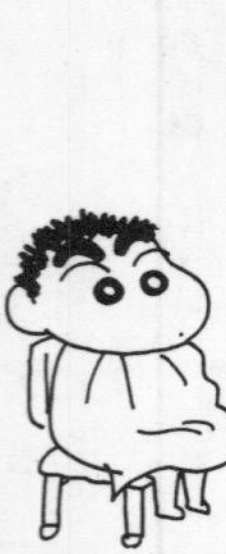

CHAPTER 8

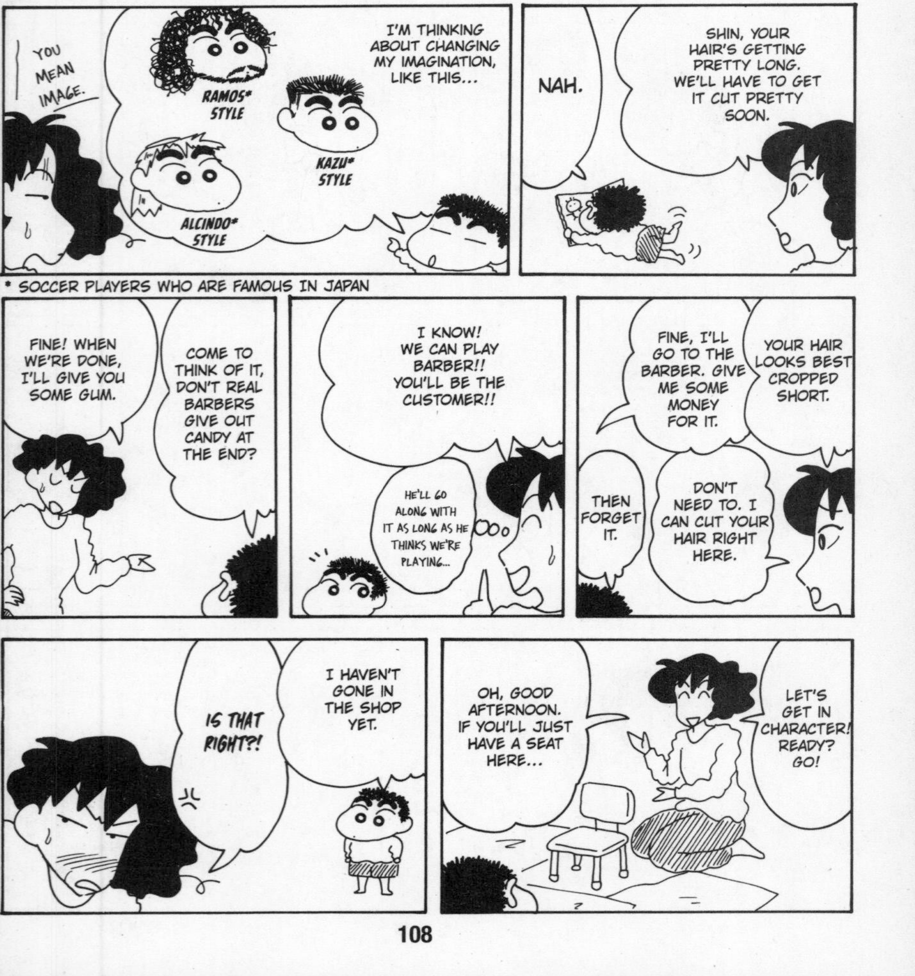
SHIN, YOUR HAIR'S GETTING PRETTY LONG. WE'LL HAVE TO GET IT CUT PRETTY SOON.
NAH.
I'M THINKING ABOUT CHANGING MY IMAGINATION, LIKE THIS...
RAMOS* STYLE
KAZU* STYLE
ALCINDO* STYLE
YOU MEAN IMAGE.
YOUR HAIR LOOKS BEST CROPPED SHORT.
FINE, I'LL GO TO THE BARBER. GIVE ME SOME MONEY FOR IT.
DON'T NEED TO. I CAN CUT YOUR HAIR RIGHT HERE.
THEN FORGET IT.
I KNOW! WE CAN PLAY BARBER!! YOU'LL BE THE CUSTOMER!!
HE'LL GO ALONG WITH IT AS LONG AS HE THINKS WE'RE PLAYING...
COME TO THINK OF IT, DON'T REAL BARBERS GIVE OUT CANDY AT THE END?
FINE! WHEN WE'RE DONE, I'LL GIVE YOU SOME GUM.
LET'S GET IN CHARACTER! READY? GO!
OH, GOOD AFTERNOON. IF YOU'LL JUST HAVE A SEAT HERE...
I HAVEN'T GONE IN THE SHOP YET.
IS THAT RIGHT?!

* SOCCER PLAYERS WHO ARE FAMOUS IN JAPAN

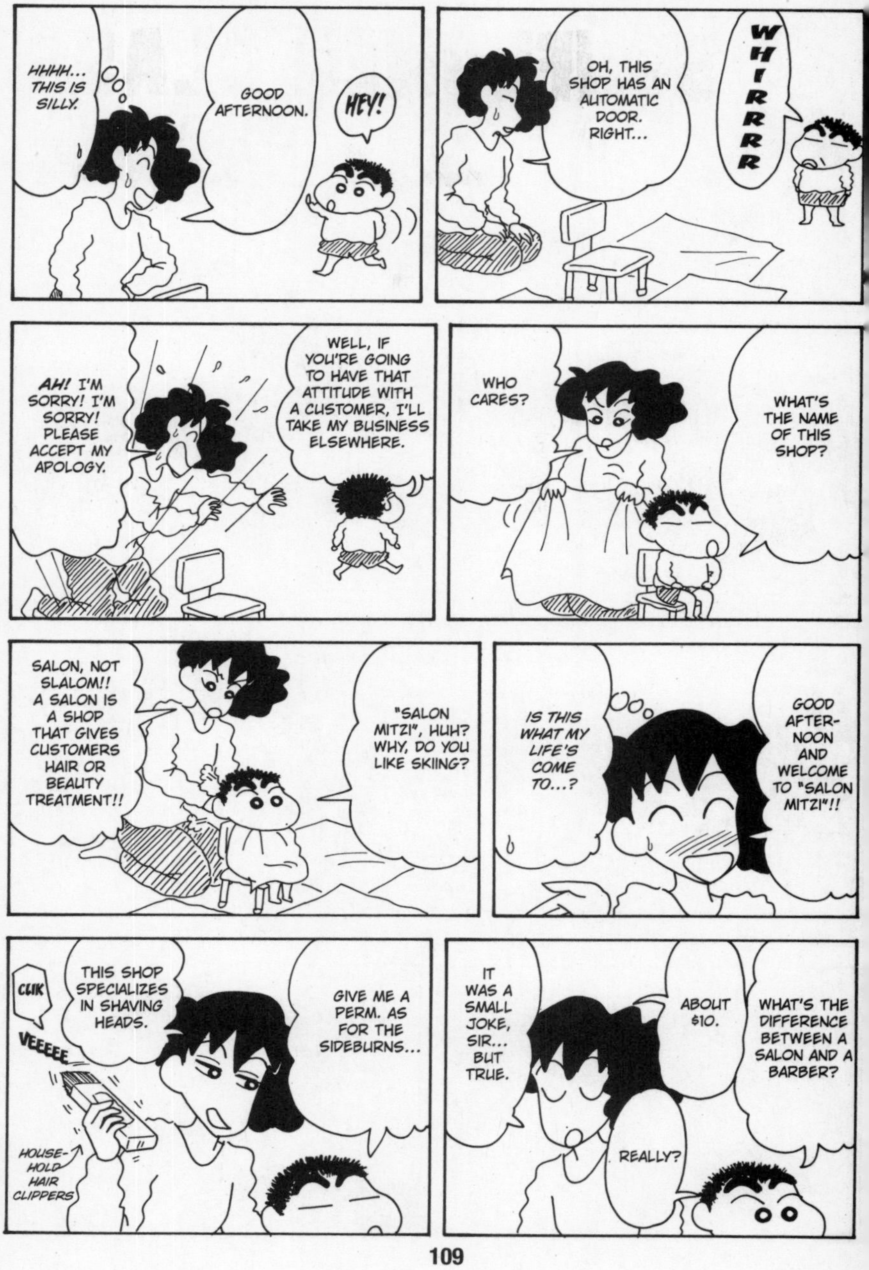
WHIRRR
OH, THIS SHOP HAS AN AUTOMATIC DOOR. RIGHT...
HEY!
GOOD AFTERNOON.
HHHH... THIS IS SILLY.
WHAT'S THE NAME OF THIS SHOP?
WHO CARES?
WELL, IF YOU'RE GOING TO HAVE THAT ATTITUDE WITH A CUSTOMER, I'LL TAKE MY BUSINESS ELSEWHERE.
AH! I'M SORRY! I'M SORRY! PLEASE ACCEPT MY APOLOGY.
GOOD AFTER-NOON AND WELCOME TO "SALON MITZI"!!
IS THIS WHAT MY LIFE'S COME TO...?
"SALON MITZI", HUH? WHY, DO YOU LIKE SKIING?
SALON, NOT SLALOM!! A SALON IS A SHOP THAT GIVES CUSTOMERS HAIR OR BEAUTY TREATMENT!!
WHAT'S THE DIFFERENCE BETWEEN A SALON AND A BARBER?
ABOUT $10.
REALLY?
IT WAS A SMALL JOKE, SIR... BUT TRUE.
GIVE ME A PERM. AS FOR THE SIDEBURNS...
THIS SHOP SPECIALIZES IN SHAVING HEADS.
CLIK
VEEEEE
HOUSE-HOLD HAIR CLIPPERS

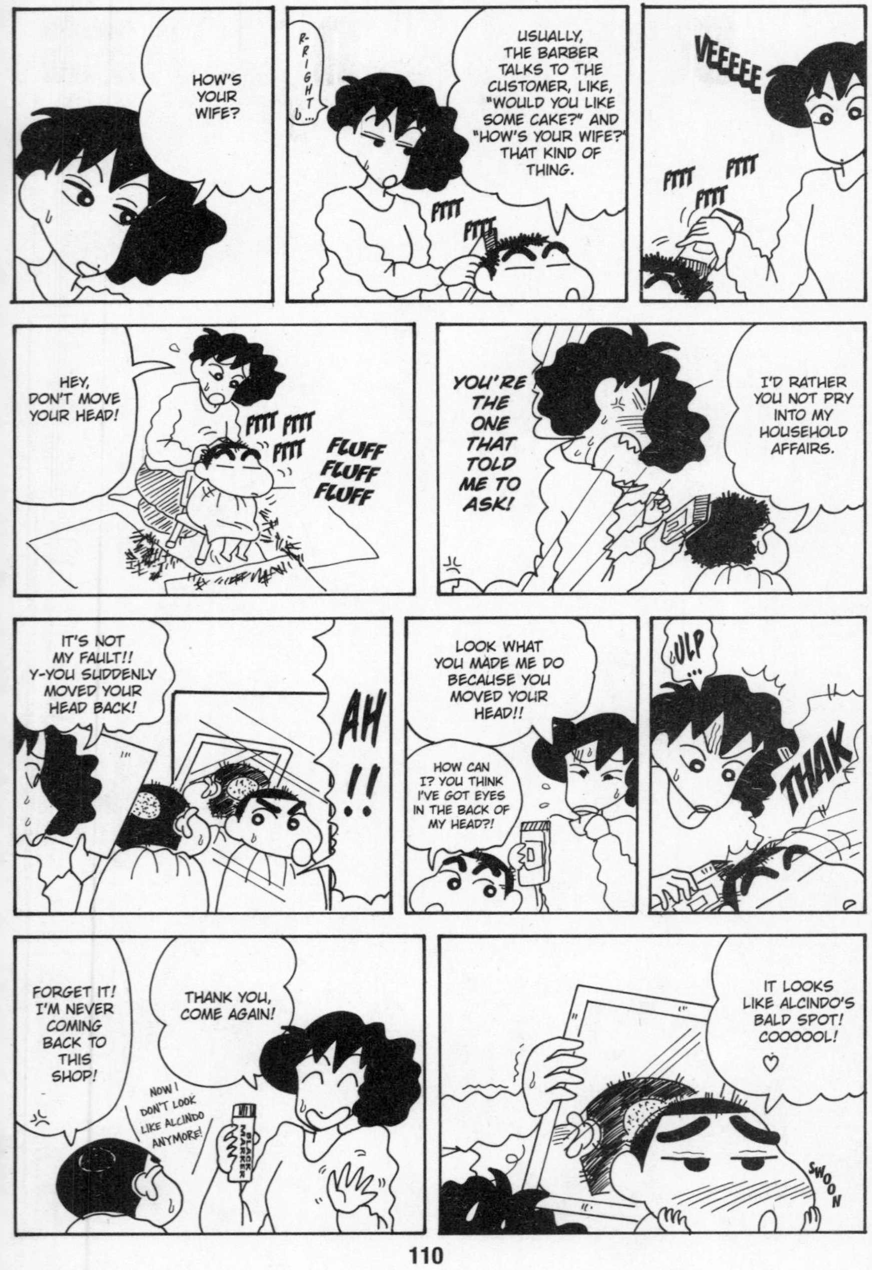
VEEEEE
PTTT PTTT PTTT
USUALLY, THE BARBER TALKS TO THE CUSTOMER, LIKE, "WOULD YOU LIKE SOME CAKE?" AND "HOW'S YOUR WIFE?" THAT KIND OF THING.
R-RIGHT...
PTTT PTTT
HOW'S YOUR WIFE?
I'D RATHER YOU NOT PRY INTO MY HOUSEHOLD AFFAIRS.
YOU'RE THE ONE THAT TOLD ME TO ASK!
HEY, DON'T MOVE YOUR HEAD!
PTTT PTTT PTTT
FLUFF FLUFF FLUFF
ULP...
THAK
LOOK WHAT YOU MADE ME DO BECAUSE YOU MOVED YOUR HEAD!!
HOW CAN I? YOU THINK I'VE GOT EYES IN THE BACK OF MY HEAD?!
AH!!
IT'S NOT MY FAULT!! Y-YOU SUDDENLY MOVED YOUR HEAD BACK!
IT LOOKS LIKE ALCINDO'S BALD SPOT! COOOOOL! ♡
SWOON
THANK YOU, COME AGAIN!
FORGET IT! I'M NEVER COMING BACK TO THIS SHOP!
NOW I DON'T LOOK LIKE ALCINDO ANYMORE!
BLACK MARKER

SUNFLOWER CLASS VS. ROSE CLASS

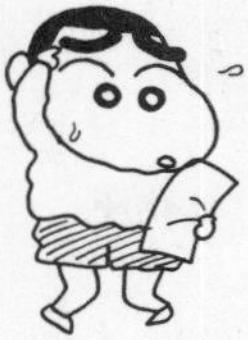

CHAPTER 9

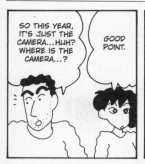

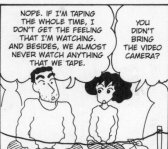

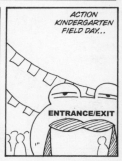

ACTION KINDERGARTEN FIELD DAY...
ENTRANCE/EXIT
YOU DIDN'T BRING THE VIDEO CAMERA?
NOPE. IF I'M TAPING THE WHOLE TIME, I DON'T GET THE FEELING THAT I'M WATCHING. AND BESIDES, WE ALMOST NEVER WATCH ANYTHING THAT WE TAPE.
GOOD POINT.
SO THIS YEAR, IT'S JUST THE CAMERA...HUH? WHERE IS THE CAMERA...?
UM... COULD YOU STOP DOING THAT?
FLASH FLASH FLASH FLASH FLASH FLASH FLASH
GET OVER HERE! JEEZ!
YOUR FATHER'S GONNA HAVE A LITTLE TALK WITH YOU.
HUH? WHERE IS HE?
SINCE HE DID ALREADY TAKE THE PHOTOS, I'LL SEND YOU COPIES WHEN THEY'RE DEVELOPED. WHAT'S YOUR NAME AND ADDRESS?
BLUSH
MAYBE I'LL TAKE ANOTHER TWO OR THREE PHOTOS OF YOU! AHAHA!

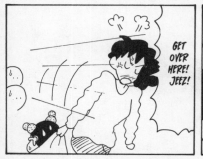

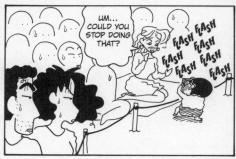

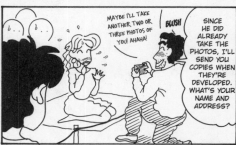

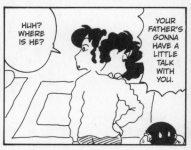

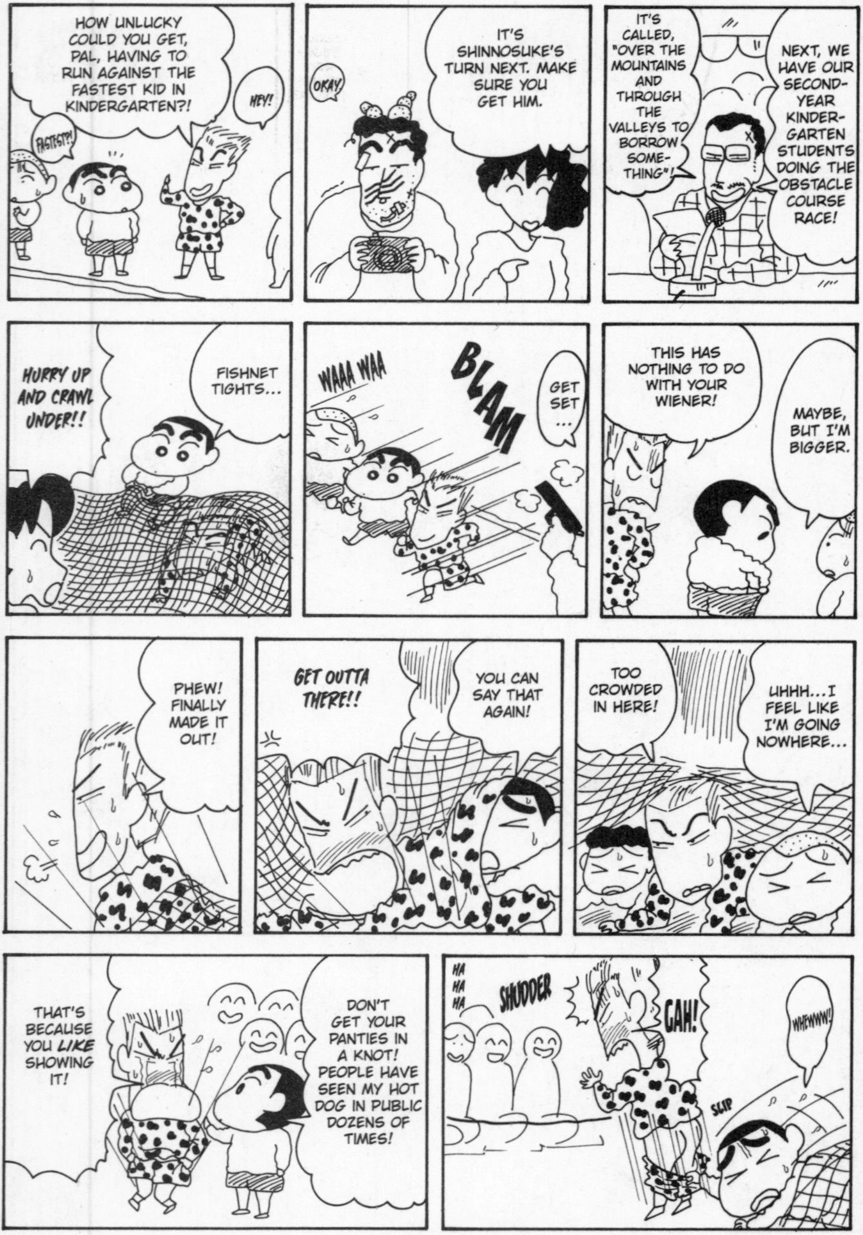
NEXT, WE HAVE OUR SECOND-YEAR KINDERGARTEN STUDENTS DOING THE OBSTACLE COURSE RACE!
IT'S CALLED, "OVER THE MOUNTAINS AND THROUGH THE VALLEYS TO BORROW SOMETHING"!
IT'S SHINNOSUKE'S TURN NEXT. MAKE SURE YOU GET HIM.
OKAY!
HOW UNLUCKY COULD YOU GET, PAL, HAVING TO RUN AGAINST THE FASTEST KID IN KINDERGARTEN?!
HEY!
FASTEST?!
THIS HAS NOTHING TO DO WITH YOUR WIENER!
MAYBE, BUT I'M BIGGER.
GET SET...
BLAM
WAAA WAA
FISHNET TIGHTS...
HURRY UP AND CRAWL UNDER!!
UHHH...I FEEL LIKE I'M GOING NOWHERE...
TOO CROWDED IN HERE!
YOU CAN SAY THAT AGAIN!
GET OUTTA THERE!!
PHEW! FINALLY MADE IT OUT!
WHEWWW!
SLIP
GAH!
SHUDDER
HA HA HA
DON'T GET YOUR PANTIES IN A KNOT! PEOPLE HAVE SEEN MY HOT DOG IN PUBLIC DOZENS OF TIMES!
THAT'S BECAUSE YOU LIKE SHOWING IT!

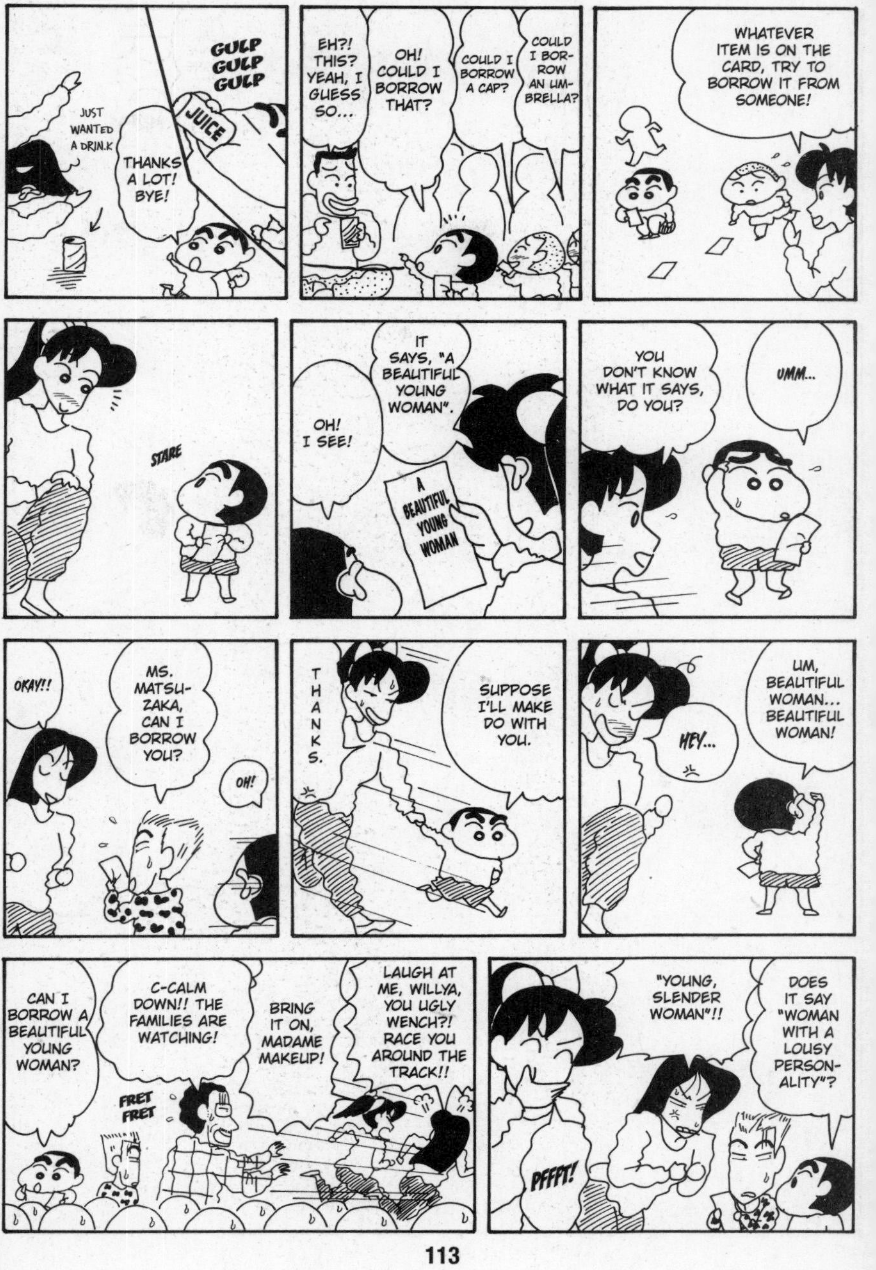
WHATEVER ITEM IS ON THE CARD, TRY TO BORROW IT FROM SOMEONE!
COULD I BORROW AN UMBRELLA?
COULD I BORROW A CAP?
OH! COULD I BORROW THAT?
EH?! THIS? YEAH, I GUESS SO...
GULP GULP GULP
JUICE
JUST WANTED A DRIN.K
THANKS A LOT! BYE!
UMM...
YOU DON'T KNOW WHAT IT SAYS, DO YOU?
IT SAYS, "A BEAUTIFUL YOUNG WOMAN".
OH! I SEE!
A BEAUTIFUL YOUNG WOMAN
STARE
UM, BEAUTIFUL WOMAN... BEAUTIFUL WOMAN!
HEY...
SUPPOSE I'LL MAKE DO WITH YOU.
THANKS.
MS. MATSUZAKA, CAN I BORROW YOU?
OKAY!!
OH!
DOES IT SAY "WOMAN WITH A LOUSY PERSONALITY"?
"YOUNG, SLENDER WOMAN"!!
PFFFT!
LAUGH AT ME, WILLYA, YOU UGLY WENCH?! RACE YOU AROUND THE TRACK!!
BRING IT ON, MADAME MAKEUP!
C-CALM DOWN!! THE FAMILIES ARE WATCHING!
FRET FRET
CAN I BORROW A BEAUTIFUL YOUNG WOMAN?

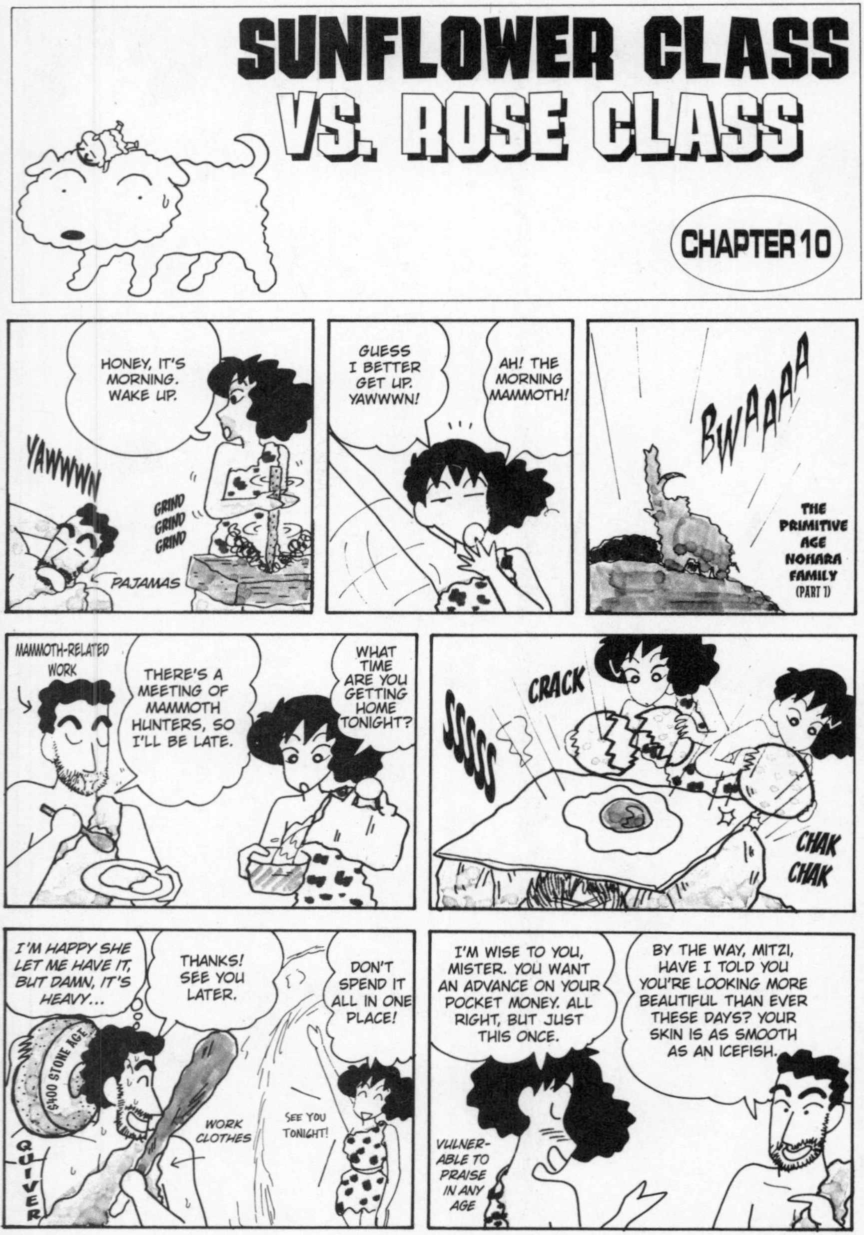
SUNFLOWER CLASS VS. ROSE CLASS
CHAPTER 10
BWAAAA
THE PRIMITIVE AGE NOHARA FAMILY (PART 1)
AH! THE MORNING MAMMOTH!
GUESS I BETTER GET UP. YAWWWN!
HONEY, IT'S MORNING. WAKE UP.
GRIND GRIND GRIND
YAWWWN
PAJAMAS
CRACK
SSSSS
CHAK CHAK
WHAT TIME ARE YOU GETTING HOME TONIGHT?
THERE'S A MEETING OF MAMMOTH HUNTERS, SO I'LL BE LATE.
MAMMOTH-RELATED WORK
BY THE WAY, MITZI, HAVE I TOLD YOU YOU'RE LOOKING MORE BEAUTIFUL THAN EVER THESE DAYS? YOUR SKIN IS AS SMOOTH AS AN ICEFISH.
I'M WISE TO YOU, MISTER. YOU WANT AN ADVANCE ON YOUR POCKET MONEY. ALL RIGHT, BUT JUST THIS ONCE.
VULNER-ABLE TO PRAISE IN ANY AGE
DON'T SPEND IT ALL IN ONE PLACE!
SEE YOU TONIGHT!
THANKS! SEE YOU LATER.
I'M HAPPY SHE LET ME HAVE IT, BUT DAMN, IT'S HEAVY...
$400 STONE AGE
WORK CLOTHES
QUIVER

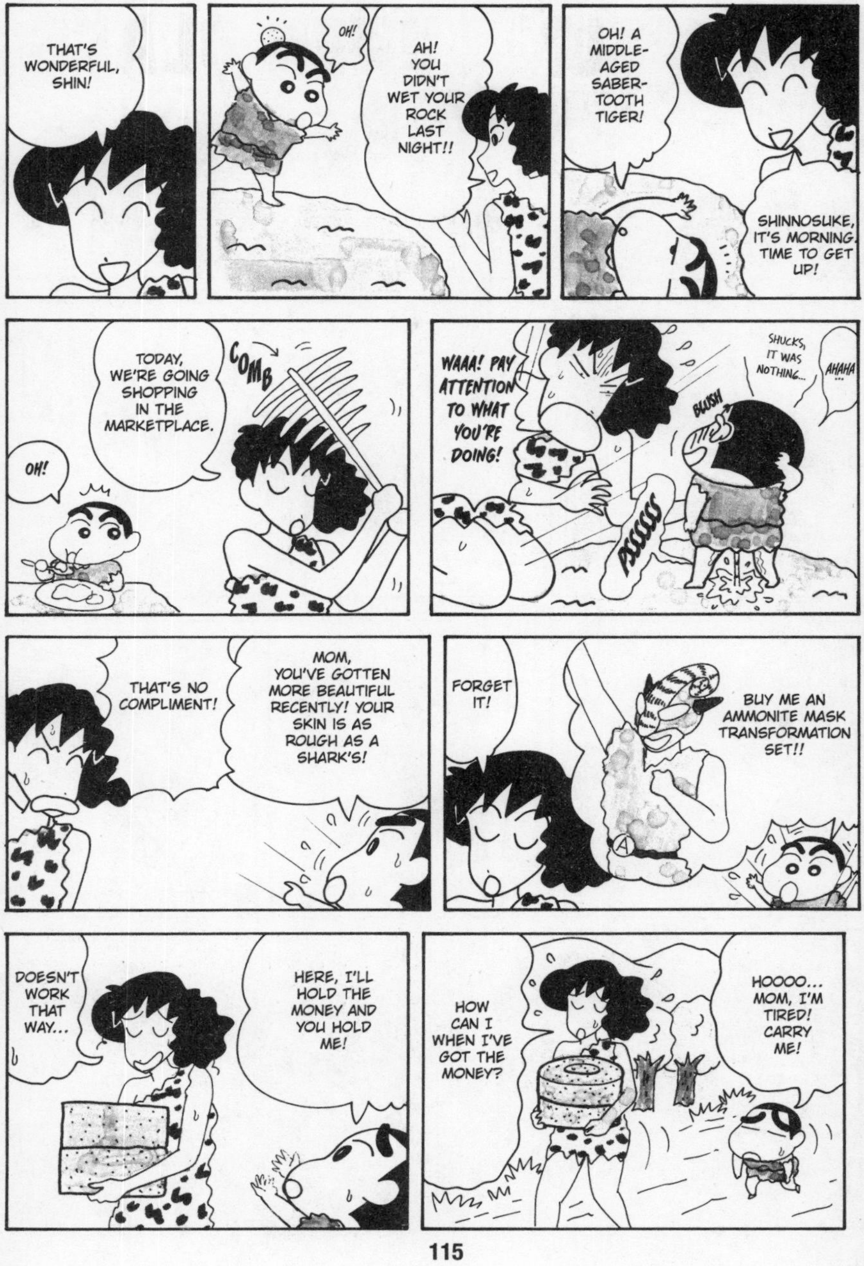
OH! A MIDDLE-AGED SABER-TOOTH TIGER!
SHINNOSUKE, IT'S MORNING. TIME TO GET UP!
OH!
AH! YOU DIDN'T WET YOUR ROCK LAST NIGHT!!
THAT'S WONDERFUL, SHIN!
WAAA! PAY ATTENTION TO WHAT YOU'RE DOING!
SHUCKS, IT WAS NOTHING...
AHAHA...
BLUSH
PSSSSSS
COMB
TODAY, WE'RE GOING SHOPPING IN THE MARKETPLACE.
OH!
BUY ME AN AMMONITE MASK TRANSFORMATION SET!!
FORGET IT!
MOM, YOU'VE GOTTEN MORE BEAUTIFUL RECENTLY! YOUR SKIN IS AS ROUGH AS A SHARK'S!
THAT'S NO COMPLIMENT!
HOOOO... MOM, I'M TIRED! CARRY ME!
HOW CAN I WHEN I'VE GOT THE MONEY?
HERE, I'LL HOLD THE MONEY AND YOU HOLD ME!
DOESN'T WORK THAT WAY...

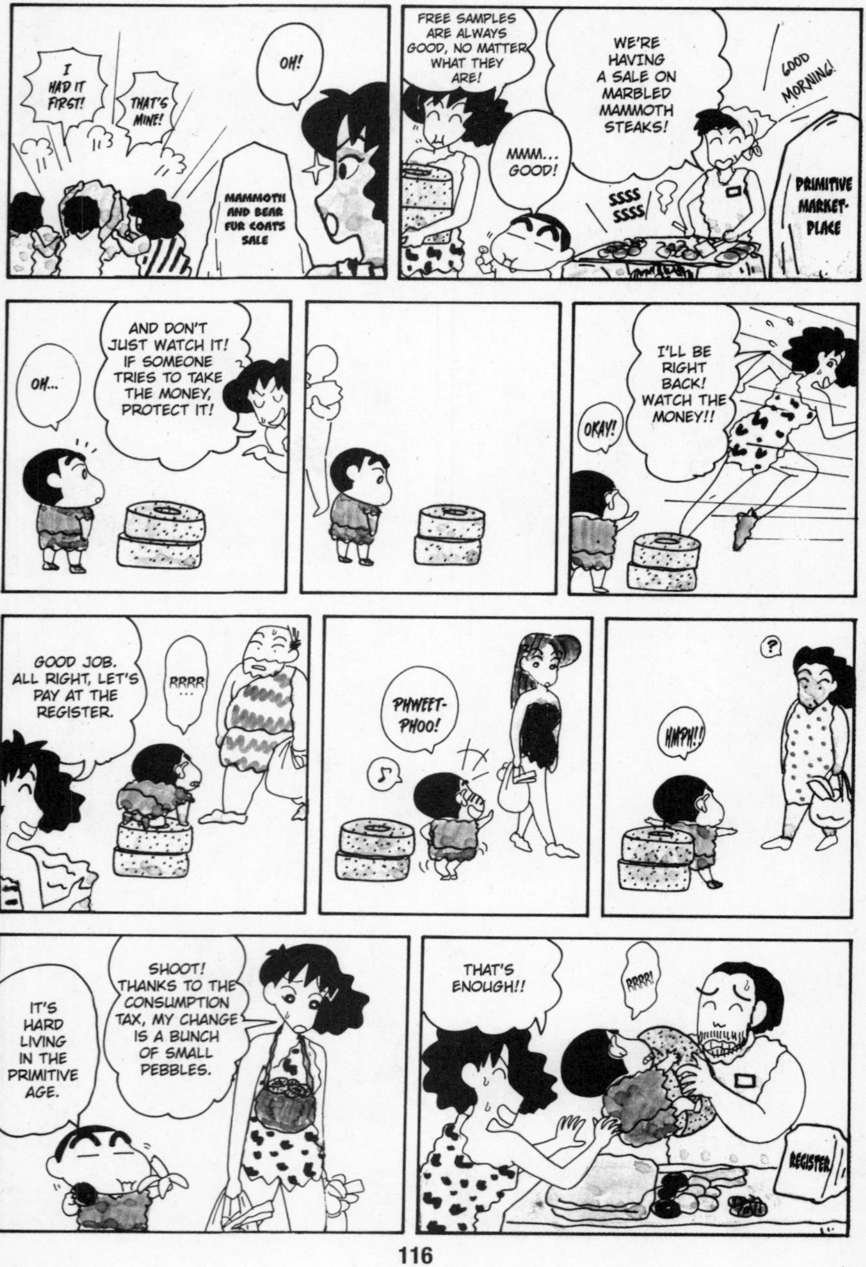
GOOD MORNING!
WE'RE HAVING A SALE ON MARBLED MAMMOTH STEAKS!
PRIMITIVE MARKET-PLACE
SSSS SSSS
MMM... GOOD!
FREE SAMPLES ARE ALWAYS GOOD, NO MATTER WHAT THEY ARE!
OH!
MAMMOTH AND BEAR FUR COATS SALE
THAT'S MINE!
I HAD IT FIRST!
I'LL BE RIGHT BACK! WATCH THE MONEY!!
OKAY!
AND DON'T JUST WATCH IT! IF SOMEONE TRIES TO TAKE THE MONEY, PROTECT IT!
OH...
?
HMPH!!
PHWEET-PHOO!
♪
RRRR...
GOOD JOB. ALL RIGHT, LET'S PAY AT THE REGISTER.
RRRR!
THAT'S ENOUGH!!
REGISTER
SHOOT! THANKS TO THE CONSUMPTION TAX, MY CHANGE IS A BUNCH OF SMALL PEBBLES.
IT'S HARD LIVING IN THE PRIMITIVE AGE.

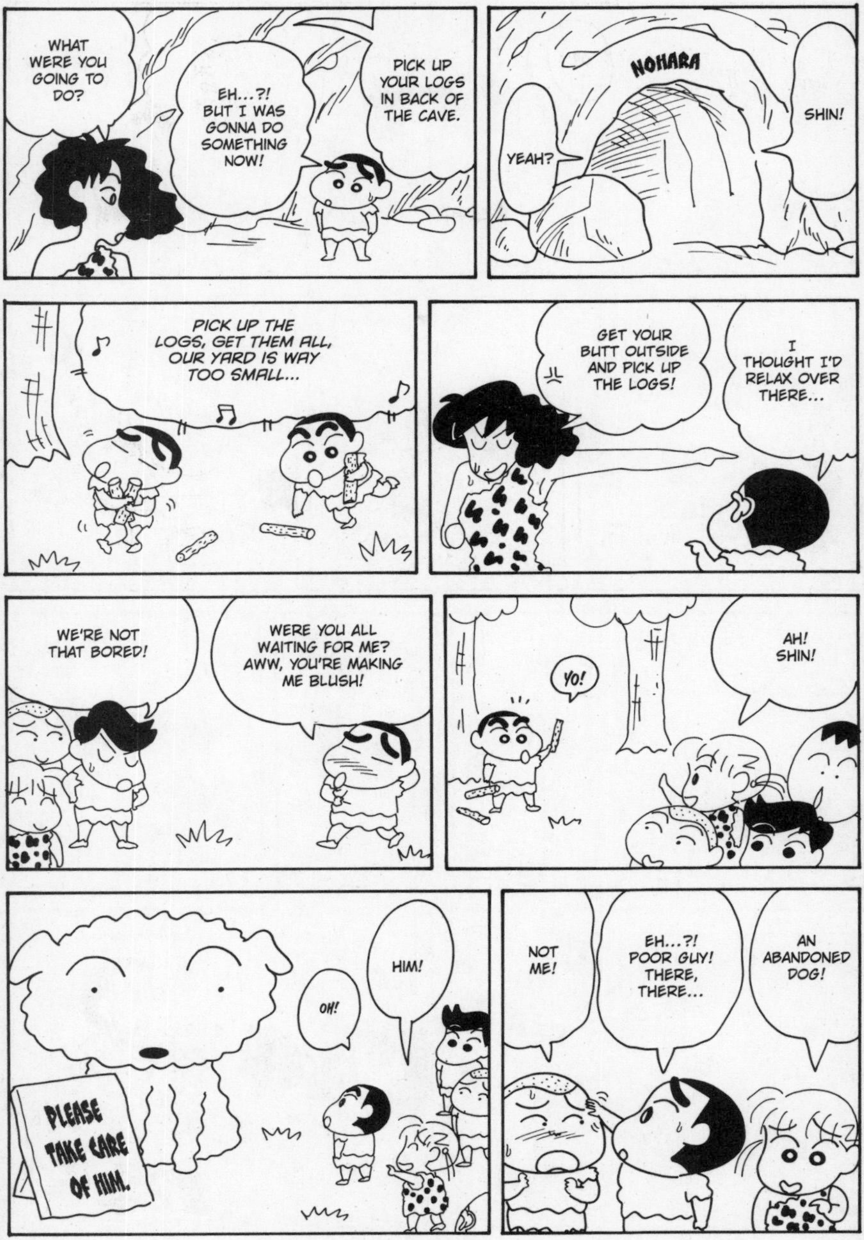
NOHARA
SHIN!
YEAH?
PICK UP YOUR LOGS IN BACK OF THE CAVE.
EH...?! BUT I WAS GONNA DO SOMETHING NOW!
WHAT WERE YOU GOING TO DO?
I THOUGHT I'D RELAX OVER THERE...
GET YOUR BUTT OUTSIDE AND PICK UP THE LOGS!
PICK UP THE LOGS, GET THEM ALL, OUR YARD IS WAY TOO SMALL...
AH! SHIN!
YO!
WERE YOU ALL WAITING FOR ME? AWW, YOU'RE MAKING ME BLUSH!
WE'RE NOT THAT BORED!
AN ABANDONED DOG!
EH...?! POOR GUY! THERE, THERE...
NOT ME!
HIM!
OH!
PLEASE TAKE CARE OF HIM.

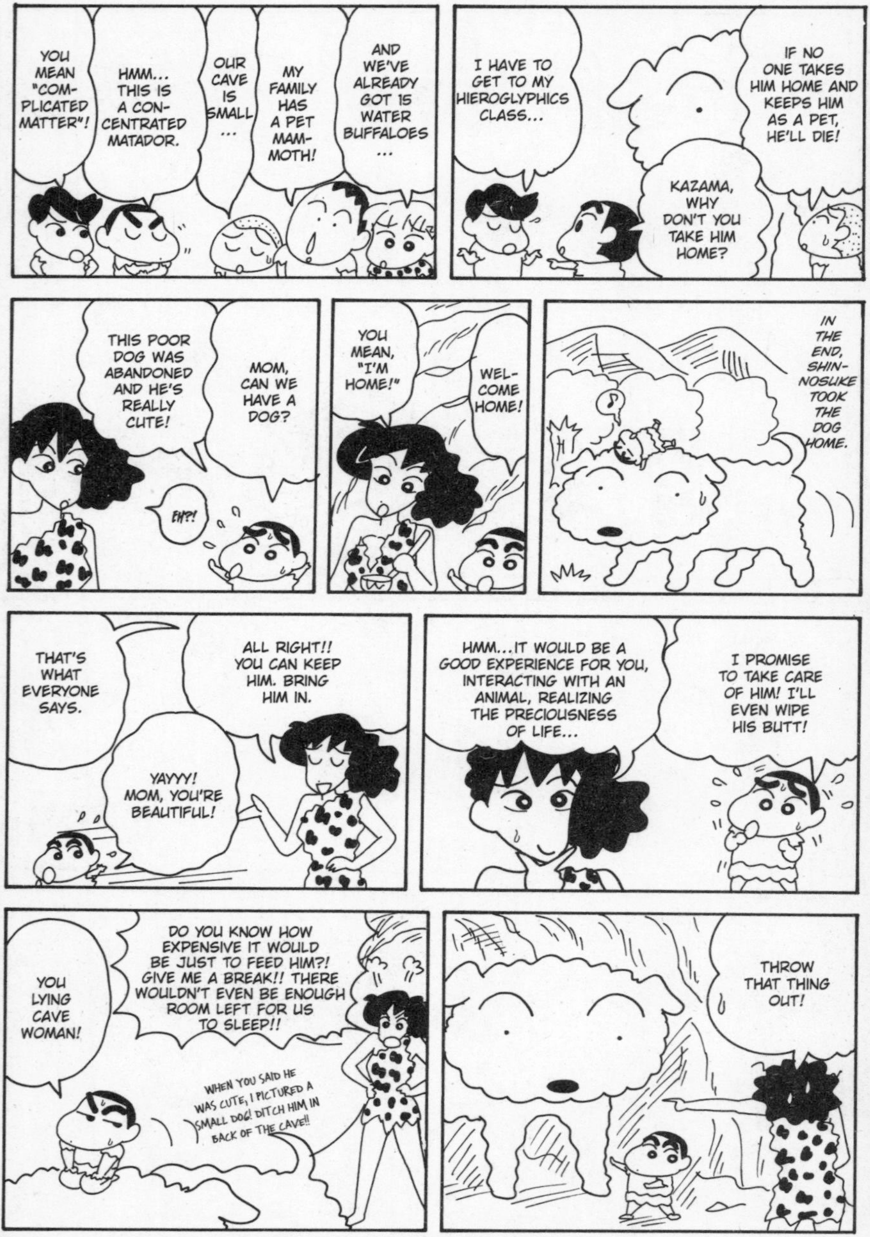
IF NO ONE TAKES HIM HOME AND KEEPS HIM AS A PET, HE'LL DIE!
I HAVE TO GET TO MY HIEROGLYPHICS CLASS...
KAZAMA, WHY DON'T YOU TAKE HIM HOME?
AND WE'VE ALREADY GOT 15 WATER BUFFALOES...
MY FAMILY HAS A PET MAMMOTH!
OUR CAVE IS SMALL...
HMM... THIS IS A CONCENTRATED MATADOR.
YOU MEAN "COMPLICATED MATTER"!
IN THE END, SHINNOSUKE TOOK THE DOG HOME.
WELCOME HOME!
YOU MEAN, "I'M HOME!"
MOM, CAN WE HAVE A DOG?
THIS POOR DOG WAS ABANDONED AND HE'S REALLY CUTE!
EH?!
I PROMISE TO TAKE CARE OF HIM! I'LL EVEN WIPE HIS BUTT!
HMM...IT WOULD BE A GOOD EXPERIENCE FOR YOU, INTERACTING WITH AN ANIMAL, REALIZING THE PRECIOUSNESS OF LIFE...
ALL RIGHT!! YOU CAN KEEP HIM. BRING HIM IN.
THAT'S WHAT EVERYONE SAYS.
YAYYY! MOM, YOU'RE BEAUTIFUL!
THROW THAT THING OUT!
DO YOU KNOW HOW EXPENSIVE IT WOULD BE JUST TO FEED HIM?! GIVE ME A BREAK!! THERE WOULDN'T EVEN BE ENOUGH ROOM LEFT FOR US TO SLEEP!!
YOU LYING CAVE WOMAN!
WHEN YOU SAID HE WAS CUTE, I PICTURED A SMALL DOG! DITCH HIM IN BACK OF THE CAVE!!

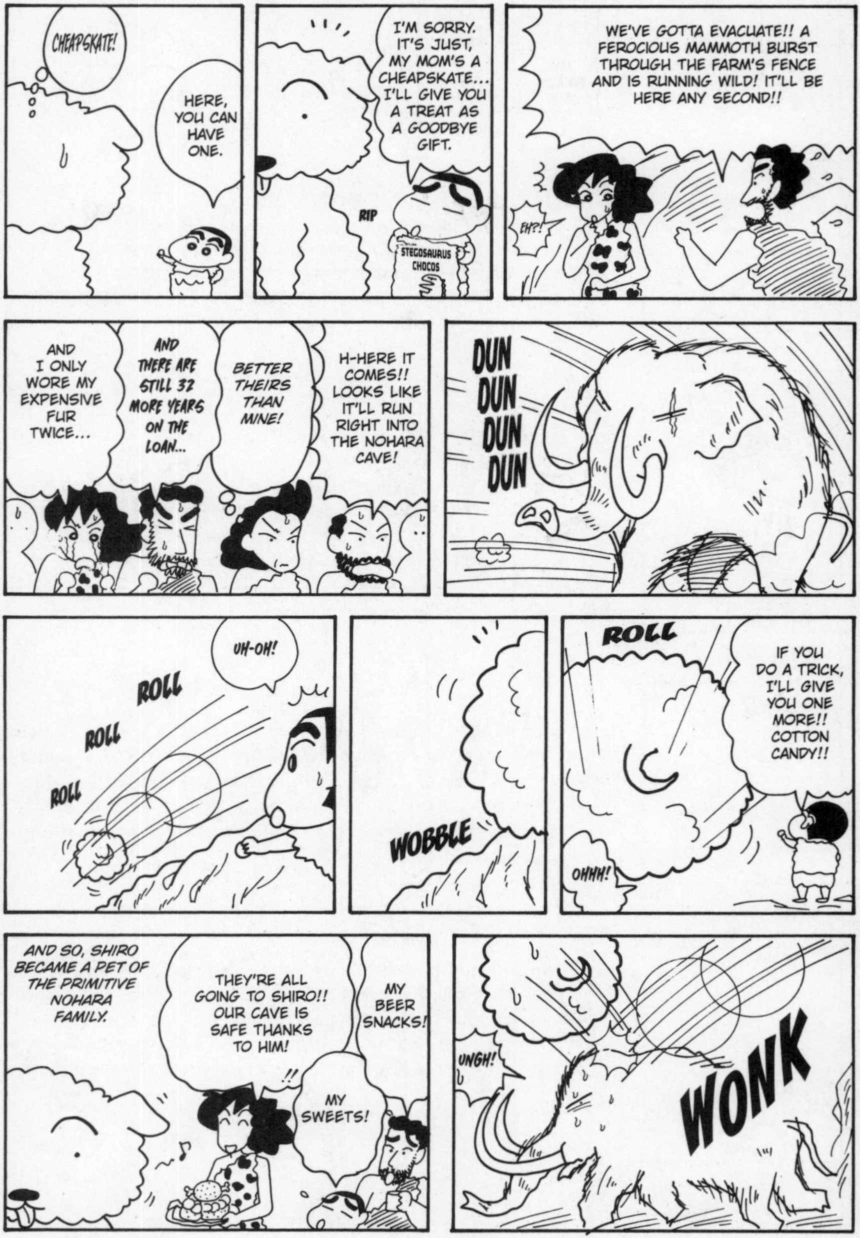
WE'VE GOTTA EVACUATE!! A FEROCIOUS MAMMOTH BURST THROUGH THE FARM'S FENCE AND IS RUNNING WILD! IT'LL BE HERE ANY SECOND!!
EH?!
I'M SORRY. IT'S JUST, MY MOM'S A CHEAPSKATE... I'LL GIVE YOU A TREAT AS A GOODBYE GIFT.
RIP
STEGOSAURUS CHOCOS
CHEAPSKATE!
HERE, YOU CAN HAVE ONE.
DUN DUN DUN DUN
H-HERE IT COMES!! LOOKS LIKE IT'LL RUN RIGHT INTO THE NOHARA CAVE!
BETTER THEIRS THAN MINE!
AND THERE ARE STILL 32 MORE YEARS ON THE LOAN...
AND I ONLY WORE MY EXPENSIVE FUR TWICE...
ROLL
IF YOU DO A TRICK, I'LL GIVE YOU ONE MORE!! COTTON CANDY!!
OHHH!
WOBBLE
UH-OH!
ROLL
ROLL
ROLL
UNGH!
WONK
MY BEER SNACKS!
THEY'RE ALL GOING TO SHIRO!! OUR CAVE IS SAFE THANKS TO HIM!
MY SWEETS!
AND SO, SHIRO BECAME A PET OF THE PRIMITIVE NOHARA FAMILY.

Meet the Noharas!

SHINNOSUKE NOHARA

(aka: Shin, Shin-chan, Shin chan, Shinchan)
5 years old. Likes pretty girls, drawing on himself, rolling around on the floor, and eating a tasty snack called Choco-bees. Frequently uses both words and his Mom's clothing in inappropriate ways. Also obsessed with bodily functions – his own and others'.

MITZI NOHARA

(aka: Misae)
Shin's easily frustrated mom. She's a stay-at-home housewife with the misfortune of being Shin's full time caretaker. Mitzi hasn't done much better in the husband department either, as Shin's Dad's behavior has to be closely monitored too. Frequently fantasizes about a better life.

HIRO NOHARA

(aka: Hiroshi)
A browbeaten "salary man" who is the family's sole breadwinner. He's low on the totem pole at work and doesn't get much respect at home either. Like son, like father: Hiro has the eye for the pretty girls too, and Mitzi's none too tolerant of it. He talks a lot in his sleep, which doesn't help things much.

SHIRO

Stray dog that Shin found and brought home. Somehow, he managed to convince Mitzi that if she let him keep the dog, he'd take care of it. Want to guess how that's working out? But taking care of Shiro is always a convenient excuse when Mom wants some even more unpleasant chore to get done.

It's Always Fun in the Sunflower Class!

Life as a kindergarten student is an adventure when Shinchan is in your class! Let's meet some of his friends…and his teacher.

NENE SAKURADA

A good little girl who tries to be patient with Shin, but who's always fearful of trouble ahead. Shin's encounters with Nene's mom usually end with Mrs. Sakurada dropping her mild-mannered exterior, leaving Nene traumatized by her sudden change in character. ("You're not my real mommy!")

TORU KAZAMA

A legend in his own mind, Kazama considers himself to be wiser, worldlier, and certainly classier than anyone else. Naturally, he regards Shin as an uncouth menace to society and criticizes him frequently—which of course just goes right over Shin's head.

MASAO

Poor Masao. He's a shy kid and a bit of a nervous wreck. Shin's influence doesn't really help him with his "issues." He always tries to draw Masao into activities that would make even stronger children cringe. Masao just cries. Destined to spend a lot of time in therapy.

MS. YOSHINAGA

Dedicated Sunflower class teacher who has been cursed to have Shin as one of her students. Other than Mitzi, no one has to put up with more abuse from Shin. Her archrival is Ms. Matsuzaka from the Rose Class.

IS THE WORLD READY FOR TWO SHINCHANS?! FIND OUT IN JUNE!

CRAYON Shinchan

Vol. 8

By Yoshito Usui. Uh-oh. Look out. The "Terminator" saleslady is back in the neighborhood and this time she's determined not to let her juvenile archenemy stop her from selling everyone products they don't need. Then Shin has another showdown with that girl gang that thinks they're a lot tougher than they really are—the Lipstick Scorpions! And get ready for an extra-long adventure, as the Nohara family wins a trip to the kingdom of Buri Buri, where Shin meets a prince who could pass for his twin.

THE REVOLU-SHIN WILL BE TELEVISED

SHIN CHAN

GO TO SHINCHANSHOW.COM FOR LOCAL LISTINGS

★ ★ ★ ★ ★ ★ ★ ★ ★ ★ ★ ★

tv asahi FUNIMATION
★ ENTERTAINMENT
A NAVARRE CORPORATION COMPANY

PRESENTED BY
YU YAGAMI

GO WEST!

Volume 2

By Yu Yagami. Naomi digs in her spurs and rides Red Bullet hard to the town of West End. It's a hard place to miss—West End's a high-rise mesa development, the likes of which no one's ever seen. Naomi gets closer to tracking down the source of the photo that she thinks shows her mother. And when this motley band of travelers encounters a native tribe, you know it's guaranteed to be anything but a peaceful cultural exchange.

ORFINA

Volume 5

By Kitsune Tennouji. Fana leads a small band of Knights and thieves on a rescue mission and finds an unexpected ally in the Granzian warrior Hyleka. They confront a band of warriors whose armor and weapons are obviously not of this world. These foes seem to know Fana's real identity, not just her publicly assumed role of Princess Orfina. What past history connects her to these alien forces? An epic struggle brings past and present players together in this action-filled, expanded volume.

KNOW WHAT'S INSIDE

With the wide variety of manga available, CMX understands it can be confusing to determine age-appropriate material. We rate our books in four categories: EVERYONE, TEEN, TEEN + and MATURE. For the TEEN, TEEN + and MATURE categories, we include additional, specific descriptions to assist consumers in determining if the book is age appropriate. (Our MATURE books are shipped shrink-wrapped with a Parental Advisory sticker affixed to the wrapper.)

EVERYONE

Titles with this rating are appropriate for all age readers. They contain no offensive material. They may contain mild violence and/or some comic mischief.

TEEN

Titles with this rating are appropriate for a teen audience and older. They may contain some violent content, language, and/or suggestive themes.

TEEN PLUS

Titles with this rating are appropriate for an audience of 16 and older. They may contain partial nudity, mild profanity and more intense violence.

MATURE

Titles with this rating are appropriate only for mature readers. They may contain graphic violence, nudity, sex and content suitable only for older readers.

CRAYON SHINCHAN Vol. 7 © Yoshito Usui 1990. All
rights reserved. First published in Japan in 1990 by
Futabasha Publishers Co., Ltd., Tokyo.

CRAYON SHINCHAN Volume 7, published by
WildStorm Productions, an imprint of DC Comics, 888
Prospect St. #240, La Jolla, CA 92037. English
Translation © 2009. All Rights Reserved. English ver-
sion published by DC COMICS. Under license from
Futabasha Publishers Co., Ltd. CMX is a trademark of
DC Comics. The stories, characters, and incidents men-
tioned in this magazine are entirely fictional. Printed on
recyclable paper. WildStorm does not read or accept
unsolicited submissions of ideas, stories or artwork.
Printed in Canada.

DC Comics, a Warner Bros. Entertainment Company.

Sheldon Drzka – Translation and Adaptation
Wilson Ramos – Lettering
Larry Berry – Design
Sarah Farber – Assistant Editor
Jim Chadwick – Editor

ISBN: 978-1-4012-2110-2

RIGHT TO LEFT?!

Traditional Japanese manga starts at the upper right-hand corner, and moves right-to-left as it goes down the page. Follow this guide for an easy understanding.

For more information and sneak previews, visit cmxmanga.com. Call 1-888-COMIC BOOK for the nearest comics shop or head to your local book store.

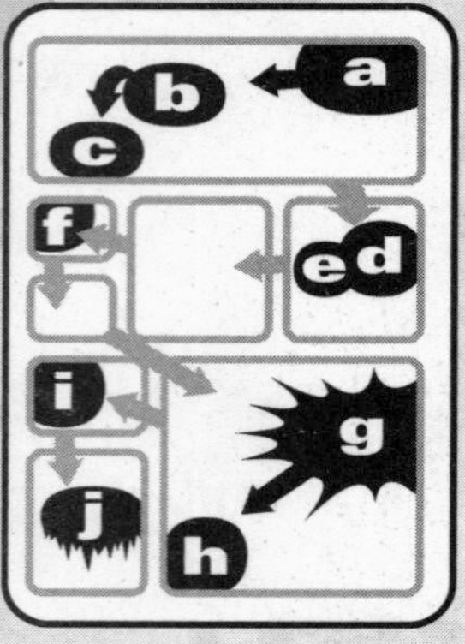
a
b
c
ed
f
g
h
i
j

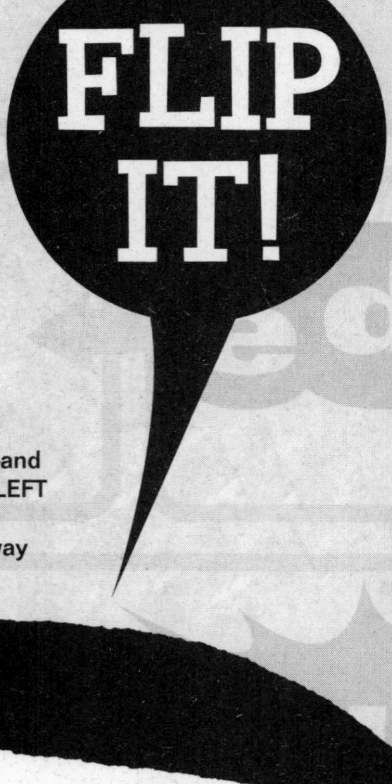
FLIP IT!

All the pages in this book were created—and are printed here—in Japanese RIGHT-to-LEFT format. No artwork has been reversed or altered, so you can read the stories the way the creators meant for them to be read.

CMX™

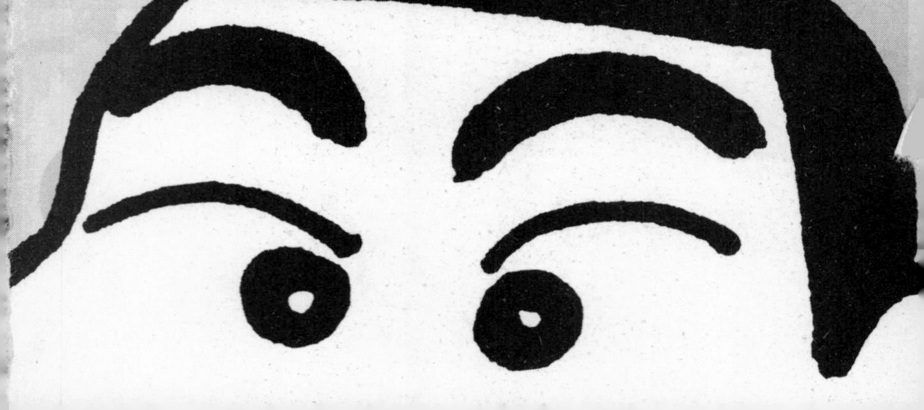